1866

The Critical Year Revisited

Patrick W. Riddleberger

UNIVERSITY
PRESS OF
AMERICA

LANHAM • NEW YORK • LONDON

To my students and faculty colleagues

Contents

Chapter 7
The Meaning of the Amendment—
For Contemporaries and Historians
162

Chapter 8
The Memphis and New Orleans Riots
177

Chapter 9
The Voice of the Electorate
202

Chapter 10
How Johnson Lost—The Historical Debate
230

Appendix
Thirteenth, Fourteenth, and Fifteenth Amendments
to the Constitution of the United States
253

Notes
255

Selected Bibliography
271

Index
279

Illustrations

Preface

PERSONS FAMILIAR with the historiography of the Reconstruction era will note the similarity of my title to that of Howard K. Beale's book, *The Critical Year*, published more than forty-five years ago. The inclusion of his title within mine is, in a way, a tribute to that important pioneering effort, as well as an affirmation of Beale's assessment of 1866, for it was indeed a critical year not only for the Reconstruction period but for the century following it. Nothing attests to this so vitally or dramatically as the adoption by Congress of the Fourteenth Amendment and the significance of that amendment in the contest for civil rights that has been going on ever since. In fact, my emphasis is on the civil rights question during the year 1866, including the Freedmen's Bureau and the Freedmen's Bureau Bill, the Civil Rights Bill, and the Fourteenth Amendment.

But a study of the politics of 1866 necessarily leads one beyond civil rights in any narrow or limited sense. Enmeshed in it is the struggle between the executive and the legislative for supremacy, a struggle that is endemic to the American political system but one that can take on a particularly virulent form under certain conditions. The conditions of 1866 were the presence of a courageous, stubborn, and overly sensitive president; a radical minority in Congress ready and willing to challenge him; and a set of problems stemming from secession and civil war that were without precedent in the American experience. The contest became one between presidential restoration—a quick and relatively easy return of the southern states to their former political place in the Union—and congressional reconstruction, involving conditions for the return of the southern states based on fundamental changes resulting from the war.

It has been suggested that the conflict between the president and Congress represented the continuation of the Civil War by other means. There is something to be said for this insight, for in the early Reconstruction era the contending political factions did turn Clausewitz on his head. The war ceased on the battlefield but continued in Washington and in parts of the South. The outcome of this phase of the war would determine what sort of reconstruction there would be—for a time if not in the long run.

My objective in writing the book has been twofold: first, to present a clear narrative of national politics during 1866 as they related to the question of restoration-reconstruction, and second, to develop a historical synthesis of Beale's work and the works of revisionist historians published in the late 1950s and the 1960s—writings by such historians as Eric McKitrick, Lawanda and John Cox, W. R. Brock, and Stanley Coben. The revisionists have made a splendid contribution to Reconstruction history and have effectively challenged the Beale thesis, which combined traditional anti-radicalism with a progressive emphasis on economic interpretation. I have felt more and more, however, that they have not said the last word, and I have therefore been led into an occasional historiographical digression from the narrative which I hope the reader will not find awkward or irrelevant. I see such digressions as intrinsically a part of the story as I perceive it and have tried to tell it.

It should not be inferred, however, that I have relied solely on these important secondary sources. Although I make no claim to having exhausted the primary sources—it will be apparent to the reader that I have not done so—it would be folly to attempt such a study as this without consulting primary sources. I might add that I have found a return to the *Congressional Globe*, after a lapse of some years, interesting and enlightening. I have been impressed with the high intellectual level of the congressional debates, with the clarity of the language and the informed resort to political theory. Of course, politicians bespoke the prejudices and the conventionalities of their era, as men of all generations do, but most of them were not simpleminded pragmatists concerned with only the immediate and the practical. Many of them thought deeply about the meaning of the cataclysm through which the nation was passing, and they sought to do what was in its best interest for the future as well as the present. To brush them aside as a "blundering generation" is to misunderstand them and grievously to underestimate them. They blundered no more than their predecessors and considerably less than their nineteenth-century successors. It was their destiny to be in national politics when the nation's constitutional and political system broke down. For good or ill, it was their lot to cope with that reality. If we are to understand them and be fair to them it is necessary never to forget the milieu in which their struggle took place.

I AM INDEBTED TO a number of persons who have helped to make possible the writing and publication of this book. Earl Beard, Nedra Branz, Suzanne Jacobitti, John Taylor, and Stuart Weiss have read parts of the manuscript and have made useful comments and suggestions. David Butler and Norman Nordhauser have read all of it; in their insights and detailed editorial suggestions they have gone far beyond what I had any right to expect. I am very grateful to them.

Joan Hewitt, Joyce Giardina, and Virginia Bradbury, and other staff members of Lovejoy Library of Southern Illinois University at Edwardsville have assisted me in innumerable ways. Robert Fortado, head of the library's documents division, has been especially helpful in making essential documents available to me when I most needed them.

The university has been generous in granting me a sabbatical leave which enabled me to start the book and released time from teaching without which it would have been difficult to finish it. Professors Samuel Pearson and Herbert Rosenthal, chairmen of the history department during the years I have been working on the book, have been consistently encouraging and helpful. William Tudor, press representative on the Edwardsville campus, and those members of the press who have worked on the book have been cooperative in every way. I am fortunate indeed to have had as my editor Stephen W. Smith, whose dedicated labor on the manuscript has made the book better than it otherwise could possibly have been.

I am indebted to Ramona Porter and Denice Taylor for typing the manuscript.

My students, through their continuing interest and encouragement, have sustained me in my efforts.

Edwardsville, Illinois　　　　　　　　　Patrick W. Riddleberger
November 17, 1978

THE READER OF *1866: The Critical Year Revisited* will readily see that the revisionist historians of Reconstruction whose books were published in the 1960s provide the genre in which my book falls. Notable among them are Kenneth M. Stampp, Eric McKitrick, William R. Brock, and Lawanda and John Cox. Subsequently, in the 1970s, young scholars began to challenge the interpretations of the older revisionists. At least two of these have written outstanding books that demand the attention of scholars and students of Reconstruction history: Michael Les Benedict's *A Compromise of Principle: Congressional Republicans and Reconstruction, 1863-1869* (1974) and Michael Perman's *Reunion Without Compromise: The South and Reconstruction, 1865-1868* (1973). Both Benedict and Perman have removed the emphasis from the struggle between Andrew Johnson and Congress and placed it elsewhere, Benedict on the divisions among the Radical Republicans in Congress and Perman on the South and its leaders, whom he designates as "Confederates."

Benedict's *A Compromise of Principle* is a large, complex, and ambitious work whose scope far exceeds my study of 1866. Using a statistical analysis of a sort usually employed by political scientists as a clarifying technique Benedict argues that Radical Reconstruction was never very radical and that the Radicals "never controlled the processes of Reconstruction." (pp. 13-14) He reiterates the argument he had made in a previous book, *The Impeachment and Trial of Andrew Johnson* (1973), that the Radicals' decision to impeach Johnson was the correct one and that the Senate ought to have convicted him. The Fessenden-Sumner juxtaposition that the reader will find in *1866* also appears in Benedict's works, but with a difference. For me Fessenden represents a practical progressive force seeking the best possible guarantee of Negro freedom against a stubborn and intractable—albeit idealist—one represented by Charles Sumner. Fessenden, as Benedict sees him, was a conservative leader ready and willing to make an unfortunate compromise with principle that Sumner would not tolerate.

Michael Perman, in what strikes me as an erroneous analogy, challenges the revisionists of the 1950s and the 1960s. "Like the Civil War revisionists of the 1940s, who argued that war was avoidable," he writes, "the Reconstruction revisionists...have suggested that radical reconstruction was not inevitable, that the differences between the sections were negotiable, and that a formula was available for reconciling the needs and fears of both Congress and the Confederate South." (p. 8) He goes on to say that the coercion of the South was necessary because the South's rulers "were not a negotiable force."

To be sure, if the coercion of the South that Perman believes to have been essential had been effected much of the suffering and turmoil that has been the legacy of the Civil War may have been avoided. We cannot know for sure because that policy was not implemented. But the notion that it could have been done in the post-Civil War milieu strikes me as unrealistic and illusory. A footnote on William R. Brock's *An American Crisis: Congress and Reconstruction, 1865-1867* may be revealing as to Perman's mind-set in the writing of history. Perman accurately paraphrases Brock's assessment as to why Reconstruction was a failure—because of the "tragic proportions of the situation in which Congress found itself, beset as it was by ideological, constitutional and institutional obstacles and limitations." With much of this Perman professed to agree, but he was "not so fatalistic as Brock in attributing Reconstruction's deficiencies to situational ironies and to tragedy." But for me, a sensitivity to the tragic theme is essential to a balanced and enlightened history of the complex Reconstruction era. Despite these reservations, *Reunion Without Compromise* is a provocative and thoroughly researched work and an important contribution to Reconstruction historiography.

Even before the appearance of the neo-revisionism of the 1970s, scholars had begun to question particular parts of the earlier revisionist argument. Notable among these was William S. McFeely, whose *Yankee Stepfather: General O. O. Howard and the Freedmen* came out in 1968. Taking his cue from W. E. B. DuBois's moving essay, "Of the Dawn of Freedom" (1903), McFeely argued that "the [Freedman's] Bureau should have been a medium of social change and not just the agent of reconciliation between ex-slaves and their former masters." The failure of the Freedmen's Bureau to live up to that standard, and its general failure, was due to the personal ineptness and the faulty administration of its commissioner, General Oliver O. Howard, whose work, according to McFeely, "seemed to preclude rather than to promote Negro freedom."

McFeely develops a strong, if not irrefutable, case against Howard— so strong, indeed, that a reader of McFeeley's book may conclude that I have been too easy on Howard in my chapter on the Freedmen's Bureau. He suggests that the "Christian General" was not above maneuvering his way into the "freedmen business" to advance his post-war career, that he was too much under the spell of his former commanding general, the racially prejudiced William T. Sherman who warned Howard against making a "New Revolution" that might bring on another war, and that there were other better qualified men for the office of commissioner. General Rufus Saxton, the commander on the Sea Islands, may have been the best qualified man for the position, but even the backing of Salmon P. Chase could not bring him the appointment. Howard was Secretary of War Stanton's man, and his appointment came in part as a reward for outstanding military service. Howard's acquiescence in the dismissal of Saxton from his post as assistant commissioner for South Carolina, Georgia, and Florida early in 1866 was a rather sorry episode. Unaccountably, also, Howard departed from his Washington headquarters at the end of July, 1865 for a month's vacation, leaving in charge his adjutant general, James Scott Fullerton, a known enemy of the Bureau who cooperated with Andrew Johnson in trying to undermine it.

The validity of many of McFeely's charges are undeniable; yet there is a flaw in his argument. An inherent weakness of the Freedmen's Bureau was the fact that it was under the control of the War Department and that many of its officials, including Howard, were military men whose subordination to the President and Commander in Chief placed them in a vulnerable position. Surely this must account for some of their attitudes and actions. Although McFeely alludes to this problem, he does not develop it or pay much attention to it. True, the Freedmen's Bureau did not come up to the standards of some contemporaries or of DuBois and McFeely. But does it necessarily follow that the Bureau was a total failure? Surely, that must remain an open question for historians. Finally, McFeely's argument is too *ad hominem* to stand as a fair and balanced account of the work of the Bureau. No one man, not even an inadequate commissioner, could have affected or controlled the total operation of an amorphous agency in the states and localities throughout the South.

Much of what I have said about the historians discussed in this essay has to do with their assumptions and presuppositions in their practice of the historian's craft. On this subject, Gordon S. Wood, in a review of Barbara Tuchman's most recent book (*The New York Review of Books*, March 29, 1984, p. 10) makes some very pertinent and useful suggestions for the historian of Reconstruction:

> Unlike sociology or political science [Wood writes] history
> is a conservative discipline—conservative of course not in
> any contemporary political sense but in the larger sense of
> inculcating skepticism about people's ability to manipulate
> and control purposefully their own destinies. By showing that
> the best-laid plans of people usually go awry, the study of
> history tends to dampen youthful enthusiasm and to restrain

the can-do, the conquer-the-future spirit that many people have. Historical knowledge takes people off a roller coaster of illusions and disillusions; it levels off emotions and gives people a perspective on what is possible and, more often, what is not possible. By this definition Americans have had almost no historical sense whatsoever; indeed such a sense seems almost un-American.

In a recent book on the Freedmen's Bureau, *To Set the Law in Motion: The Freedmen's Bureau and the Legal Rights of Blacks, 1865-1868* (1979) Donald G. Nieman writes as though he is aware of Professor Wood's caveat. Allowing the evidence to speak for itself, and without excessive interpretation, Nieman reveals a Bureau whose members are frequently—though not always—dedicated to the fulfillment of their charge, but with the odds overwhelmingly against them. "In the face of massive resistance from white Southerners," Nieman concludes, "a temporary and poorly staffed agency which possessed only limited authority could not perform the herculean task of providing blacks with a firm basis of freedom." Avoiding unnecessary polemics, Nieman never loses sight of the tragic element in the history of the Freedmen's Bureau, or of the Reconstruction.

Although the emphasis of my book is not on the South, per se, I have included a chapter on the Memphis and New Orleans race riots because they were the most serious outbreaks of racial violence during the year and because of their bearing on the election of 1866. Because the antecedents of the New Orleans riot lay in wartime reconstruction in Louisiana and the constitutional convention of 1864, the historian is confronted with the problem of how much of this earlier history he should relate, and my treatment of it may seem rather minimal. For a more penetrating and more complete analysis the reader should consult two books, Peyton McCrary's *Abraham Lincoln and Reconstruction, the Louisiana Experiment* (1978) and Lawanda Cox's *Lincoln and Black Freedom: A Study in Presidential Leadership* (1981). McCrary and Cox agree that Lincoln was eager to have the state assure civil rights and suffrage to Negroes and that he used the power of his office in an abortive effort to achieve that end. They differ in their estimates of General Nathaniel P. Banks and the radical leader Thomas J. Durant. If their treatment of these men is only indirectly related to the 1866 riot, Cox's contrast between Lincoln and Johnson and the impact of Johnson's presidency on the Louisiana situation is most relevant. A more detailed account of the history of wartime reconstruction in Louisiana would have led me also to a more complete coverage of the Wade-Davis Bill of 1864, which I have given rather short shrift in my introductory chapter.

Neither James L. Roark's *Masters Without Slaves: Southern Planters in the Civil War and Reconstruction* (1977) nor Leon Litwack's *Been in the Storm So Long: The Aftermath of Slavery* (1979) is oriented toward politics, but they are invaluable as treatments of white and black attitudes and the conditions under which the members of each race lived during the reconstruction era in the South.

The few books mentioned here, in this supplementary historiographical essay, are only a few of those being published in a veritable outpouring of reconstruction history that has been in progress since the late 1950s and the early 1960s. It is not strange that this is so, for in these decades the nation has returned to the deferred commitment of the reconstruction experiment of a century ago, under vastly more favorable circumstances. It is a well known axiom that historians are influenced by the milieu in which they live and work, so we should expect that the history of the first notable effort to wipe out the most glaring flaw and inconsistency in the theory and practice of American democracy by bringing Negroes into a position of civil and political equality would be examined and reexamined. The ever changing interpretations and emphases show that, whatever validity there may be in a cyclical view of history, there are visible cycles in the interpretation of history.

As I have reread *1866: The Critical Year Revisited* in preparation for its reprinting, I have been moved by the generosity of many reviewers of the original volume. I express my gratitude to them. But I want to thank those who were not always generous, who gave of their time and energy to read the book carefully and to give me the advantage of their incisive criticism. Their reviews are of inestimable value to me as I continue with the difficult and exhilarating task of writing on the history of the Reconstruction era.

Edwardsville, Illinois   Patrick W. Riddleberger
May, 1984

1866

Chapter 1

Andrew Johnson Tries Restoration

THE CIVIL WAR tested the American nation in painful and profound ways, beyond the comprehension or the imagination of persons who saw it coming or experienced its beginning. But the crucible of war did not prepare it for coping successfully with the aftermath. Even the term *reconstruction* is in a sense inaccurate, for there could be no reestablishment of the nation as it had been in the antebellum days. The effect of the war on institutions, ideas, the power structure, indeed on the whole culture was unfathomable or even revolutionary, and it had come so rapidly and in such a way that many had no awareness or understanding of the nature and magnitude of the change. Of all the problems and issues facing the nation the necessity for a political reconstruction of the broken Union was only the most immediate and pressing. And it was unprecedented. After all, political leaders had had no little experience with matters such as banking and currency, tariffs, transportation, and public land policy. But despite these issues and others, including nullification and states' rights, despite differences about the meaning of the Constitution, experience could not be an adequate guide for coping with the problems emanating from eleven states lying prostrate in the South without governments and subject only to the nation's military power. It was even worse than that, because there was no substantial agreement among those who would be called on to formulate a policy as to what ought to be done.

The Republican party, whose success in 1860 had been the occasion for the secession of the southern states, though unified in its determination to preserve the Union by force, was divided as to the purposes and meaning of the war and as to the status of the former Confederate states under the Constitution. At the beginning of the war Congress and the president had agreed that its basic objective was to preserve the Union and that the war should cease when that objective had been won. But the radical faction in the party had taken the position that the war was also a crusade against slavery, thus making mandatory the destruction of the "peculiar institution" and the social and economic system that rested on it. Perhaps because the war was so prolonged and bitter, becoming before the end a war against land and people and property, the objective changed, so that even Lincoln could say in his second inaugural, "One-eighth of the whole population were colored slaves, not distributed generally over the Union, but localized in the southern part of it. These slaves constituted a peculiar and powerful interest. All knew that this interest was, somehow, the cause of the war." This merging of moderate and radical thinking about slavery was in a way a recognition of the revolutionary nature of the struggle.

The agreement that slavery had been dealt a mortal blow did not mean that there was accord on what should now be done for the freedman, on the constitutional status of the former Confederate states, or on how the executive and the legislative branches of government would use their powers in the reconstruction of the nation. Each side developed a theory as to what had happened between 1861 and 1865 on which it would build its case. Each argument was cogent enough, given its basic premises, but each was designed to give credence and support to the actions its authors were determined to take.

Lincoln's theory was that there was no such thing as constitutional secession and thus that no state had really seceded from the Union. An insurrection in the southern portion of the nation had taken place, and the president, with the sanction of Congress, had subdued it. It followed that the president would have a great deal to say about subsequent federal actions. The matter was not really that simple, of course, and Lincoln knew it. The southern states had gone through a process of separating themselves from the Union and had joined together in a southern confederacy, and in most respects the war that ensued was carried on as though it was a war between foreign nations. Clearly then these states were not functioning in the customary way in relation to the federal government, and Lincoln was forced to state in more precise terms just what was their constitutional standing. He came up with the perfect answer to serve his purposes. The southern states, he said, were merely out of their proper practical relationship to the Union, and the task of government was to reestablish that proper relationship as quickly and easily as possible. This notion of state-federal relations was still vague enough to give the president the leeway to proceed in his usual pragmatic fashion. As the executive he could, and did, make the first move and thereby tried to establish the preeminence of executive power. If Congress should move to check him, he was still left with leverage and maneuverability. He was too much the politician to engage in a fight to the finish with Congress or to state categorically that Congress had no role to play. Lincoln and the radicals were playing a game of chess, and before the end of the war Lincoln had made the first move.

The radical position concerning the status of the southern states was more precise than Lincoln's and probably more in accord with existing conditions at the end of the war. The two great radical leaders, Charles Sumner in the Senate and Thaddeus Stevens in the House of Representatives, held that the southern states had indeed seceded and formed themselves into a confederacy which was now a conquered province. The members of this confederacy had committed "state suicide" and could now be organized into territories over which Congress would have major control.

Moving from theory to practical application, Lincoln, more than a year before the end of the war, in December 1863, set forth his 10 percent plan. Essentially this plan provided a way to find a core of loyal persons in the southern states who could commence the process of reconstruction along presidential lines. He offered amnesty to all persons, except for high-ranking military and civilian officials in the Confederacy and those who had left Congress or the armed forces of the United States to join the Confederacy, who would take an oath of loyalty to the United States and would accept whatever policies might be forthcoming from Washington with respect to slavery. When the number of persons taking this oath in any state equaled one tenth of the voters of 1860, this small minority might organize a government that would be accorded presidential recognition. Except for modifications made necessary by the war, these states would be reconstituted as they had been, with the same legal codes, the same names, the same boundaries, in line with Lincoln's theory of the continuity and indivisibility of the Union.

In taking this action without the advice or consent of Congress Lincoln was stretching executive power to the limit. It is unlikely that he could have gotten by with it had the war not still been going on. However, so long as the war continued he could take all sorts of political actions that might be justified as war measures by the commander in chief to subdue the rebellion. Even so, he was careful not to give any guarantees to the South about congressional recognition of the state governments. He conceded that his plan was only a beginning, like the "egg to the fowl." But he preferred "having the fowl by hatching the egg rather than by smashing it."

In July 1864, Congress made its reply to Lincoln's reconstruction plan with the passage of the Wade-Davis Bill. Not only did this measure set forth a more stringent procedure for the return of the southern states to the Union, it also represented a reassertion of the power of Congress in the matter. It provided for a military governor in each state who would be responsible for the enrollment of all white, male citizens. When a majority of these enrollees had taken an oath of loyalty to the United States the governors were to call for constitutional conventions to prepare new state constitutions that would abolish slavery and repudiate state debts in support of the Confederacy. To participate in the election of these conventions as a voter or in its work as a delegate another oath, the "ironclad oath," was required. Under this oath the person could never have voluntarily borne arms against the United States or supported the Confederacy.

Lincoln retaliated against this radical measure with a pocket veto, but he did not terminate the matter merely by letting the bill die for want of his signature. He explained that he did not wish to be tied to a plan so specific or final as this. But he would accept the Wade-Davis Bill as an alterative plan if any southern state preferred it. Everybody knew, of course, that no southern state would take the radical plan over Lincoln's lenient one, and the radicals were understandably angered by the president's clever finesse. They now lashed out at him in the Wade-Davis Manifesto, in which they lectured him on the powers of Congress and the limitations of the executive power. Congress would not submit to impeachment by the president, said the manifesto, "and if he wishes our support, he must confine himself to his executive duties—to obey and execute, not make the laws—to suppress by arms armed rebellion, and to leave political organization to Congress."

The legislative-executive conflict over reconstruction, which would ultimately reach its climax with the impeachment of Andrew Johnson, thus began nine months before Lincoln's death. Despite the rebuke from Congress, Lincoln went ahead with his plan, and at the time of his death in April 1865 Virginia, Arkansas, Tennessee, and Louisiana had established governments under it.

The temptation to speculate about what would have happened if Lincoln had lived in almost irresistable to the historian of the Civil War and Reconstruction. It is inconceivable that Lincoln's continuation in the White House could have led to impeachment. To imagine such a thing is to misconceive the character and the political acumen of the man. Nothing in his past performance could lead to such a conclusion. Even though he found the radicals difficult and sometimes clashed with them, Lincoln never resorted to the name-calling and the invective that his successor did. He was careful to keep his communications open to the radical camp and often enjoyed cordial personal relations with it.

Charles Sumner, for example, was not an easy man to get along with; he could be arrogant and condescending, but this did not destroy the friendship of the two men. Sumner did not believe Lincoln was the best qualified man in the Republican party for the presidency and hoped that a better one would be nominated in 1864. But despite their disagreements the White House was always open to Sumner, and eventually the two men came to have respect for one another and even to enjoy each other's company.

George W. Julian, radical Indiana congressman, opposed almost everything Lincoln did with respect to the conduct of the war and the formulation of Reconstruction policy. He was bitterly disappointed with several executive actions and policies, for example, the president's border state policy in 1861, especially the dismissal of John Frémont from his command in St. Louis for attempting to free the slaves of the state of Missouri; his toleration of General McClellan long after the radicals thought he should have been dismissed; and his refusal to permit the confiscation of land owned by southern planters—which Julian believed to be an essential to the accomplishment of the aims of the war. Yet Julian could not develop the sort of hatred of Lincoln he felt for other moderates, and found Lincoln's manner and charm irresistible.

In his cabinet Lincoln managed to use the considerable talents of radicals such as Salmon P. Chase, who always believed that he was better qualified for the presidency than Lincoln and permitted the development of a movement to bring him the nomination in 1864 while he was still in the cabinet, and Edwin M. Stanton, a not altogether trustworthy prima donna whose superb administration of the War Department was vital to the war effort.

Lincoln's adroit handling of these difficult men was made possible by his supreme self-confidence which made it unnecessary for him to posture or make a display of his power so long as he actually wielded it. Without such a man at the helm the underlying divisions within the Republican party would undoubtedly have broken out into the open long before the end of the war. Having managed so well politically during the war, it is unlikely that he would not have continued to do so during Reconstruction.

To be sure, Lincoln was no revolutionary, as were some of the radicals. Rather he was in the tradition of nineteenth-century democratic liberalism, and while the differences with the radicals would have continued, it is likely that Lincoln would have moved toward the radical position as he had done during the war on the slavery issue. He was astute enough to know that, whatever his plan for the quick and easy restitution of the Union, the nation after 1865 was not and could not be the nation of 1860. He would have recognized some responsibility on the part of the federal government for the freedmen, and he might well have helped the radicals work out a more successful plan in the long run than the one they eventually resorted to under the presidency of Andrew Johnson.

One interpretation of Lincoln's plan of reconstruction holds that, in addition to his views about the nature of the Union and the meaning of the compact under the Constitution, the president was preparing a foundation for the Republican party to become a truly national party. This interpretation emphasizes Lincoln's Whig antecedents, especially his commitment to the party of Henry Clay which had been strong in the North and the South before southern Whigs had been driven by the sectional controversy of the 1840s and 1850s into the ranks of the Democrats. If this was indeed one of his purposes, he had much in common with some leading radicals. Twelve years after his death, this very effort, through the rejuvenation of Whiggery, would bring the end of military rule in the South.

It follows from all this that there would have been no breakdown in the executive-legislative relationship as occurred under Andrew Johnson, but this leads us to another conjecture. Without the breakdown and the application of radical rule there may have been no Fourteenth Amendment, that keystone of civil rights for blacks, not just during Reconstruction but in the twentieth century.

In venturing into one final speculation we are most certainly on more solid ground than in the preceding ones. If Lincoln had continued as president into the Reconstruction period, it is unlikely that there would have been a Lincoln legend. Historians would have eventually placed him among our great presidents—at or near the top. But the demands of Reconstruction would have reduced him to the proportions of a man.

The bullet that found its mark in the body of Abraham Lincoln on the evening of April 14, 1865, brought to the presidency a very different kind of leader. Andrew Johnson's theory of reconstruction, especially his belief in the predominant role of the executive, was very similar to Lincoln's, and his plan of reconstruction was in some respects a continuation of Lincoln's plan. The great difference between the two men lay in their capacity for leadership, the way in which they responded to problems and issues, indeed in their very personalities.

If background and environment are significant forces shaping the careers of political leaders, Lincoln and Johnson should have been very similar. Both were born in slave states of the upper South—Johnson in North Carolina and Lincoln in Kentucky; both were of humble origins and exemplars of the concept of the self-made man. Neither had the advantages of formal education, even by the rudimentary standards of the mid-nineteenth century. But where Lincoln's upward struggle led to self-confidence, wit, a sensitivity to the nuances of public opinion and the trend of events, Johnson's led to defensive overreaction and an obstinacy which, although courageous, could reach the point of political obtuseness.

Born into an impoverished family in North Carolina in 1808, Johnson migrated in 1826 to eastern Tennessee, where he settled in the village of Greeneville. Here he became a tailor, married, and soon entered local politics. His wife taught him to read and write. He soon discovered that he had a flare for politics as it was practiced in the region, and he began a climb up the political ladder that was remarkably unhampered by failure—from alderman to mayor, to the state legislature, to the House of Representatives in Washington, where he served for a decade, from

ANDREW JOHNSON
Reproduced from the collection of the Library of Congress

1843 to 1853. This was followed by a term as governor of Tennessee, and in 1857 he returned to Washington again, this time as United States senator. When the Civil War came Johnson was the only senator from the seceded states to remain at his post in Washington.

Johnson's party was the Democracy of Jefferson and Jackson. He was one of those who clung to the Jeffersonian tradition on into mid-century, especially Jefferson's agrarianism, and he acted on that principle in Congress in his continuing efforts for a homestead act, to assure the rural yeomanry of its place in American society. Actually Johnson had never abandoned these principles and objectives. His nomination on the ticket with Abraham Lincoln in 1864 was the nomination of the Union party, not the Whiggish Republican party, summoning support from any quarter where it might be found, including the Democracy, in an election year that was very uncertain. As a reflection of his Jacksonian heritage, Johnson detested monopoly in any form, believing that wherever monopolies gained a foothold they were "sure to be a source of danger, discord, and trouble." Had he lived into the 1880s and 1890s he would very likely have found a place in the antimonopoly movement and the Populist party.

The town of Greeneville, Tennessee, located in a region of small farms and few slaves, was not dominated by the large slaveholders whose power Johnson resented. But if he resented the inordinate power of the planter class it did not follow that he was a champion of black slaves or that he opposed the institution of slavery. On the contrary, he seems to have accepted that part of the antebellum proslavery argument linking slavery and democracy. If slaves were more widely dispersed and if every man could own a slave or two, the argument went, the "peculiar institution" might be a liberating institution for whites from hard menial labor. Johnson's objections, then, were not to the institution of slavery per se but to the way in which it served the interests of the planter class.

It is hardly strange, therefore, that this lone courageous southern senator, whose life was threatened as he took his stand against the Confederacy, should be appointed to the Joint Committee on the Conduct of the War and should serve there with such radicals as Benjamin Wade and Zachariah Chandler. If he had remained as a member of the committee the radicals might have learned more about Johnson, and as the war became more of a contest against slavery, they might well have blocked his nomination for vice-president in 1864. But early in 1862 the Union armies broke the southern defensive line in northern Tennessee and occupied much of the state, and in March Lincoln appointed him military governor of the state with the rank of brigadier general.

As military governor of Tennessee Johnson did an effective job in lining up and protecting loyal people for the Union cause, and he eventually succeeded in establishing a Union government. During the 1864 campaign he made statements about secessionists that seemed to place him clearly within the radical camp. The traitor, said Johnson, "has ceased to be a citizen, and in joining the rebellion has become a public enemy. He forfeited his right to vote with loyal men when he renounced his citizenship and sought to destroy our government. Treason must be made odious, and traitors must be punished and impoverished. Their great plantations must be seized, and divided into small farms, and sold to honest, industrious men."

During the weeks immediately following the assassination of Lincoln the radicals rallied around Johnson. He listened quietly to the radicals and appeared to share their ideas about reconstruction policy. With such a man at the helm they did not long lament the murdered president. Johnson was their man, and they were jubilant. But as the unfolding history of Reconstruction would show, never had a group or faction of politicians made such an egregious miscalculation in their assessment of one of their number. This same fraternity of radicals, so hopeful of good things to come under their new president, would only three years later impeach him.

There is no simple or final explanation as to why the radicals had gone so far astray in their judgement of the president. The nature of the conflict between executive and Congress can only be understood by examining it as it developed in 1866 and after. It is clear, however, that the radicals' views of Johnson were based on what they had seen of him during the war years. The urgency of the push for victory among those who joined together to accomplish that goal covered up a good many differences among individuals and factions. Once the victory had been won there would be a return to other issues where the disagreements would be all too apparent. Within a few years even the radical phalanx which had seemed so solid would begin to disintegrate. There was, of course, some area of agreement between Johnson and the radicals in 1865. What both sides discovered was that the area of agreement was narrower than either had believed possible at the end of the war.

When Johnson came to the presidency Congress was not in session, and would not normally be for another eight months. The radicals fully expected that he would call a special session, or at least that he would await the return of Congress before beginning with reconstruction. With good reason they expected to share with the president the formulation and implementation of a reconstruction policy. But Johnson saw the eight months lying ahead of him as a time when he, as chief executive, could carry out a policy, and have political reconstruction—

restoration he habitually called it—completed by the return of Congress in December. All that would be left to Congress would be approval of what the president had done.

Even if we accept his view of the validity of a primary executive role, it is still difficult to comprehend what went through Johnson's mind during those months. Could he have really believed that Ben Wade, Zach Chandler, Thaddeus Stevens, and Charles Sumner would stand idly by and allow him to bring the southern states back into the Union on terms that were a direct violation of their whole approach to the war and reconstruction? Whatever Johnson may have thought, this effort at presidential restoration was the first in a series of blunders which, more than anything else, was to undermine his effectiveness as president.

On May 9, Johnson gave recognition to the governments established by Lincoln in Virginia, Tennessee, Arkansas, and Louisiana. Then on May 29 he issued two proclamations that set forth his restoration policy. The first of these was an amnesty to all persons in the former Confederate states who would take a simple oath of loyalty to the Union, based not on past affiliations but on an affirmation "henceforth faithfully [to] support, protect, and defend the Constitution of the United States." Fourteen classes of persons were exempted from the privilege of taking the oath; they were almost identical with Lincoln's exempted classes. But Johnson included one class not included in the Lincoln plan, namely all persons who had voluntarily participated in the rebellion and whose estimated taxable property exceeded $20,000 in value. This last provision was designed, it seems, to exclude the planter class, which Johnson held responsible for secession, from any participation in political reconstruction. No such restriction against the planters ever became effective, however, because of yet another provision in Johnson's plan, which permitted persons not included in the amnesty to apply for special pardons. Thousands of requests came in and Johnson, perhaps enjoying his power over the aristocrats, dispensed pardons liberally.

The second proclamation of May 29 established a procedure for the restoration of North Carolina, including the appointment of William H. Holden as provisional governor, and served as a model for the remaining southern states, those that had not already begun reconstruction under the Lincoln plan. Provisional governors were charged with the responsibility of convening conventions in the several states, "composed of delegates to be chosen by that portion of the people . . . who are loyal to the United States . . . for the purpose of altering or amending the constitutions thereof" in order to restore the states to their "constitutional relation to the Federal Government." No person would be allowed to vote or to serve as a member of the convention who had not taken the president's amnesty oath. Either the convention or the legislature established under the new constitution would prescribe qualifications for voting and office holding, "a power the people of the several States composing the Federal Union have rightfully exercised from the origin of the Government to the present time." Military commanders were made subordinate to the provisional governors and were instructed to "aid and assist" them in carrying out their duties.

State debts incurred under the Confederacy were to be repudiated, ordinances of secession declared null and void, and slavery abolished. After the newly created state legislatures had ratified the Thirteenth Amendment the new governments could take control of the states, representatives and senators would take their seats in Congress, and restoration would be completed.

Such a plan was not, of course, what the radicals had in mind; but the president might have used it in such a way as to strengthen his position, win the support of the northern people, including moderate Republicans, and thus expedite the whole process. Some of the provisions of Johnson's plan were, in fact, similar to those of the Wade-Davis plan of 1864. The exclusion of the large planters might well have been a step toward redistributing political power in the South and toward the granting of land to freedmen, all very much in accord with Johnson's traditional role of champion of the yeomanry through the homestead principle. True, Johnson's states' rights view of the constitution would have made it difficult for him to provide for black suffrage under federal law, but he might well have used presidential leverage to establish the right to vote for a substantial number of freedmen. He could have begun his administration with a display of firm and evenhanded leadership. The absence of such leadership was to be crucial in the months ahead. It was what Southerners did and Johnson condoned or supported that spelled doom for presidential reconstruction.

As Andrew Johnson understood and interpreted the Constitution the states should decide such matters as qualifications for voting and holding office, and this concept was written into his reconstruction plan. When Johnson saw that the people in charge of the new state governments in the South were making no provision for black suffrage, he appealed to them to do so. But it was an appeal without conviction and without force, anything but the sort of action that would be effective with recalcitrant Southerners. "If you could extend the elective franchise to all persons of Color who can read the Constitution . . . and write their names . . . [and] who own real estate valued at not less than two hundred and fifty dollars," he wrote Governor W. L. Sharkey of Mississippi, "you would completely disarm the adversary and set an example for other states to follow. . . . And as a consequence the radicals, who are wild upon negro franchise, will be completely foiled in their attempts to keep the Southern States from renewing their relationship to the Union by not accepting their Senators and Representatives."

The message indicates that there was a vast gulf between Johnson and the radicals on the question of Negro suffrage. Johnson did not envision that suffrage for the blacks would automatically accompany their emancipation. No wonder the white South, which clung to its antebellum notions about blacks and was still determined to keep the South a white man's country, ignored the president's plea and let him take care of his own problems with the radicals. The letter to Governor Sharkey, dated August 15, 1865, is instructive in yet another way. It shows that within ninety days of his reconstruction proclamations Johnson had moved into the camp of the conservative South and that in his mind the radicals were the adversary. It also shows that nearly four months before the assembling of the Thirty-ninth Congress in December Johnson feared that members of Congress elected under his plan might be rejected.

Even more ominous than the rejection of black suffrage, from the Republican point of view, was the enactment of Black Codes in all the states of the former Confederacy, laws that, in effect, kept the freedmen in a state of semislavery. Blacks were accorded certain rights under the laws that they had not had as slaves. They could enter into legal marriages, but only with persons of their own race; they could be witnesses in court, if one party to the case was a black; they could sue and be sued and could hold property. But for the most part the codes limited freedom more than they expanded it. Freedmen were subject to fines for a number of petty offenses such as trespassing, seditious speech, and preaching without a license. Most serious were the vagrancy clauses under which unemployed blacks or those without visible means of support could be placed under the control of white employers. Orphans and children who could not be supported by their parents were also made the apprentices of whites who became their virtual masters. Some states and municipalities forbade blacks from handling or possessing firearms or using alcoholic beverages. Others limited the movement of blacks by means of curfews or laws requiring blacks to have passes from their employers to be absent from their place of employment. No doubt some Southerners were convinced that such laws were necessary to get their labor force back to work or to cope with the race problem, but the laws were an anathema to many Northerners who saw in them an ebbing away of their hard-won and costly victory. The reaction of the *Chicago Tribune* to the Black Code of Mississippi was a warning to that state that Northerners would see the state turned into a "frog pond" before permitting its codes to "disgrace one foot of soil in which the bones of our soldiers sleep and over which the flag of freedom waves."

Some insight into the attitudes of Southerners at the end of the war and the reaction in the South to defeat is essential to an understanding of the policies and practices of 1866. A number of persons traveled through the South in 1865 and reported on conditions there. Some went individually, some were sent by newspapers and journals, and others were sent by President Johnson himself. General Grant made a brief and very optimistic report which shows the continuing magnanimity of the victorious general toward the defeated enemy. Grant was satisfied that "the mass of thinking men accepted the present situation of affairs in good faith." Such difficult questions as slavery, states' rights, and the right of secession "they regard as having been settled forever by the highest tribunal—arms—that man can resort to." He concluded that "the citizens of the Southern States were anxious to return to self-government . . . as soon as possible . . . [and] in earnest in wishing to do what they think is required by the government . . . and that if such a course were pointed out they would pursue it in good faith."[1]

The report of Benjamin Truman was as much a defense of Johnson's policy and an answer to his critics as it was a report on conditions in the South. Rather than the reported disloyalty, which critics had attributed to "an ill-timed, ill-advised leniency," said Truman, the South was more loyal in April 1866 than at the end of the war, "more loyal today than yesterday, and . . . it will be more loyal tomorrow than today." A moderate government had brought hope where there was despair and order where there had been chaos.[2] Of course, such a report was manna for Johnson in making his case against the radicals.

Carl Schurz, sent by Johnson into the South to gather information, wrote the longest and most detailed report, but letters to the president and to the press indicated that it was not what Johnson wanted to believe, and he rejected it. Later it became an important document to the radical cause.

Schurz divided the southern people into four classes with respect to their attitudes and beliefs. First, there were those who "having yielded submission to the national government only when obliged to do so, have a clear perception of the irreversible change produced by the war, and honestly endeavor to accommodate themselves to the new order of things." Second, those who would make some concessions to the federal power in order "to have the States without delay restored to their position and influence in the Union and the people of the States to the absolute control of their concerns." In this class were to be found a number of professional politicians who were active in the restoration movement, "loud in their praise of the President's reconstruction policy, and clamorous for the withdrawal of the federal troops and the abolition of the Freedmen's Bureau." Third, were those who still hoped that a time would come when the southern confederacy would achieve its independence and who still "indulge in the swagger which was so customary before and during the war." These people, said Schurz, persecuted Union men and Negroes whenever they dared to do so, and insisted "clamorously upon their 'rights'." Despite the boastfulness and clamor of this class, many had taken the president's amnesty oath. The fourth class comprised the great majority who had "no definite ideas about the circumstances under which they live and about the course they have to follow; whose intellects are weak, but whose prejudices and impulses are strong, and who are apt to be carried along by those who know how to appeal to the latter."

CARL SCHURZ
Reproduced from the collection of the Library of Congress

Despite the differences represented by these classes, Schurz found a general agreement that "further resistance to the power of the national government was useless, and submission to its authority a matter of necessity." In the South he found an "utter absence of national feeling"; thus Southerners submitted to national authority because, for the moment, they could do no better and because it was "the only means by which they could rid themselves of the federal soldiers and obtain more control of their own affairs." Nor did Southerners, according to Schurz, fully accept the end of slavery as a system of bondage. True, they no longer considered the freedman to be the property of the individual master, but he was "considered the slave of society, and all independent State legislation will share the tendency to make him such." If the freedman were to be protected against "oppressive class legislation and private persecution" it would be necessary to endow him with a measure of political power. Schurz therefore called for a determined policy on the part of the national government, which should exercise "lenity as to persons such as is demanded by the humane and enlightened spirit of our times, and vigor and firmness in carrying out the principles, such as is demanded by the national sense of justice and the exigencies of our situation."[3]

The attitudes of Southerners reported by Schurz were those that might have been expected. A proud people who in the defense of their anachronistic institution had increasingly isolated themselves would, of course, react bitterly to defeat, would justify the righteousness of their cause, and would begin to enshrine their heroes. In the humiliation of defeat Southerners would naturally try to minimize the effects of war and reestablish the status quo ante bellum as quickly and painlessly as possible. It would be expecting too much of them to change overnight the premises of race relations and class division that had become the foundation of their culture. Less explicable, however, is the way in which Andrew Johnson played into the hands of these recalcitrant elements described by Schurz and indeed encouraged them to proceed along lines that were in defiance of his own restoration plan.

In addition to the Black Codes enacted in the southern states, some states refused to repudiate the Confederate debt. Objections were also raised to ratification of the Thirteenth Amendment and at least one state refused such action. Even more serious was the election of former Confederate political and military officials to public offices, men who did not qualify even under the provisions of the Johnson plan. Among those elected were Alexander H. Stephens, former Confederate vice-president, to the United States Senate from Georgia and Benjamin G. Humphries, an unpardoned brigadier general, to the governorship of

Mississippi. The case of Humphries is instructive: He was elected on October 2, 1865; in his inaugural address a short time later he promised an administration based on white supremacy that would encourage the passage of laws to keep blacks in their place. A week later Johnson pardoned him and thus not only legalized his election but sanctioned his program as well. Soon the president entered upon a policy of granting pardons wholesale to other questionable southern leaders, a policy that was to continue through the period of presidential reconstruction to the point where Johnson had granted 13,500 pardons.

In his conduct of affairs in 1865 Johnson not only permitted the South to make a shambles of his program; he set in motion events that would assure his failure. Any president during the Reconstruction period would have needed all the support he could get, from the public, from state officials, and from Congress, and Johnson was destroying the very base of that support. In placing his reliance almost solely on southern conservatives, he took a path that would make his administration untenable. Yet despite this unexpected and questionable restoration policy, Johnson enjoyed for some months a substantial goodwill from the people of the North and its political leaders. Almost everybody, it seemed, desired the success of the president and his policies. Not even all the radicals turned away from him immediately. Some northern Democrats may have felt that Johnson had deserted his party in running on the ticket with Lincoln, but it was to their advantage to reestablish the Union as quickly as possible; so they praised him and invited him back into their party. But the most important political faction standing with the president were the moderate Republicans. Led by such men as William Pitt Fessenden and Lyman Trumbull in the Senate and James G. Blaine, Elihu Washburne, and James A. Garfield in the House of Representatives, these Republicans were willing to go a long way with Johnson so long as he protected the freedmen from oppression from their former masters and preserved the northern victory by maintaining the supremacy of persons of unquestioned loyalty in the southern states. If Johnson could guarantee that the victory would not be thrown away through a frivolous reconstruction policy the moderates would agree to the return of the southern states to the Union and of their senators and representatives to Congress. But in late 1865 and early 1866 the moderates were becoming disenchanted with presidential reconstruction. Soon many of them would move toward the radicals and some into their ranks.

We can see in retrospect that by the end of 1865 the conduct of affairs by the Johnson administration contained all the elements of a classic failure. The nation was not united either politically or spiritually; slaves had been made legally free but were not free from a system of bondage; and the government was about to enter into the most critical conflict between the executive and legislative branches in the nation's history. And perhaps most tragic of all was the president's abandonment of his own cherished principles and objectives—his championship of the yeomanry and the rearrangement of power in the South by redistribution of land—principles and convictions that had led him to defy his state and had thus brought him to the presidency.

The reasons for this metamorphosis of Andrew Johnson have not yet been found. A part of the explanation undoubtedly lies in Johnson's stubborn courage combined with his fundamentalist states' rights doctrine with respect to the Constitution. As Rembert W. Patrick has pointed out, "For strict construction of the Constitution, preservation of the Union, state rights, and local self-rule, [Johnson] was willing to face personal danger and bear insults; but he would not yield to compromise on principles."[4] It would follow from this interpretation that Johnson was caught between two sets of criteria and that his constitutional principles finally prevailed over his democratic Jeffersonian predilections.

Another historian of Reconstruction, Kenneth M. Stampp, presents a more complex explanation, stressing the enigmatic and psychic in Johnson's character. Much of the answer, says Stampp, is to be found in a weakness in Johnson that is common among men of his background and experience.

> The memory of his early poverty, the scars he bore from his political battles, the snubs he had received from the haughty planter aristocracy, all had left him with a raw ego and a craving for recognition and respect. Like the southern common people for whom he spoke, Johnson's resentment of the planter class was . . . combined with a certain grudging admiration. If his vanity demanded that he gain recognition and respect, then nothing could satisfy him more than forcing this class to seek mercy at his hands. By denying amnesty to all Confederate leaders and large property-holders and requiring them to apply to him for special pardons, this is precisely what he obliged them to do. Those who had scorned him were now flattering him, appealing to his generosity, begging for the franchise and the protection of their property—but influencing policy as well. [For Johnson this was] an intoxicating experience, and he became a little giddy as delegation after delegation of contrite Southerners assured him that the fate of the South was in his hands. [Perceiving his weakness, southern

planters] exploited his vanity and defeated him with remarkable ease.[5]

Revisionist historians have been very harsh in their criticism of Andrew Johnson—and not without some reason. They have shown us that he was no tragic hero who sacrificed himself for the nation in challenging the satanic power of the radicals, but that he was a literal-minded, shortsighted, egotistical blunderer who probably did more harm to himself than others did. With considerable justification they have condemned him, especially for his failure to use executive power in the cause of civil rights for blacks. However, the frustrations, the mistakes, and the failures of the Reconstruction era through 1866 cannot be related accurately simply by making a bête noire of Andrew Johnson. Men of all factions and parties shared in the responsibility for neglect of civil rights and the failure to emancipate the slaves in the fullest sense of the word. These politicians were not necessarily vicious or malicious—although a few of them might have been—but they were human, and thus not always rational. Men of all factions had their prejudices, their axes to grind, and their demanding constituencies to serve. The story of 1866 is the story of the struggle of men to do more than could properly be expected of them.

Chapter 2

The Assembling

IN DECEMBER 1865, Charles Sumner published an article in the *Atlantic Monthly* that no other senator could have written. It dealt with the fable of Scylla and Charybdis—the rock and the whirlpool—between which Ulysses, by "prudence and the counsels of Circe," had maneuvered his tortuous course back to Ithaca. Sumner found the theme recurring in *The Aeneid, Paradise Lost, The Merchant of Venice*, and a poetic history of Alexander the Great.

In the last few pages of the article Sumner revealed his purposes in writing it. "I should have little heart for any literary diversion," he said, "if I did not hope to make it contribute to those just principles which are essential to the well-being, if not the safety of the Republic." To him, the lesson for America emerging from the Civil War was clear: "You are now escaping from the whirlpool of war, which has threatened to absorb and engulf the Republic. Do not rush upon the opposite terror, where another shipwreck of another kind awaits you, while Sirens tempt with their 'song of death.' . . . Alas! the Scylla on which our Republic is now driving is that old rock of *concession and compromise* which from the beginning of our history has been a constant peril."

In more specific terms, Sumner warned of the dangers of permitting the quick return of the old "Rebel Oligarchy with a new lease of immense power, including the control over local citizens, whose fidelity to the Republic had been without question." If there was to be a policy of pardoning "belligerent traitors," let it come only after the assurance of equal civil and political rights, in accord with the principles of the Declaration of Independence. The foremost duty of the moment was to pay the national debt, a twofold debt, "first to the . . . freedmen; and, secondly to the national creditor."[1]

The *Atlantic* article was not the first public warning by Sumner as to President Johnson's restoration policy. Less than two months earlier he had presided over the Massachusetts state Republican convention at

Worcester, where he had spoken out against Johnson's policies, while taking care not to attack the president personally. Johnson, he said, claimed that the former Confederate states were now peaceful. But Sumner's correspondence from the South proved him wrong, that the "rebel spirit still prevails." Reconstruction could not properly be left to the president, for Congress had "plenary power over the whole subject." If the president had the power to require the rebel states to ratify the Thirteenth Amendment and to repudiate the Confederate debt, why did he not have the power to compel Negro suffrage? In any case, Congress would certainly give the vote to blacks under the constitutional guarantee of a republican form of government to all the states. Sumner then warned holders of government bonds that "not a single ex-Rebel . . . would vote to pay the interest on the national debt," a point he dramatized by holding up a Treasury note which, he said, would be worthless under the Johnson plan. It was clear that, for Sumner, the

CHARLES SUMNER
Reproduced from the collection of the Library of Congress

antislavery crusade was far from over. "This is not the first time . . . I have battled with the barbarism of slavery," he declared. "I battle still, as the bloody monster retreats to its citadel; and, God willing, I mean to hold on, if it takes what remains of my life."[2]

Some weeks before the appointed day for the convening of the Thirty-ninth Congress in early December, then, Sumner had all but given up on the president and had placed his hope for saving the nation in Congress. One might wonder why Sumner would seek an appointment with Johnson, or why the president would grant it. Apparently each was seeking a tactical advantage. If a presidential-congressional conflict was inevitable, each would try to maneuver the other into firing the first shot. They met at the White House on Saturday evening, December 2, the day of Sumner's return to Washington. Johnson gave the senator a cool reception, and the atmosphere was tense throughout the conversation of two and a half hours. Sumner made the first thrust, accusing the president of throwing away the hard-won Union victory and charging that rebels in Alabama and Georgia were mistreating the freedmen. Johnson maneuvered Sumner into admitting that even in Massachusetts people sometimes knocked each other down, and he conceded that on that ground the state ought not to be excluded from the Union. On taking his leave, Sumner picked up his top hat which he had laid on the floor near Johnson only to discover that the president had used it for a spittoon.[3]

Just a few days before Sumner's appearance at Worcester Thaddeus Stevens, in a speech at Lancaster, Pennsylvania, made his first public challenge to Johnson's restoration policy. The program he set forth was more extreme and more specific than the senator's proposals. At the time, the speech attracted little attention. Even some of Stevens's friends dismissed it as the fantasy of a quixotic old man and not to be taken seriously as reconstruction policy. The *Lancaster Intelligencer* called it "a tissue of sophistical fallacies." Only the *New York Tribune* printed the whole speech at the time, but after Congress assembled in December and Stevens's power became more evident other editors did recall the speech and commented on it.

The victory of the Union armies over the Confederate states, said Stevens, had brought their territory into the possession of the United States, and it was now "necessary to establish Governments therein" which would be "republican in form and principles. . . . Every vestige of human bondage" should be excluded and rendered "forever impossible in this nation." Stevens hoped that "no provision of the Constitution [would] be infringed, and no principle of the law of nations disregarded."[4] Care should be taken that "the authorities of the Union [should] indulge in no acts of usurpation which may tend to impair the stability and permanency of the nation." Within the broad, and not altogether clear, limits thus established lay the power of the government to act. Now it was "the duty of the Government to inflict condign punishment on the rebel belligerents, and so weaken their hands that they can never again endanger the Union." Their municipal institutions must be so reformed as to "make them republican in spirit as well as in name."

"The property of the chief rebels," Stevens insisted, "should be seized and appropriated to the payment of the national debt, caused by the unjust and wicked war which they instigated." There were two opposing principles, he said: *"First*—to treat those states as never having been out of the Union. . . . *Second*—to accept the position in which they placed themselves as severed from the Union, an independent government *de facto*, and an alien enemy to be dealt with according to the laws of war." A reformation in the southern states "must be effected; the foundation of their institutions, . . . political, municipal, and social, *must* be broken up and *relaid*, or all our blood and treasure have been spent in vain." Only by adhering to the second theoretical position, "by treating them as a conquered people" could the reformation be accomplished.

In contrast to Sumner, Stevens was willing to postpone Negro suffrage, which would come in due time. The essence of Stevens's plan was confiscation and redistribution of land:

> There are some 6,000,000 of freedmen in the South. The number of acres of land is 465,000,000. Of this those who own above 200 acres each, number about 70,000 persons, holding in the aggregate (together with the States) about 394,000,000 acres, leaving for all the others below 200 each, about 71,000,000 of acres. By thus forfeiting the estates of the leading Rebels, the Government would have 394,000,000 of acres beside their town property, and yet nine-tenths of the people would remain untouched. Divide this land into convenient farms. Give, if you please, forty acres to each adult male freedman. Suppose there are 1,000,000 of them. That would require 40,000,000 of acres, which deducted from 394,000,000 leaves 354,000,000 of acres for sale. Divide it into suitable farms and sell it to the highest bidders. I think it, including town property, would average at least $10 per acre. That would produce $3,540,000,000.
>
> Let that be applied as follows, to wit: 1. Invest $300,000,000 in six per cent government bonds, and add the interest semi-

annually to the pensions of those who have become entitled by this villainous war. 2. Appropriate $200,000,000 to pay the damage done to loyal men, North and South, by the Rebellion. 3. Pay the residue, being $3,040,000,000 toward the payment of the National Debt. . . .

If the South is ever to be made a safe Republic, let her lands be cultivated by the toil of the owners, or the free labor of intelligent citizens. This must be done even though it drive her nobility into exile.

The colonization of emancipated slaves, which Lincoln had tried with miserable results, was for Stevens no solution at all. It would be "far easier and more beneficial to exile 70,000 proud, bloated, and defiant Rebels than to expropriate 4,000,000 of laborers, native to the soil and loyal to the Government."

Stevens's message was directed to an audience far larger than the one gathered in the courthouse square in Lancaster. And his concluding remarks left no doubt that he was looking three months ahead, to the Thirty-ninth Congress: "Is this great conquest to be in vain? That will depend upon . . . the next Congress. To Congress alone belongs the power of Reconstruction, of giving law to the vanquished. . . . Under 'Restoration' every Rebel State will send Rebels to Congress, and they, with their allies in the North, will control Congress, and will occupy the White House."[5]

If Sumner and Stevens, and the radicals for whom they spoke, could have had their way in the Thirty-ninth Congress, they would undoubtedly have wrested control of the South from Johnson, placed it in the hands of Congress, and gone on to replace the presidential restoration policy with a reconstruction even more far-reaching than the one they adopted in 1867. But the radicals were not in control of their party, either in 1865 or in 1867. Their influence was indeed great, and they gave direction to reconstruction that led to the acts of 1867. But the demands of Sumner and Stevens, especially the latter, were never realized.

In December 1865, the radicals were one of three Republican factions in Congress. More numerous and equally as influential were the moderates, led by such men as William Pitt Fessenden, Lyman Trumbull, and John Sherman in the Senate and John Bingham, James A. Garfield, and Rutherford B. Hayes in the House. On some important points the moderates were in substantial agreement with the radicals. They agreed that Congress must have an important, if not an exclusive, part in reconstruction. Freedmen and loyal whites in the South must be protected against physical molestation and in their civil rights by federal legislation, by the continued presence of the military, and if necessary by another constitutional amendment. It was by no means certain that the Thirteenth Amendment, whose final ratification was announced in mid-December, would be enough to guarantee freedom to the former slaves. It would be well, also, for the South and its leaders to show some remorse about the war, to show some awareness of who had been the victor and who the vanquished, to demonstrate a modicum of penitence and humility. It was this sense of contrition on the part of the South that seemed to be so totally missing, so that well before the end of 1865 Northerners of the moderate persuasion began to wonder whether the Southerners merited the concern and leniency Johnson was according them. But the moderates were unalterably opposed to the confiscation policy recommended by Stevens, and they were very dubious of Sumner's Negro suffrage.

An important point of difference between moderates and radicals was that the former had not given up on Andrew Johnson. Granted, he had made some mistakes and had gone further than the president should go without consulting Congress. But now that Congress was back in session again there was no reason why executive and legislative could not work together toward an orderly restoration of the Union. After all, Johnson was not only the president, he was the leader of their party, the great Union party whose victory in 1864 had set it on the road to continued national political dominance and had raised their hopes that it would be transformed from the sectional party of the prewar and the war years to a truly national one. Understandably, such men were less concerned than either the president or the radicals with abstract arguments about the status of the former Confederate states. Taking a cue from their marytred leader they would, if possible, avoid entanglement in such "pernicious abstractions" and get on with the practical work of restoration.

To a considerable extent, the role and impact of the moderates would depend on Andrew Johnson. If he could maintain some flexibility in his program and show a little adroitness in playing the game of politics with Congress, he might drive a wedge between the radical and moderate factions. Doing this, he might sacrifice a little of what he wanted and deprive the radicals of most, if not all, of what they wanted. This is why 1866 was indeed a critical year. Probably at no other time has the conduct of politics at the highest level had so much to do with vital decisions affecting future generations.

In the third faction in the Thirty-ninth Congress were the followers of Johnson, the conservatives. They were on the other extreme of the

Republican party spectrum from the radicals, for whom they had almost unbounded contempt. Their leader was Senator James R. Doolittle of Wisconsin, joined by Edgar Cowan of Pennsylvania and James Dixon of Connecticut and in the House of Representatives by Henry J. Raymond of New York. In their way they were more dogmatic than the most extreme radicals. For them Andrew Johnson was the savior of the nation and his doctrine that the purpose of the Constitution was to preserve states' rights—short of secession of course—was the only true doctrine. Social and political changes in the wake of costly and bloodly civil war had left their minds almost untouched. Doolittle went so far as to say that if border slave states, like Kentucky and Delaware, did not ratify the Thirteenth Amendment they still had the right to maintain the institution of slavery.[6] Their loyalties were to Andrew Johnson and his program of restoration rather than to the Republican or Union party. Ideologically they were closer to the Democrats, with whom they were already collaborating whenever it appeared to be to their advantage to do so.

This Johnson faction in Congress was virtually powerless, but the coterie around the president included cabinet members and other men of affairs who gave him unstinting support. There was no more ardent defender of Johnson or his policies than Secretary of the Navy Gideon Welles, a caustic critic of the radicals whom he saw as wild revolutionaries bent on destroying the country. Secretary of the Treasury Hugh McCulloch was less caustic than Welles, but he too could be counted on by the president. Secretary of State William Seward, an experienced and skillful political leader, might have given much needed guidance if it had been requested or if he had been more forceful. But he was no longer young, had lost his influence in the party counsels of New York, and had never fully recovered from the wounds he received at the time of Lincoln's assassination. Outside the cabinet there were Gen. William T. Sherman; former Attorney General Edward Bates; Charles Francis Adams, Minister to Great Britain; and former Senator Orville H. Browning of Illinois, soon to be appointed to the cabinet.

Finally, there were the Democrats, weaker and more disorganized than they had ever been, with the halcyon days of Jefferson and Jackson as only fond memories. Never had a party been so discredited as were the Democrats by secession and civil war, by the labels of copperheadism and treason that were pinned on them. They held less than one-third of the seats in Congress, and the elections of 1865 were a disaster for them in the states. But presidential restoration was an unexpected fillip for them; if they could attract Andrew Johnson back to his ancient party and help him succeed in returning southern representation to Congress, they might look to the future with some hope. States' rights, restoration, and Negro suffrage (which they would, of course, oppose) were the issues that might bring a resurgence in their party fortunes.

The most immediate problem confronting the Thirty-ninth Congress when it convened on December 4, 1865, was whether or not to accord recognition to representatives from the former Confederate states. It was resolved when Edward McPherson, clerk of the House of Representatives, simply did not list them on the rolls or call their names. Horace Maynard of Tennessee, bearing a certificate of election from Governor "Parson" Brownlow, protested the omission of his name. Three times he demanded recognition by the clerk only to be refused each time. McPherson's decision was neither difficult nor precipitous. Nor did it come out of a radical plot to make war on the president. It was a decision agreed to by a large Republican majority, including some conservatives, and the matter had been debated in the northern press for at least five months before Congress assembled. It was really the only decision open to McPherson. Had he taken it upon himself to place the Southerners' names on the rolls he would have been usurping the power of Congress to pass on the qualifications of its own members. Such an action, especially at such a time, would have been unthinkable. As the pro-Johnson *New York Herald* had pointed out, the clerk of the House had a "golden opportunity for a brilliant coup d'état in support of President Johnson," and by taking advantage of it could "play a leading role in one of the most important revolutions of the nineteenth century." According to one of the best authorities on the subject, "He [McPherson] would have been pronouncing a judgment . . . more explicit than any President Johnson himself had announced."[7] Even without the Southerners there was a quorum, and the House proceeded to organize itself and to make Schuyler Colfax its Speaker.

Five days before Congress met, Thaddeus Stevens and the president had met to discuss reconstruction policy. Stevens warned him that unless there was a drastic change in his policies he could expect little support from the Union party in Congress. Two days later, on Friday, December 1, a caucus of radicals met to discuss their line of action on Reconstruction. The establishment of a joint congressional committee to deal with the question was suggested and was adopted unanimously the next day by the Republican party caucus. Then, on the first day of the session, after the organization of the House and the election of the Speaker, Stevens introduced a resolution calling for the establishment of a Joint Committee of Fifteen, with nine members from the House and six from the Senate who shall inquire into the condition of the states which formed the so-called Confederate States of America, and report whether they, or any of them are entitled to be represented in either House of Congress, with leave to report at any time, by bill or otherwise; and until such report shall have been made, and finally acted on by Congress, no member shall be received into either House from any of the so-called Confederate States: and all papers relating to the representation of said states shall be referred to the said committee without debate.[8]

Congressman James Brooks of New York tried to postpone action on the resolution until after the president's message, which was to be sent to Congress the next day, but he was overridden and the House went on to adopt it by a vote of 133 to 36. On December 12 the Senate passed a resolution accepting the establishment of the committee, but it would not be bound, as was the House, to exclude members from the former Confederate states until the committee had reported.[9] Before the end of December the committee had been appointed, and in early January it began its deliberations under the leadership of Senator Fessenden and Congressman Stevens. It made its most notable contribution through its authorship of the Fourteenth Amendment. Before entering into a more detailed examination of the committee's operations, it is necessary to consider other developments that had a bearing on them.

With the assembling of Congress Andrew Johnson's plan of presidential restoration had been in operation for six months. In his first annual message, which Congress heard on December 5, he presented his first public explanation and the theoretical justification of it. The message, in its organization and style an admirable document, was written by George Bancroft, the old Jacksonian Democrat and historian. In explaining his actions, Johnson said that he had "found the States suffering from the effects of a civil war" and that "resistance to the General Government appeared to have exhausted itself"; forts and arsenals had been recovered and the United States Army was in occupation of every state that had attempted to secede. But military governments over an indefinite period, said Johnson, "would have offered no security for the early suppression of discontent, would have divided the people into the vanquisher and the vanquished, and would have envenomed hatred rather than have restored affection. They would have occasioned an incalculable and exhausting expense." Peaceful emigration to and from the South, one of the best means for the restoration of harmony, would have been prevented. Under continued military rule only those who "would have been dependent on the General Government or . . . who expected profit from the miseries of their erring fellow-citizens" would have been attracted to the South. "The powers of patronage and rule" exercised by the president under these circumstances "I could never, unless on occasion of great emergency, consent to exercise."

"The States attempting to secede," he continued, had "placed themselves in a condition where their vitality was impaired, but not extinguished; their functions suspended, but not destroyed." On this principle he had acted in order "to restore the rightful energy of the General Government and of the States." His whole plan of provisional governors, conventions, and elections of local legislatures as well as senators and representatives to Congress had been directed to that end. United States courts had been reopened, customs houses reestablished, post offices made functional, and the blockade removed. Such a "restoration" was a blessing to the states and a "sure promise of harmony and renewed attachment to the Union."

To this point the president had made a good case that his actions had been wise ones on the part of an executive confronted with a crisis in which there were no clear precedents. When he turned to his exercise of the pardon he was on much shakier ground. His language was less precise, and he was less sure of himself. His policy, he conceded, involved some risk, for to succeed it needed the acquiescence of the southern states. The very purpose in resorting to that "one other power of the General Government" was to diminish and if possible to remove all danger. It was in the exercise of his power to pardon, which his critics thought was excessive, that he was most vulnerable. His explanation can hardly have been reassuring to the skeptics. "As no State can throw a defense over the crime of treason," he said, "the power of pardon is *exclusively vested in the executive government of the United States.*"[10]

In order further to "restore the Constitutional relations" of the former Confederate states, he had invited them "to participate in the high office of amending the Constitution." This action would "efface the sad memory of the past" and be "a pledge of perpetual loyalty and peace." Once the Thirteenth Amendment was adopted, "it would remain for the States whose powers had been so long in abeyance to resume their places in the two branches of the National Legislature, and thereby complete the work of restoration. Here it is for you, fellow-citizens of the Senate, and for you, fellow-citizens of the House of Representatives, to judge, each for yourselves, of the elections, returns, and qualifications of your own members." The statement bears careful reading, lest it imply an admission on the part of the president that Congress had the power to reject these persons for any reason other than irregular election procedures or improper personal credentials. In no sense was it an admission that Congress could exclude the representatives in accordance with a congressional policy of reconstruction that differed essentially from Johnson's.

At the end of May 1865, when he had announced his plan and appointed his first provisional governor, Johnson had said in a personal conversation, "there's no such thing as reconstruction. These States have not gone out of the Union. Therefore reconstruction is unnecessary."[11] There is little in this first message or in subsequent ones to indicate that he ever deviated from this belief. His fixed idea was that the solution was to be found in the Constitution, and to him the Constitution meant states' rights. The opening passages of the address are a paean to the founding fathers and the excellence of their work in framing the Constitution, a work so enduring that the framers themselves could not have fully comprehended it: "The hand of Divine Providence was never more plainly visible in the affairs of men than in the framing and adopting of that instrument."

Johnson's assertion of the states' rights theory in the preservation and restoration of the Union posed a dilemma, for it was this theory that Confederate leaders had used in justifying secession. Just what did states' rights mean if they did not mean that at some point a state could defy the Union? How could states' rights square with the concept of a perpetual Union? Just how far could a state go in applying the theory? The answer that Johnson and the other advocates of "restoration" came up with was in effect a denial that the theory could ever be carried to its logical conclusion. Although the maintenance of the Union was based on "the support of the State governments and all their rights," said Johnson, it did not follow that any state "could renounce its place in the Union" or nullify its laws. States' rights was not state sovereignty. But the character of the country, "its capacity for comprehending within its jurisdiction a vast continental empire is due to the system of States. The perpetuity of the Constitution brings with it the perpetuity of the States; their mutual relation makes us what we are, and in our political system this connection is indissoluble. The whole cannot exist without the parts, nor the parts without the whole. . . . The destruction of one is the destruction of the other; the preservation of the one is the preservation of the other." These were the principles on which he "had sought to solve the momentous questions and overcome the appalling difficulties that met [him] at the . . . commencement of [his] Administration."[12]

Finally Johnson turned to the freedmen. Guided by the Constitution and long established custom, he had rejected the granting of Negro suffrage by executive proclamation. It had long since become "the uniform usage for each State to enlarge the body of its electors according to its own judgment." Neither president nor Congress during the war had in any way sanctioned a departure from this principle.

> Moreover, a concession of the elective franchise to the freedmen by act of the President of the United States must have been extended to all colored men, wherever found, and so must have established a change of suffrage in the Northern, Middle, and Western States, not less than in the Southern and Southwestern. Such an act would have created a new class of voters, and would have been an assumption of power by the President which nothing in the Constitution or laws of the United States would have warranted.[13]

Either by conscious design or because he was so fundamentally in agreement with racist views in the North as well as in the South, this was a strong appeal for sympathy and support. It was a rare northern senator or congressman indeed who could have ignored with impunity the pervading racism among his constituents and the widespread opposition to Negro suffrage.

If the federal government was powerless to extend the elective franchise to blacks, Johnson continued, "good faith" required "the security of the freedmen in their liberty and their property, their right to labor, and their right to claim the just return of their labor." But again, the federal government was virtually absolved of responsibility, since the "public interest [would] be best promoted if the several States [would] provide adequate protection and remedies for the freedmen." Slavery, according to Johnson, was essentially a monopoly of labor and had thus blocked the development of free industry in the South. "With the destruction of the monopoly free labor will hasten from all parts of the civilized world to assist in developing various and immeasurable resources which have hitherto lain dormant." If the blacks would not rise to a position of freedom and dignity in this new Eden of individual competition and free enterprise, "let us be careful that the failure shall not be attributable to any denial of justice."[14]

For the freedmen, as well as for the radicals, this credo of social and economic liberalism applied to reconstruction could have been only a message of despair. They were left with no other alternative than to oppose it. Wendell Phillips's *National Anti-Slavery Standard* found Johnson's attitude toward the freedmen "utterly repulsive." A less radical paper, the *Brooklyn Daily American*, raised some incisive questions about the president's message:

If the nation is bound to defend the rights of the blacks, why has not the President incorporated such a defense in the conditions of readmission? If justice only is the thing which can save us from suffering in the solution of the negro problem, why has the President quietly ignored justice just at the point where it becomes most absolutely essential that it should be observed? Just when the President proposes to establish each State securely and impregnably behind the banners of resumed Statehood, why does he leave the negro helpless?[15]

For the most part, however, reaction to the message was favorable. James A. Garfield wrote to a friend that the message was much better than expected, and that there was reason to be hopeful now that Congress would be able to work with the president despite some "bristling" on the part of foolish men who seemed "anxious to make a

WENDELL PHILLIPS
Reproduced from the collection of the Library of Congress

rupture" with him.[16] Senator Shelby M. Cullom remembered the message as an "admirable state document, one of the finest from a literary and probably from every other standpoint that ever came from an Executive to Congress. . . . Aside from the worst radicals, the message pleased every one, the country at large and the majority in Congress; and there was a general disposition to give the President a reasonably free hand in working out his plan of reconstruction."[17] Republican papers generally said that the address augured well for accord between Johnson and Congress, while the Democratic press also expressed encouragement because the address portended a conflict between them.

As these diverse reactions suggest, there were ambiguities in the message, giving rise to the question of whether Johnson was intentionally abstruse in order to place himself in a more favorable political position. Lawanda and John Cox have examined the question thoroughly and have concluded that this is exactly what he was doing. His explanations of his actions, they say, rested on a vague pragmatism that precluded the development of a logical theory. Finding in the message an implied theory that did not square with the facts, their case is strengthened by a comparison of the message with a draft prepared by Secretary of State William Seward which Johnson could have used if he had wished to be unequivocal.[18]

Although this interpretation has merit, it does not seem to conform with Johnson's personality or his intellectual habits. It casts Johnson too much in the mold of Lincoln who really meant it when he referred to the theoretical status of the former Confederate states as a "pernicious abstraction" which could only hinder the search for a practical solution to the problems of reconstruction through political compromise and experimentation. Johnson, on the other hand, a states' righter to the core, did not present his plan of restoration as an experiment, as a starting point for continuing discussion and ultimate compromise. He was deadly serious, and he would not budge.[19] A progressive understanding of this reality, more than anything else, would lead to the ultimate break between the president and Congress. Much has been made by historians of the Civil War and Reconstruction of the misunderstanding of Johnson by the radicals, their dismaying discovery that he was not one of them. Equally as important was the miscalculation of Johnson by the moderates, and even by some conservatives. The disenchantment emerged in direct ratio to the president's intractability and the fading hope of a reconstruction settlement through the combined efforts of the executive and the legislative.

It would have been strange indeed if Johnson's message had not evoked an answer. It came from Thaddeus Stevens, now indisputably the radical leader in the House, if not in Congress, in a speech on December 18, the day of the announcement of the ratification of the Thirteenth Amendment. Stevens offered a number of resolutions to refer each part of the president's message to an appropriate House committee. The last one proposed that "so much of the President's message . . . as relates to the subject of reconstruction be referred to the joint committee on reconstruction." Stevens's explanation of this resolution provided the occasion for the speech, which turned out to be a challenge to the president's whole theoretical argument. It will be recalled how, in his Lancaster speech, Stevens had outlined his program of confiscation of land in the South and the banishment of the top ranks of the planter class. Now he examined the nature of the Civil War as it related to political and constitutional theory. Although showing due deference to the Constitution, Stevens's argument led him on beyond it to an invocation of the law of nations. His analysis was his justification for the primacy of Congress and the actions it would be obliged to take in the reconstruction of the nation. Once the president and Stevens had both spoken the limits were established within which the prolonged debate on reconstruction would develop. Whatever settlement might be made, it would lie within those boundaries.

Nobody could pretend, Stevens asserted, that the "late rebel States" could claim their old rights under the Constitution. They had "torn the constitutional States into atoms, and built on their foundation fabrics of a totally different character. Dead men cannot raise themselves. Dead States cannot restore their own existence." In whom, then, did the Constitution place the power to restore them? To Stevens's mind there was no difficulty in finding an answer. It lay in a combination of Article IV, giving Congress the power to admit new states into the Union, and the "law of nations." Under this concept "the late war between two acknowledged belligerents severed their original compacts, and broke all the ties that bound them together." But even if those states had never been out of the Union, he continued, "as some dreaming theorists imagine," then that section of Article IV which said, "The United States shall guarantee to every State . . . a republican form of government," would grant the power to Congress in concurrence with the executive.

The theory that the rebel states, which for four years were unrepresented in Congress while they carried on a war with the Union, were all the while in it was "a good deal less ingenious and respectable than the metaphysics of Berkeley, which proved that neither the world nor any human being was in existence." Such a notion, said Stevens, was not simply ridiculous but "deeply injurious to the stability of the nation." To strengthen his case Stevens cited the South Carolina resolution of 1861 which said, "That the separation of South Carolina from the Federal Union is final, and she has no further interest in the Constitution of the United States; and that the only appropriate negotiations between her and the Federal Government are as to the mutual relations of foreign States." He reminded his fellow congressmen that similar resolutions had been passed by other rebel states and similar proclamations made by political and military leaders of the Confederacy.

The validity of the law of nations to the American Civil War, Stevens continued, was also decreed by the United States Supreme Court in the *Prize Cases* of 1863. This decision involved the legality of President Lincoln's blockade of April 1861, and the related question of whether this act was the official beginning of the war. It also bore directly on the question of the belligerency of the Confederate States. Stevens's citation came from the opinion of Justice Grier who spoke for the majority of the Court in a divided decision:

> In organizing this rebellion, they have acted as States claiming to be sovereign over all persons and property within their respective limits, and asserting a right to absolve their citizens from their allegience to the Federal Government. Several of these States have combined to form a new confederacy, claiming to be acknowledged by the world as a sovereign State. Their right to do so is now being decided by wager of battle. The ports and territory of each of these States are held in hostility to the General Government. It is no loose, unorganized insurrection, having no defined boundary or possession. It has a boundary marked by lines of bayonets, and which can be crossed only by force. South of this line is enemies' territory, because it is claimed and held in possession by an organized hostile and belligerent power.

Going beyond the Supreme Court, Stevens turned to an even more substantial authority whose treatise he had read at least as early as 1861, Emmerich de Vattel, an eighteenth-century Swiss political theorist whose *Le Droit des gens, ou principes de la loi naturelle, appliqués à la conduite et aux affaires des nations et des souverains* was in the tradition of Grotius, but in some respects went beyond him. Vattel's comments on the nature of civil war were apposite to Stevens's argument, and it was from this part of the work that Stevens quoted:

> A civil war breaks the bands of society and government, or at least suspends their force and effect; it produces in the nation two independent parties, who consider each other as enemies, and

acknowledge no common judge. These two parties must therefore be considered as thenceforward constituting, at least for a time, two separate bodies; two distinct societies. They stand, therefore, in precisely the same predicament as two nations who engage in a contest, and being unable to come to an agreement, have recourse to arms. . . . And when a nation becomes divided into two parties absolutely independent, and no longer acknowledge a common superior, the State is dissolved, and the war between the two parties stands on the same ground, in every respect, as a public war between two different nations.[20]

Although the law of nations as defined by Vattel strengthened Stevens's theoretical position, there were passages that might have been useful in refuting his reconstruction program. Vattel suggested, for example, that peace should be made through compromise under which neither party should be condemned as unjust. Nor does ont find in Vattel any justification for the sort of confiscation Stevens was advocating for the South. It does not appear, however, that Stevens's opponents ever cited these passages in making their case.[21]

With its authority to act clearly established, Stevens turned next to the duties incumbent on Congress. The first was to pass a law declaring the condition of the "defunct States and providing proper civil governments for them." This could be done by establishing territorial governments under which they could "learn the principles of freedom and eat the fruit of foul rebellion." Second, Congress should initiate the adoption of a constitutional amendment to change the basis of representation from "Federal numbers to actual voters," and thus abolish the obnoxious three-fifths provision. This would "secure the perpetual ascendency of the party of the Union and . . . render our republican government stable forever." Stevens had no doubt that "the amendment must be consummated before the defunct States are admitted to be capable of State action," or republican ascendancy could never be established and maintained. The proposed amendment should include a provision for the federal taxation of exports as the only feasible way to raise any considerable revenue in the South. It would also be a form of protection for domestic manufactures.[22] Third, Congress was bound to provide for the freedmen until they could take care of themselves. Four millions of them were about to be turned loose "without a hut to shelter them or a cent in their pockets. The infernal laws of slavery [had] prevented them from acquiring an education, [from] understanding the commonest laws of contract, or of managing the ordinary business of life." If they were not furnished with homesteads or protected under law, "if we leave them to the legislation of their late masters, we had better leave them in bondage," for their condition would be "worse than that of the prisoners at Andersonville." "If we fail in this great duty now, when we have the power, we shall deserve and receive the execration of history and of all future ages."

If Congress was to fulfill its responsibilities and do its duty, Stevens continued, it was of vital importance that no rebel state should be counted in the ratification of any amendments to the Constitution "until . . . duly admitted into the family of States by the law-making power of their conqueror." There was no such thing as a legal legislature under the president's plan in the rebel states, nor was there any legal basis for the claim of some of these states that they had ratified the Thirteenth Amendment. Those "extinct States" were no more legally existent "than the revolted cities of Latium, two thirds of whose people were colonized and their property confiscated, and their right to citizenship withdrawn by conquering and avenging Rome." It was time "that Congress should assert its sovereignty, and assume something of the dignity of a Roman senate." It was also time, he said, for Congress to "set the seal of reprobation" on the prevailing racism, couched in phrases coming from the provisional governors and from the copperhead party. "Wherein does this differ from slavery except in degree?" he pleaded. "Does not this contradict all the distinctive principles of the Declaration of Independence?"

As Johnson had done, Stevens turned back to the founding fathers and the era of the Revolution and the Constitution. There was nothing new about this: it had been common practice in constitutional debate between North and South since 1830. But, with the possible exception of the secession crisis, the two sides had never been more contrasting than now. Johnson had found the essence of that period in the Constitution. Stevens found it in the Declaration of Independence and the revolutionary spirit: "Our fathers repudiated the whole doctrine of the legal superiority of families or races, and proclaimed the equality of men before the law. Upon that they created a revolution and built the Republic. They were prevented by slavery from perfecting the superstructure whose foundation they had thus broadly laid. For the sake of the Union they consented to wait, but never relinquished the idea of its final completion."[23]

The use of theory and history by the two men harmonized with their understanding of the nature of the American experiment and in turn of the Civil War. For Johnson and those of his persuasion the war simply confirmed the concept of the compact as a binding rather than a dividing force; the logic of this belief compelled them to differentiate between states' rights and state sovereignty. With the war over, they could return to one of the debates of the antebellum era—not that between North and Souhth but the one between Abraham Lincoln and Stephen A. Douglas. The charges they made against the radicals (and eventually against the Republicans) were almost identical with those made by Douglas against Lincoln: that he was disturbing the delicate balance between the states and the federal government and destroying the very essence of American democracy, the control of their own affairs by the local communities. The course the Civil War had taken had led to the end of slavery under the Constitution, but the question of what to do about the freedmen was not a matter of high priority.

Stevens and his followers, on the other hand, saw the war as a truly revolutionary force. They would seek ways and means to act under the Constitution, but they were prepared to go beyond it. Their appeal to the Declaration and the law of nations was an appeal to a higher law, reminiscent of the argument of the political abolitionists in the 1850s. For them, the condition and the fate of the freedmen were paramount. This was the question, above all others, that divided the generation of the Civil War and Reconstruction. It has also been the dividing line among historians and their interpretations up to the present time.

The members of the Joint Committee on Reconstruction were appointed and the committee was ready to commence its work early in January 1866. William Pitt Fessenden of Maine was chairman of the committee on the part of the Senate and thereby, in accordance with Congressional custom, became chairman of the whole committee. Except for a brief tenure as secretary of the treasury under Lincoln, Fessenden's career in the Senate was continuous from 1854 to his death in 1869. At the time of his appointment to the committee he was fifty-nine years of age and in somewhat frail health. Although not one of the great dramatic leaders of the Senate, he was widely respected as a logical and persuasive debater and as chairman of the Senate Finance Committee. His strength as a debater lay in his avoidance of histrionic oratory and his ability to get to the essentials of a question. He could hardly abide the ponderous verbosity of Charles Sumner, with whom he was not always on speaking terms. In one exchange with Sumner, Fessenden exclaimed, "My constituents did not send me here to philosophize. They sent me here to act, to find out, if I could, what is best, and to do it, and they were not so short-sighted as to resolve that if they cannot do what they would, therefore they would do nothing."[24]

Fessenden anticipated that the work of the committee would be "severe and onerous" and that it would last for some weeks. He was concerned that Congress should play its necessary role and at the same time avoid a rupture with the executive. "My belief," said Fessenden, "is . . . that the President is as anxious as we are on that point. . . . He manifests no desire to interfere with the proper prerogatives of Congress, and appears willing to yield much to its opinions." Fessenden believed it was necessary for him to accept the chairmanship of the committee in order to prevent Sumner, who was "very anxious for the place," from getting it. Fessenden would soon find his role as mediator more difficult than he had imagined it would be and that the president was at least as intractable as the radicals. As time passed Fessenden would on some points lean more and more toward the radical position. There were some signs of this even before the establishment of the committee. He had been skeptical of Lincoln's 10 percent plan and had voted against the admission of senators from Arkansas under it, preferring that the governments where the Lincoln plan was in effect rest on a majority of loyal citizens rather than a mere 10 percent. Also, Fessenden believed that Congress had the sole authority to determine what constituted a state for purposes of representation. Apparently he was one of those persons who had misread the President's annual message.

The radical Theodore Tilton, who was no special friend of Fessenden's, said of him: "I believe that on the whole Fessenden has more continuous influence in the Senate than belongs to any other Senator. He is the best debater in the body—a complete parliamentarian—a recognized authority in many and varied subjects of legislation and an incorruptible man. If he were less conservative and more bold, he would approach my ideal of an American legislator."[25]

Thaddeus Stevens shared with Fessenden the leadership of the committee. In his Lancaster speech Stevens had appealed to young men to do the duty that had now fallen upon them. "Would to God," he lamented, "I were still in the prime of life, that I might aid you to fight through this last, greatest battle of freedom."[26] Yet at the age of seventy-three, as the leader of the radical ranks and chairman of the House portion of the committee, Stevens had reached the apogee of his power and influence. Friend and foe alike recognized him as the guiding force of the radical movement. Fifteen years earlier Howell Cobb of Georgia, speaking of Stevens, had commented on those qualities that now became apparent to others. "Our enemy has a general now," Cobb had commented. "This man is rich, therefore we cannot buy him. He does not want higher office, therefore we cannot allure him. He is not vicious, therefore we cannot seduce him. He is in earnest. He means what he says. He is bold. He cannot be flattered or frightened."[27] Stevens did want higher office—he longed to be a senator but never

made it. And not everybody agreed that Stevens was not vicious.
Senator John Sherman described him as a man "of great intellect, with a
controlling will, and the dangerous power of great sarcasm, which he
wields against friend and foe, cutting like a Damascus blade."[28]

Stevens's effectiveness as a parliamentarian was legendary. It appears, however, that his techniques were often directed to the enforcement of harsh party discipline rather than to manipulative legerdemain.
In commenting on his parliamentary methods a contemporary said that
in times of emergency Stevens "would call on every Republican in the
House to sustain the party measures, and boldly defy any conservative
to oppose them on pain of being 'read out' of the Republican organization." At such times, said the same observer, Stevens would resort to
"the bitterest sarcasm and his voice cold and trenchant as steel, would
strike terror to the hearts of his weaker followers."[29]

From the standpoint of his earlier life and career Stevens appears as a

THADDEUS STEVENS
Reproduced from the collection of the Library of Congress

somewhat unlikely candidate for his leadership role in reconstruction. There were early events and conditions of life that undoubtedly had a continuing effect and to which some of his biographers have attached much importance. First, he was born with a clubfoot, for which he may have compensated in ways that might in part explain certain personality traits. One of Stevens's congressional colleagues remarked that he seemed to feel that "every wrong inflicted upon the human race was a blow struck at himself."[30] Second, his father, Joshua Stevens, deserted the family some time during Thaddeus's early adolescence, never to return. Perhaps there is something to be said for the interpretation that Stevens's vindictiveness was an expression of a persistent and unexpressed hatred for his father, but it would be hard to prove. There is no doubt, however, that he had an abiding love and concern for his mother. Eventually he was able to end the state of poverty in which her husband had left her. She remained for him an "extraordinary woman" who had worked day and night to educate him. "That one devotion," said Alexander McClure, "was like an oasis in the desert of his affections, and, regardless of his individual convictions, he revered everything taught him by his mother."[31]

This mother, Sarah Stevens, was no ordinary woman. She recognized her son's unusual intellectual qualities and in some way raised the money to send him to Peacham Academy and then to Dartmouth College. In both he made a good record, but at Dartmouth he was rejected for membership in Phi Beta Kappa, a disappointment he never forgot. Learning of the selection of another student for the fraternity, Stevens wrote in anger that this fellow student had "entered into the service of the aristocracy, in the capacity of scullion." Those elected were "fawning parasites" seeking unmerited honors. Even before he had left college, then, Stevens had learned the art of vituperation. And the attacks could be devastating, for he was able to combine courage and conviction with a keen and frequently punishing wit. Another characteristic that remained with him from his youth was an inability to curry favor with those above him, a trait that sometimes weakened him politically because he frequently chose the side not destined for power. The strength of his personality and his crusading zeal had their effect, but because he commanded little or no patronage his power was limited.[32]

When he was about forty years old, Stevens suffered an attack of fever, probably typhoid, that left him without any hair, and from that time on he wore a ridiculous reddish wig that could not be kept in place. His clubfoot and his baldness made him the butt of many jokes that were not always good-natured. Before this misfortune he was regarded as a handsome man, standing six feet tall and with a full head of chestnut hair. Perhaps owing to his fear of passing on his clubfoot to children or to humiliation because of his physical appearance, Stevens remained a bachelor.

In 1815, at age twenty-three, Stevens moved from Vermont to York, Pennsylvania, where he taught for a year in an academy while studying law. The following year he opened up a law office in Gettysburg. His adroitness as a defense attorney in a hopeless case, which he did not win, helped to establish his reputation throughout the state and launched him on a successful and lucrative career. Later there were dark rumors in the Gettysburg area linking his name to the murder of a young black woman, rumors that may have been started by Freemasons trying to punish Stevens for his affiliation with the Antimasonic party or by persons jealous of his success as a lawyer.

With the demise of the Antimasonic party Stevens became more deeply involved in the antislavery movement, first as an attorney defending fugitive slaves and then as an active political abolitionist of the Whig persuasion. In 1838, a member of a Pennsylvania constitutional convention, he refused to sign the constitution because it denied the vote to blacks. Meanwhile, he had become the champion of the free school movement in Pennsylvania and was largely responsible for the establishment of free schools in that state. Here was a tangible victory in his war against privilege, one that gave him satisfaction to the end of his life. A short time before his death he had copies of his moving speech for free schools in the Pennsylvania legislature printed and gave a copy to his friend McClure, saying, "That was the proudest effort of my life."[33]

Stevens moved in 1842 to Lancaster, where he was elected in 1848 as a Whig to the Thirty-first Congress. From this moment he was in the front rank of the political antislavery movement; he was not long in launching his attack, not only on the votaries of the institution of slavery in the South but on its northern defenders. "Any northern man," he charged, "enlightened by a northern education, who would, directly or indirectly, by omission or commission, by basely voting or cowardly skulking, permit it to spread over one rood of God's free earth," should be looked upon "as a traitor to liberty and a recreant to God!" Reelected in 1850, Stevens went down to defeat in the Whig debacle of 1852 and was not elected again until 1858, but from that time until his death in 1868 he remained the representative of the Lancaster district.

He opposed the compromise efforts of 1860 and 1861 and was one of four representatives to vote against the Crittenden Resolution, which stated that the objective of the war was the preservation of the Union and not "for any purpose of conquest or subjugation [or of] overthrowing or interfering with the rights or established institutions of" the seceded states. He would never agree that "slaves should be returned again to their masters and that you should rivet again the chain which you have once broken." Instead, the policy of the administration should be "to free the slaves, enlist and drill them, and set them to shooting their masters if they do not submit." As early as 1861, he introduced his "laws-of-war" thesis, on which he elaborated in his December 1865 address.[34]

In 1863 a Confederate cavalry unit under the command of General Jubal Early, en route to Gettysburg, destroyed Stevens's ironworks at Caledonia, Pennsylvania. The assertion of his traducers that from this incident stemmed Stevens's confiscation policy for the South is without substance. Although he did not eschew wealth and property, their preservation was not a matter of first priority with him. His own account of his reaction to the raid seems accurate enough: "As to my personal wants nature will soon take care of them. We must all expect to suffer by this wicked war. I have not felt a moment's trouble for my share of it. If, finally, the government shall be reestablished over our whole territory, and not a vestige of slavery left, I shall deem it a cheap purchase."[35]

In his attack on slavery Stevens was a true representative of the nineteenth-century reformer, but his was no narrow or parochial brand of reformism; it was tempered with an intense nationalism that gave it strength and direction. Slavery in itself was bad enough but slavery as a cause for breaking the Union made it all the more intolerable. He warned that "if this nation were broken into fragments, and two or three republics were to arise upon its ruins, we would be a feeble people, incapable of self-defense. The Old World would shape our institutions, regulate our commerce, and control all our interests."[36]

If we recognize that in Stevens there was, along with his reformism, a strain of Calvinist elitism and thus a conviction that the South might have to be told what was good for it, we can better understand that he was trying less to harm the South than to redeem it. He opposed Abraham Lincoln's colonization schemes not only on moral grounds but because he believed that the deportation of the South's black labor force would mean the ruination of the region. If the strength and unity of the nation, resting on the sovereignty of the people and exercised through the legislative power, could not be managed under the Constitution, then Stevens was ready to abandon it in favor of a parliamentary system along the lines of the British government. In this sense he was, indeed, a revolutionist, but one seeking to establish the power of the central government rather than to overthrow it.

If Stevens's mother was the first woman in his life, Mrs. Lydia Smith, a mulatto woman who came to live with him as a housekeeper in 1848, was the second. At the time, she was thirty-five and he was fifty-six. It really makes little difference whether Lydia was merely his housekeeper, his common-law wife, or his mistress except for the inevitable rumors about their relationship and their effect on an already controversial personality. It was impossible for Stevens to marry her, and he could not even introduce her to social life. But she became a part of the growing Stevens legend. In Thomas Dixon's novel of 1905, *The Clansman*, the villain is a radical congressman with a mulatto mistress "of extraordinary animal beauty . . . and fiery temper," a temptress who dominated the politician and dictated his political actions.[37] There is little evidence that Lydia had either great beauty or a fiery temper. What seems to be true is that Stevens had affection and respect for her. In his will he provided for her continuing comfort and financial security. Two years before his death Stevens purchased a cemetery lot in Lancaster but returned it when he discovered that it was located in a segregated cemetery. Ultimately he found a lot in a cemetery where whites and blacks could be buried together.

Senatorial members of the joint committee, in addition to Fessenden, were James W. Grimes of Iowa, Ira Harris of New York, Jacob M. Howard of Michigan, George H. Williams of Oregon, and Reverdy Johnson of Maryland. Members from the House of Representatives, along with Stevens, were John A. Bingham of Ohio, Henry T. Blow of Missouri, George S. Boutwell of Massachusetts, Roscoe Conkling of New York, Justin Morrill of Vermont, Elihu B. Washburne of Illinois, Henry Girder of Kentucky, and Andrew J. Rogers of New Jersey.

After Stevens, Boutwell was the most radical member of the committee. Like Sumner, he came from the Massachusetts abolitionist tradition, and he agreed with the senator that Negro suffrage was a necessity. He was a man of recognized ability, but without Sumner's eloquence or Stevens's wit and intellect. Howard, a cultivated senator from Michigan, could also be counted upon to take a consistent stand with the radicals. He had been a leader in the organization of the Republican party and the author of its first national platform. Roscoe Conkling also ranged himself on the side of the radicals, but primarily for political purposes. He was already preparing himself as the "Stalwart" leader, on which his fame chiefly rests. Later he would subvert the Fourteenth Amendment through a unique interpretation of its "due process" clause to protect corporate railroad interests.

Standing with Fessenden in the moderate group was J. W. Grimes, a close friend of Fessenden's, whose opinions undoubtedly carried weight

with the chairman. John A. Bingham was more truly representative of
the moderate position than any other member of the committee. In
agreement with the necessity for protection of loyal whites and freedmen and an advocate of civil rights on a national rather than a sectional
basis, he had more faith than most Republicans that there were ways of
treating with southern leaders. Anxious to avoid a rupture with the
president, Bingham sought a quick solution to the reconstruction process. He played an especially important part in hammering out the
resolution that emerged from the committee as the Fourteenth
Amendment.

Among the three Democrats on the committee Reverdy Johnson was
the only one of influence and reputation. His politics at this point was a
somewhat strange amalgam. A former Whig and attorney general in
Zachary Taylor's cabinet, he had turned Democrat in the mid-fifties,
and now defended the states' rights arguments of Andrew Johnson. He

REVERDY JOHNSON
Reproduced from the collection of the Library of Congress

had voted for the Thirteenth Amendment and was remarkably free of racial bias. "I believe that [Negroes] are capable of as much and as high civilization as the white race. I have seen as much native talent exhibited in the black race as I have seen exhibited in the white race," he had said in the Senate.[38] He voted against the Fourteenth Amendment, but felt that it would be wise for the southern states to ratify it. He then voted for the Reconstruction Acts of 1867 in order to stave off a more "thorough" radical program. Although an experienced and highly respected lawyer, he was the author of the weak and legally flawed minority report of the committee.[39]

Andrew Jackson Rogers of New Jersey deserves mention only because of his extreme racism, which he expressed publicly in such violent negrophobic language that it did only harm to the cause of white supremacy which he championed. After one of his diatribes, during the debate on Negro suffrage in the District of Columbia, Stevens said, "I move that he be allowed to go on for the rest of the session!"[40]

The only congressional faction not represented on the committee was the Johnson Republicans, but the Democrats more than adequately filled that vacuum. The committee was therefore well balanced with respect to differing congressional opinions. It was so well balanced, indeed, that it was impossible for extreme radicals or extreme conservatives to win any substantial victories. The votes of the moderate Grimes were, on occasion, the determining ones. Also, because a constitutional amendment recommended by the committee required a two-thirds vote of Congress for approval, any substantial minority could defeat proposed amendments of which it disapproved.[41]

One of the first acts of the committee was to create from its ranks four subcommittees, each charged with examining conditions in a designated region of the late Confederacy.[42] Organized in this way, the committee took testimony from 145 witnesses, including Union Army officers, Freedmen's Bureau officers, avowed ex-Confederates, black and white southern loyalists, and northern travelers in the South. The information gleaned from these testimonies became the basis of the final report which the committee published June 18, 1866.

The work of the Committee, especially the testimony of witnesses, has been a major point of contention among historians of Reconstruction. Howard K. Beale, writing in 1930, condemned the committee as "a great American Court of Star Chamber sitting for the conviction of the South in an ex parte case. The Committee sought not to learn the truth about the South, but to convince the people of the efficacy of the Radical program. The examination of witnesses was no taking of testimony, for the South unheard stood precondemned."[43]

The usually fair-minded Rembert W. Patrick, whose *Reconstruction of the Nation* was published in 1967, also charges the committee with advancing the radical cause, for "while the Committee investigated, Radicals had time to formulate their plan of reconstructing the southern states and appeal to northern voters for support. . . . Undoubtedly, a majority of the committee members were biased." "Witness after witness," Patrick continues, "declared the enfranchisement of Negroes the only hope for political reform in the South and the development of a Republican organization in that region. This testimony appealed to committee members who knew the South would pick up twelve seats in the House with the elimination of the three-fifths compromise of the Constitution."[44]

Eric McKitrick concedes that the testimony was to prepare an indictment of the South, but this very fact, he suggests, "has prevented its ever being analyzed for any other purpose." He is "convinced that, properly weighed and classified, the material constitutes an extremely valuable body of source documents for judging the state of Southern feeling at this period, quite aside from the 'badness' or 'goodness' of that feeling."[45]

That the committee members were biased is incontrovertible. In the atmosphere of post–Civil War America it would have been difficult indeed to find anybody free of bias on the subject of reconstruction. Certainly it would have been too much to expect of members of Congress in either party. Andrew J. Rogers, the obstinate and dogmatic Negrophobe, was undoubtedly the most biased member of the committee. But searching for the degree of bias of committee members does not lead us very far toward an understanding of the committee's role. More important and more revealing are the assumptions and objectives of the committee members and their assessment of the evidence presented to them. The lawyers who had won places on the committee were, indeed, skilled in extracting from witnesses what they wanted to hear. There was testimony supporting all shades of opinion for whatever use the members might make of it.

Blacks testified that they wanted their personal and civil rights and tried to assuage the fears of whites with assurances that with these rights there would be no more amalgamation than there had been under slavery. "I suppose that if the colored race get all their rights before the law," said Richard R. Hill, "it would not hurt . . . or trouble the nation."[46] Asked what he would anticipate if the military were removed from the South, another black man replied, "Nothing shorter than death; that has been promised to me by the rebels."[47] John Minor Botts of Virginia was a well known southern white Unionist who had been imprisoned during the war. The committee asked him about the feeling of ex-rebels toward the government of the United States. At the time of Lee's surrender, he said, "there was an almost universal acquiescence and congratulations among the people that the war had been terminated, and a large majority . . . were at least contented, if not gratified, that it had terminated by the restoration of the State to the Union." They then became uneasy and apprehensive about their security when Johnson came in, with his declarations about punishing traitors. But with Johnson's "indiscriminate system of pardoning . . . they became bold, insolent, and defiant." Were there any schemes, secret or open, among the rebel leaders "for renewing the war or again asserting the principle of secession"? he was asked. He replied that without money, arms, and the materials of war such action would be difficult, but Botts was certain that there were many political leaders who, in the event of a foreign war, "would throw every obstacle and every impediment in the way of the success of the United States." He believed "that the most constant and earnest prayer" of many political leaders was "that the United States [should] be involved in a foreign war." Botts knew of the proposed Fourteenth Amendment pending in the Senate, but he did not believe that any legislature in the southern states, given the prevailing temper, would ratify it. He thought that while the Freedmen's Bureau was a proper and in some localities an indispensable institution it was in need of reform because some persons connected with it did not understand "the true relation of the original master to the slave" and held out promises to the former slaves that could never be realized.[48]

Caleb G. Forshey, founder and superintendent of the Texas Military Institute and a former engineer in the Confederate army, was a spokesman for the die-hard secessionist party. Confederates did not return to the Union out of any feeling for it, Forshey asserted, but from a "sense of necessity." Texans expected that there would be a "speedy and immediate restoration," apparently without conditions. There was no need for the presence of the military in Texas to protect anybody; not only was it unnecessary, it was "very pernicious everywhere, and without exception." The local authorities and public sentiment were "ample for protection." The Freedmen's Bureau was an irritant that prevented blacks from working out contracts with their former masters.

This witness, so certain of his recititude, was left virtually unmoved by four years of war. He conceded that the South had lost and secession had failed, but otherwise almost nothing had changed. Asked for his opinion "as to the respective advantages to the white and black races of the . . . free system of labor [and] , . . . slavery" he replied, "I think freedom is very unfortunate for the negro; . . . his present helpless condition touches my heart more than anything else I ever contemplate. . . . The poor negro is dying at a rate fearful to relate. . . . My judgment is that the highest condition the black race has ever reached or can reach, is one where he is provided for by a master race." He had arrived at this conclusion, he said, after "a great deal of scientific investigation and observation of the negro character."[49]

One of the best informed of the former Confederate witnesses was James D. B. De Bow of New Orleans. Publisher of the influential *De Bow's Review* and an advocate of the development of southern commerce in the prewar era, at the time of his appearance before the committee he had just completed a tour of the South. The tone of his testimony was moderate and conciliatory. He thought everybody now accepted the outcome of the war and was ready to accept policies the government might adopt on the Negro and other questions. A free labor system, he conceded, might be more advantageous to the South if the Negro could be made to work as efficiently as he had before the war. Negroes had not been disposed to work so long as the promise of land grants was held out to them, but with the end of that expectation around January 1, they had returned to work. But in his answers to questions about reconstruction policies and agencies De Bow presented the routine argument of former Confederates. The army was not needed for the protection of blacks or loyal whites; the Freedmen's Bureau, or any other agency that intervened between former masters and slaves, was "only productive of mischief."[50]

General Robert E. Lee and Alexander Stephens were the most illustrious of the Confederate leaders to appear before the committee. Lee came up to Washington from Lexington, Virginia, where he was president of Washington College (later to be named Washington and Lee University). He was a very reluctant witness whose answers were extracted from him by many questions from the interrogators through two hours of testimony. Senator Howard asked whether he was acquainted with the feeling among Virginia secessionists toward the United States government. "I do not know that I am," the general replied. "I have been living very retired, and have had but little communication with politicians." He did not even know of the proposed Fourteenth Amendment then before the Senate. He "scarcely ever read a paper." Questioned about acts of treason on the part of Confederate leaders and whether a Virginia jury would find them guilty of treason, Lee answered that such a jury would not consider that treason had been committed. The state, in withdrawing from the United States, had carried the individuals of the state along with it; thus the state—not the

individual—was responsible for the act. Secession was one of the legitimate rights reserved to the states, and his view was "that the act of
Virginia, in withdrawing herself from the United States, carried me
along as a citizen of Virginia, and that her laws and her acts were
binding on me."

Lee did not believe blacks were as capable of acquiring knowledge as
whites, although he had had "servants" who learned to read and write
very well. They were "an amiable and social race" who liked their ease
and comfort and looked "more to their present than their future condition." But it was no new opinion with him, he said, that Virginia would
be better off to be rid of its black people.[51]

Alexander Stephens, former vice-president of the Confederacy now
waiting to be seated as a senator from Georgia, was a witness of a
different order. Where Lee was modest and guarded in his testimony,
Stephens talked effusively and dogmatically. An opponent of secession
in Georgia in 1861, Stephens nonetheless clung to his conviction of the
right of secession under the Constitution. John C. Calhoun could not
have presented a stronger argument for the theory of a compact among
sovereign states. Boutwell asked whether his opinion on this subject
had undergone any change during the war. On the original abstract
question his convictions had not changed, he said, but "I accept the
issues of the war and the result as a practical settlement of that question. The sword was appealed to to decide the question, and by the
decision of the sword I am willing to abide." Did Stephens mean to
assert that "there [was] no constitutional power in the government
[without the southern states being represented] to exact conditions
precedent to the restoration to political power of the eleven states that
have been in rebellion?" "That is my opinion," Stephens replied. Georgia, then, acting in accord with these constitutional principles, would
not ratify the Fourteenth Amendment with Negro suffrage or reduced
representation, and no other southern state should do so either.[52] Such
ideas, flung at the committee by the man who had held the second
political office of the Confederacy, a man only recently released from
imprisonment in Boston's Fort Warren, must have been depressing to
members of Congress looking for some sign of contrition, some small
admission of wrongdoing from former rebels, some basis upon which
they could deal realistically with southern leaders.

Whatever the purposes of the committee may have been, the report
they published on June 18, 1866, which accompanied the testimony of all
the witnesses, was not a brief for the radical case. Rather, it was an
eclectic statement, establishing an important role for Congress, to be
sure, but embracing many ideas. Its conclusions were those of the

Republican majority in Congress, and its author was Fessenden. Although the committee rejected Andrew Johnson's plan of restoration, there was no personal attack on the president, and it agreed with him that reconstruction should not be unnecessarily delayed. "It is most desirable," the report read, "that the Union of all the states shall become perfect at the earliest moment consistent with the peace and welfare of the nation; that all these States shall become fully represented in the national councils, and take their share in the legislation of the country."[53] The president's appointment of provisional governors had been proper under his "military authority." "But it was not for him to decide upon the nature or effect of any system of government which the people of the States might see fit to adopt. This power is lodged by the Constitution in the Congress of the United States, that branch of the government in which is vested the authority to fix the political relations of the States to the Union, whose duty is to guarantee to each State a republican form of government."

Johnson had claimed that the condition of the late Confederate states was such as to justify their restoration, but he had presented no evidence of the loyalty of those who had participated in the southern state conventions. "The impropriety of proceeding wholly on the judgement of any one man, however exalted his station, in a matter involving the welfare of the republic in all future time . . . without fully understanding all its bearings and comprehending its full effect, was apparent." The only recourse left to the committee, then, was the examination of witnesses.[54]

The hand of Thaddeus Stevens can occasionally be seen in the report. The recent war was a civil war "of the greatest magnitude," and "the people waging it were . . . subject to all the rules which, by the law of nations, control a contest of that character." Congress must decide whether "conquered enemies have the right, and shall be permitted at their own pleasure and on their own terms, to participate in making laws for their conquerors." Yet other passages were closer to Lincoln's views. Whether the former Confederate states were still states in the Union, or had ever been otherwise, was a "profitless abstraction about which . . . many words [had] been wasted." (Lincoln had called it a "pernicious abstraction.") It did not follow, however, "that the people of those States may not place themselves in a condition to abrogate the powers and privileges incident to a State in the Union."[55]

Although there is nothing in the report remotely endorsing Stevens's plan for confiscating southern land for the benefit of the freedmen, the committee recognized the obligation to protect the former slaves, many of whom had remained loyal to the Union and fought for it. The committee did have doubts, however, about the power of Congress to prescribe the qualifications of voters or whether the states would surrender "a power they had always exercised, and to which they were attached." The dilemma of the committee, and of Congress, on the question of Negro suffrage is indicated in Section 2 of the Fourteenth Amendment, which provides that representation in the states will be determined by population and that when the vote is denied to any male portion of the population representation shall be reduced proportionally. Thus the rebel states would be able to exercise this traditional power, but not without paying a price for denial of Negro suffrage.

Of the 145 witnesses to appear before the committee, Alexander Stephens is the only one whose name is mentioned in the summary report. His testimony and his asserted right to a Senate seat was just the kind of evidence the committee needed to show the danger of a resurgence of "unrepentant and unpardoned" rebel leaders under the Johnson plan:

> It is only necessary to instance the election to the Senate of the late vice-president of the confederacy, a man who, against his own declared convictions, had lent all the weight of his acknowledged ability and of his influence as a most prominent public man to the cause of the rebellion, and who, unpardoned rebel as he is, with that oath staring him in the face, had the assurance to lay his credentials on the table of the Senate. Other rebels of scarcely less note or notoriety were selected from other quarters. Professing no repentance, glorying apparently in the crime they had committed, avowing still, as the uncontradicted testimony of Mr. Stephens and many others proves, an adherence to the pernicious doctrine of secession, and declaring that they yielded only to necessity, they insist, with unanimous voice, upon their rights as States, and proclaim that they will submit to no conditions whatever as preliminary to their resumption of power under that Constitution which they still claim the right to repudiate.[56]

The committee concluded that "the States lately in rebellion were, at the close of the war, disorganized communities, without civil governments, and without constituencies or other forms, by virtue of which political relations could legally exist between them and the federal government." Congress could not be expected to recognize the election of representatives from such communities and

> would not be justified in admitting [them] to a participation in the government of the country without first providing such constitu-

tional or other guarantees as will tend to secure the civil rights of all citizens of the republic; a just equality of representation; protection against claims founded in rebellion and crime; a temporary restoration of the right of suffrage to those who have not actively participated in the efforts to destroy the Union and overthrow the government, and the exclusion from positions of public trust of, at least, a portion of those whose crimes have proved them to be enemies to the Union, and unworthy of public confidence.

The late rebel states had "deprived themselves" of representation in Congress "for the criminal purpose of destroying the federal Union." The burden, therefore, rested upon them "to show that they are qualified to resume federal relations."[57]

The three Democrats on the committee submitted a minority report, written by Reverdy Johnson, which was in essence a restatement of the doctrine of state sovereignty. The comment of John W. Burgess, writing in 1902 in the genre of the Dunning school and no friend of radical or congressional reconstruction, on this minority report is instructive. Although it was an able "lawyer's brief," said Burgess, it was "the veriest dry bones of legal reasoning, the veriest sophistry of juristic abstraction. There was no political science in it, and it ended with an unfortunate and irritating defence of President Johnson's personal loyalty, which had not been in the slightest degree impugned by the majority."[58]

The Joint Committee on Reconstruction did not at first envision itself as an agency to confront the president or to undermine his policies. Soon after organizing itself it had sent a delegation of its moderate leaders to assure Johnson of its goodwill, but within a matter of weeks Johnson had decided that the committee was a cabal whose purpose was to dictate the policy of his administration. It soon became a focal point in the emerging executive-legislative conflict.

Chapter 3

Howard, Trumbull, and the Freedmen

THE JOINT COMMITTEE was soon engaged in the prolonged and tedious work of framing the Fourteenth Amendment, its major contribution to Reconstruction. The first direct clash between the president and Congress was to come, however, not from the Reconstruction committee but from the standing judiciary committee of the Senate under the chairmanship of Lyman Trumbull of Illinois.

Trumbull, a former Democrat who had joined the Republicans following the Kansas-Nebraska Act in 1854, was not one of the popular leaders of his era in or out of Congress. One associate described him as "deliberate, cool, and calculating"; another spoke of his "reserved manners, his abstemious habits," and his lack of "geniality of temperament." He seems to have been somewhat straitlaced, and he could be condescending, even toward Abraham Lincoln, whose policies he generally supported. He had introduced the Thirteenth Amendment and was instrumental in pushing it through to adoption. His reputation rested mainly on his hard work and ability, especially in legal and constitutional matters. He had no intention of upsetting the president's restoration program, but for months he had been receiving reports from the South of oppression of blacks and loyal whites for whom he would now provide legal protection. In mid-Devember, invoking the Thirteenth Amendment, he announced his intention of introducing legislation to curb the abuses. He had no doubt, he said, that under the provisions of that amendment "it would be competent for Congress to protect every person in the United States in all the rights of person and property belonging to the free citizen." To secure these rights was the purpose of the legislation he proposed to introduce.

On January 5, 1866, Trumbull presented the Freedmen's Bureau Bill and the Civil Rights Bill. The measures were passed by substantial majorities in both houses, the former on February 6 and the latter on March 11. Johnson vetoed both! Congress reacted by passing the Civil

Rights Bill over his veto. However, it sustained his veto of the Freedmen's Bureau Bill, adopting instead a modified bill in July which it passed over his veto. With the two vetoes, which came as a shock to the majority of Congress, the president had thrown down the gauntlet to the legislative branch. Congressional Republicans felt that they had no choice but to accept the challenge.[1] These measures and the debates on them, including the veto messages, illuminate the process of political reconstruction as well as racist attitudes north and south, concepts and concerns about centralized government, and the fear of paternalism under American institutions. It is worthwhile, therefore, to examine them in some detail.

The Freedmen's Bureau Bill, the first of the two measures passed by Congress, was in the most specific sense simply an extension of the already existing bureau (the Bureau of Refugees, Freedmen, and Abandoned Lands) which had been enacted in March 1865, and immediately approved by Lincoln in one of the last acts of his presidency. In a broader context, the establishment of a Freedmen's Bureau was one of many measures called forth as the war was transformed from a conflict to preserve the Union to a war of attrition leading, perforce, to the destruction of the institution of slavery. Actually, the slaves themselves had forced a new policy on the government by going over to the areas occupied by Union armies and creating problems that could not be solved under the terms of the Crittenden Resolution of 1861, which stated that the war was "not waged . . . in any spirit of oppression, or for any purpose of conquest or subjugation, or . . . of overthrowing or interfering with the rights or established institutions of [the] States." As the war progressed the number of such refugee slaves steadily increased until near the end the refugees became a "dark and human cloud that clung like remorse on the rear of [the] swift columns, swelling at times to half their size, almost engulfing and choking them."[2]

Individual commanding generals dealt with the problem in their own ways, but the most notable experiment and one that established an important precedent was adopted by Gen. Benjamin Butler at Fort Monroe, Virginia. Butler designated slaves as contraband of war and put them to work as a labor force in building fortifications for the Union instead of for the Confederacy. Butler's policy was given legislative sanction by the Confiscation Acts of 1861 and 1862, the first of which provided for the seizure of property being used for "insurrectionary purposes" and the second for the forfeiture of property of persons supporting the rebellion. Meanwhile, Congress had enacted a new Article of War which prohibited military commanders from using the forces under their command to return refugee slaves to their masters.

These initial steps, taken nearly three years before the end of the war, together with Lincoln's Emancipation Proclamation and the decision to enlist black troops in the armed forces of the United States, would lead necessarily to some plan for more centralized control.

Other field experiments also had a bearing on the establishment of the Freedmen's Bureau as well as on the whole vexing question of the role of the freedmen in reconstruction. By far the most important of these was the Sea Islands experiment, which was begun following the capture of Port Royal, South Carolina, in November 1861. The planters there made a hasty exit, taking their more skilled slaves with them but abandoning their lands and some 8,000 field hands, constituting one of the most culturally isolated and backward slave communities in the whole South. Although these slaves could not be emancipated under any existing law, their very isolation provided an unusual opportunity to apply the contraband policy. The initial effort was to maximize the production of cotton, first under the control of the army and later under Treasury agents, without much concern for the welfare of the slaves. But some northern abolitionists saw other possibilities in the Sea Island situation. If these unfortunate blacks could be organized as freedmen capable of producing cotton on a large scale, what a fillip it would be to the antislavery cause and how damaging to the whole proslavery argument, especially that part of it contending that blacks could work effectively only in a system of bondage, a view that was by no means confined to the South. "Here," said the *National Anti-Slavery Standard*, "within the protection of the arms of the United States, might a new experiment of tropical culture be tried. Succeeding there, . . . how simple the process by which it might be extended wherever the arms of the nation may be predominant."[3] Acting on the appeal of the abolitionists, Secretary of the Treasury Salmon P. Chase sent his friend Edward L. Pierce to investigate the Sea Islands and somewhat later appointed him a special Treasury Department agent with authority to select superintendents and teachers to carry on the experiment. Freedmen's aid societies now emerged in the northeastern states to provide the superintendents and teachers and pay their salaries. In June 1862, Pierce submitted a glowing report of the work of the "Gideonites" who accompanied him to the Islands. The success of the movement, said Pierce, had exceeded his "most sanguine expectation."

Despite Pierce's optimistic report, he had his problems on the Sea Islands, especially with officials who gave little consideration to anything except cotton, men who worked the "contrabands" almost as slave labor and resented even the small wage Pierce paid the blacks in preparing them for ultimate freedom. Soon Pierce was ready to depart and to relinquish his responsibilities to Gen. Rufus Saxton, who was placed in command of the area by Chase and Secretary of War Edwin Stanton. Since Saxton was in general agreement with Pierce as to the conduct of the experiment, many of the teachers brought in by Pierce remained after his departure.[4]

Saxton was still in command when Gen. William T. Sherman made his march to the sea at the end of 1864. Following Sherman's army were thousands of slaves who knew that by then the war was one of liberation for them. Stanton came down from Washington and, after a conference with Sherman and a spokesman for the blacks, Sherman issued, on January 15, 1865, his famous Special Field Order Number 15. The order placed Saxton in command of an area embracing the Sea Islands and a coastal region extending thirty miles inland from Charleston south to the St. John's River. Here Saxton was to implement a colonization scheme, not in some distant foreign land but in a former stronghold of the slave system. Freedmen could occupy "abandoned lands" in tracts of forty acres or less with "possesory" titles as a means of protection "until such time as they [could] protect themselves, or until Congress [might] regulate their title."[5] As the language of the order suggests, this was to be no scheme of permanent colonization but rather a step toward protecting the freedmen in such a way that their emancipation would be more than a legal technicality or a token gesture. Indeed, the Sea Island experiment is an example of what might have been done with respect to freedmen during reconstruction. Its ultimate failure, which came with Johnson's restoration of the land to the original owners, is a landmark in the history of the abandonment of the Negro at that crucial time.

In the Mississippi Valley there were similar efforts to cope with the problem of black refugees. Throughout the first year of the war General Grant tried to avoid the problem and issued orders that blacks were to be treated as vagrants and turned out of military encampments. But confronted with growing numbers of refugees and backed by the authority of the Confiscation Acts, in November 1862 he appointed Chaplain John Eaton to take charge of the freedmen, with instructions to establish them in separate encampments and to put them to work producing cotton. Clothing and tools were provided by the army quartermaster and food by the commissary. Further contributions came from the Western Freedmen's Aid Commission. By April 1863, Eaton had assembled some 20,000 blacks in his contraband camps, where they were paid wages to work for the government and for individual investors who had leased abandoned plantations. Before the end of the war Eaton organized a black colony at Davis Bend, Mississippi, the estate of the Confederate president, where blacks not only worked on the land but,

under military control, served as sheriffs and judges.[6] Field commanders, then, in both major theaters of war, were forced to cope, in
one way or another, with blacks who "had drifted into nooks and corners
like *debris* into sloughs and eddies; and were soon to be found, ill-
conditioned masses, all the way from Maryland to Mexico, from the Gulf
to the Ohio River."[7]

Meanwhile, there were pressures from the northeastern states and
from Washington for a more unified national plan for the freedmen, one
that would not only meet the exigencies of war but would continue to
operate during reconstruction as well. Under the guidance of Secretary
of War Stanton and Senator Sumner, in March 1863, the War Department created the American Freedmen's Inquiry Commission "to investigate the condition of the colored population emancipated by acts of
Congress" and the Emancipation Proclamation and "to report what
measures will best contribute to their protection and improvement, so
that they may support and defend themselves."[8] The three-man commission, under the chairmanship of Robert Dale Owen, after extensive
journeys through the South, made two reports to the Secretary of War,
in which it recommended the establishment of a bureau of emancipation
or freedmen, preferably under the War Department, to be a friend and
counselor to freedmen, to protect them in legal matters, and with the
aid of benevolent agencies to provide for their education. Blacks were to
be established on the abandoned lands of planters, where they would
work for regular wages and have an opportunity to purchase land. The
commission made it clear that the bureau was not to be an agency of
permanent guardianship and emphasized the importance of teaching
self-reliance to the freedmen.[9]

The movement in Congress to create such a bureau began before the
end of 1863, when Thomas D. Eliot of Massachusetts introduced in the
House a bill along the lines of the American Freedmen's Inquiry Commission's recommendations. Charles Sumner, chairman of the newly
created Senate Committee on Emancipation, worked with Eliot in
preparing the legislation that would emerge as the bill establishing the
Bureau of Refugees, Freedmen, and Abandoned Lands (the Freedmen's Bureau), on March 3, 1865. The bureau, under the control of the
War Department, was charged with the "supervision and management
of all abandoned lands, and the control of all subjects relating to refugees and freedmen"; it was to continue in force for one year after the
end of the war. At the head of the bureau was to be a commissioner,
appointed by the president with the consent of the Senate, along with
assistant commissioners in the states. The commissioner, under the
direction of the president, was authorized to "set apart, for the use of

loyal refugees and freedmen, such tracts of land . . . as shall have been abandoned, or to which the United States shall have acquired title by confiscation, or sale, or otherwise." Every male, whether refugee or freedman, might be assigned not more than forty acres for a term of three years at a nominal rent and was to be protected in its use and enjoyment. At the end of the three years the occupants were to be allowed to purchase the land at its appraised value. It will be noted that no land was to be given to freedmen; they would gain possession by the application of their labor to it, a point that is relevant to the criticism of the bureau as a paternalistic institution.

Nor was there to be a direct appropriation for the support of the bureau. It was expected to be self-supporting, except that the secretary of war might issue to it "provisions, clothing and fuel as he may deem needful for the immediate and temporary shelter and supply of destitute and suffering refugees and freedmen, and their wives and children."

O. O. HOWARD
Reproduced from the collection of the Library of Congress

The commissioner and assistant commissioners were to receive modest salaries, paid by the War Department through assigning them as military officers to the bureau without increased pay or allowances.

The herculean task of administering the amorphous Freedmen's Bureau fell to a thirty-five-year-old major general, Oliver Otis Howard, a courageous if not always astute battle commander. He had served in McClellan's Army of the Potomac early in the war, losing his right arm at Fair Oaks; at the end of the war he was in command of the Army of the Tennessee. Converted to Methodism in the 1850s, Howard had all the zeal of the true convert. His abstemiousness and abhorrence of profanity were well known throughout the army. Stanton, trusting in Howard's radicalism, recommended him to Lincoln, who agreed to the appointment but died before it could be made, leaving it to Andrew Johnson to make the appointment in May 1865.

On learning of Howard's appointment General Sherman, in whose army Howard had been a corps commander, wrote him a congratulatory message which was a remarkably accurate estimate of the man and the task confronting him.

> I hardly know whether to congratulate you or not, but of one thing you may rest assured, that you possess my entire confidence, and I cannot imagine that matters that involve the future of 4,000,000 souls could be put in more charitable and more conscientious hands. So far as man can do, I believe you will; but I fear you have Hercules' task. God has limited the power of man, and though in the kindness of your heart you would alleviate all the ills of humanity, it is not in your power to fulfill one tenth part of the expectation of those who formed the Bureau for the Freedmen and Refugees and Abandoned Estates. It is simply impracticable. Yet you can and will do all the good one man may, and that is all you are called on as a man and a Christian to do, and to that extent count on me as a friend and fellow soldier for counsel and assistance.[10]

If we consider the magnitude and complexity of the work undertaken by the bureau, it is difficult to see how a better administrator than Howard could have been found. The fact that he remained as commissioner throughout its turbulent life, to 1872, in the face of obloquy and censure, attests to his commitment and untiring effort. His limited experience as a bureaucrat, even his reputed naïveté, may have been an advantage in the long run, for more experienced and less dedicated men might have given up early in the game. John A. Andrew, the astute and practical war governor of Massachusetts, would not consider the job because of his distrust of Stanton.[11]

The bureau meant different things to different groups or factions. A few extreme radicals hoped that it would be the instrument for the settlement of freedmen on confiscated land; other radicals saw it as necessary in the short run but feared that it might be too paternalistic and might thwart the "manhood" of newly emancipated blacks. Even some black leaders, convinced that the best policy for the freedmen was simply to leave them alone, feared that the bureau might impose a kind of governmental slavery replacing the old master-slave relationship.[12] Democrats were threatened by the bureau as an adjunct of the Republican party in the South, southern whites saw it as an instrusion into their affairs. Well before the end of 1865 Andrew Johnson and his party were convinced that the bureau was an enemy of presidential restoration and were undermining it wherever they could without making an outright public attack on it.

The most critical and telling attack was that launched against the Bureau's agents, those officers operating at the local level within the states. The attack was a two-edged one, coming from Southerners who hated the bureau and from Northerners who favored it. Southerners made a general attack on the agents, denouncing not only their poor management and administration but their lack of "character" and the "despicable class" from which they were presumed to have come. Some Northerners felt that the agents too often neglected blacks in favor of whites. Gen. Clinton B. Fisk, the assistant commissioner in Tennessee, complained to John T. Trowbridge that he was not permitted to select his own agents and that some of those sent to him were prejudiced against blacks and too subject to the flattery and favors of the planter and to the "attentions and smiles of his fair daughter."[13] Other agents were alleged to be negligent in their paper work, especially in making reports and keeping financial accounts. While these reports were not altogether inaccurate, it is important to remember that these agents were on the outposts of the whole operation, the second lieutenants, sergeants, and corporals, so to speak, who would bear the brunt of criticism from superiors and fly-by-night reporters traveling through the South in search of material for the books and articles they expected to publish.

Many of the critics failed to consider the fact that there were never enough agents to go around. But Commissioner Howard never minimized or oversimplified the onerous work of the agent who, he said, was at once "a magistrate with extraordinary judicial power—overseer of the poor of all classes in his district, agent to take care of abandoned lands, and required to settle, in a few days, most intricate questions with reference to labor, political economy, &c, that have puzzled the world for ages."

This estimate is borne out by a Florida agent who reported that during the season for making contracts he was kept at work in his crowded office from early morning until late in the evening. Among his duties were "Reading and approving contracts [,] visiting the various plantations—allaying strife between husband and wife—deciding the ownership of a hog and last but not least—answering questions with reference to Rations."[14] Sometimes what was expected of bureau officials was absurd and displayed an abysmal ignorance of conditions in the postwar South. John R. Dennett was present in a Freedmen's Bureau office in Virginia when two planters from Mississippi appeared and requested of the bureau "about a hundred Virginia Negroes to be taken down to Mississippi to work on cotton." Informed that the bureau had no authority to send blacks away without their consent, the planters asked whether they might take a hundred paupers or criminals. When this request was also denied, the planters asked that the blacks be apprenticed to them for a number of years. When the agent also rejected this proposal, one of the planters, explaining that he had the land and the capital to raise cotton, continued, "What I want to know is this,—you say you can't use compulsion to make these Virginia niggers go down there—what compulsion will the Government let me use to make them work when I've got them there anyhow?" The Mississippian, said the agent, seemed to believe that "all Negro labor must be compulsory." "Why, of course it must," the planter replied. "How long have you lived in the South, Sir?" The agent admitted that he was not from a slave state, but he related the experience of a Virginia planter in the vicinity who had done well with a large number of free black workers. The Mississippian would not be convinced: "The employer must have some sort of punishment. I don't care what it is."[15]

The most persistent accusation against the bureau was that by dangling the expectation of government largess in the form of land grants for freedmen agents were discouraging blacks from working and thus critically delaying the economic recovery of the South. By the end of 1865 this complaint had become a cliché, repeated not only by Southerners but by many Northerners as well.[16]

Undoubtedly many freedmen did hope for free land from the government, their expectations might have been excessive, and the effect probably was in some cases to discourage them from making contracts, especially with former masters. It would have been strange indeed if such hopes and aspirations had been absent from their minds, if they

had not expected more than a token emancipation. Many had learned of
the arrangements on the Sea Islands and at Davis Bend and gravitated
toward those places. Surely the efforts of radicals such as Stevens and
George W. Julian for confiscation of land and homesteads for freedmen
were not unknown among them. Also, they had passed their lives in a
region where freedom was closely identified with land ownership. But
there is little evidence supporting the charge that the Freedmen's
Bureau or its agents encouraged these attitudes. If anything, the effect
of the bureau was just the opposite. The instructions of General Howard
to his subordinates, the policies of the assistant commissioners, and the
actions of the agents all attest to the high priority given to placing the
freedmen in productive jobs under equitable contracts. The bureau
agents were in the difficult position of adjudicators responsible for
arranging contracts acceptable to both sides. There were instances
where planters who had taken advantage of ignorant freedmen were
forced to make restitution to them; there were others where freedmen
were required to remain in the employ of planters until the expiration of
the terms of their contracts. The assistant commissioner in Texas
authorized his agents to fine freedmen for breaking contracts and levied
heavy fines for enticing blacks to break contracts. It was not unknown
for agents to blacklist persons who broke contracts, to prevent their
being hired by other employers. Insofar as either planter or freedman
received favored treatment in the matter of contracts, it is difficult to
arrive at any conclusion other than that it was usually the planter and
not the freedman who was favored.[17]

Stories of vagrancy among southern blacks, which was reported to be
rampant, were also exaggerated. Sidney Andrews, in his journey
through South Carolina toward the end of 1865, saw a great many
migrants who were seeking work other than on the plantations. But he
thought it "both absurd and wicked to charge that negroes, as a class,
[were] not at work."[18]

A young southern white man, discussing the whole question of defeat
and emancipation and the white reaction to it, may have summed up
southern attitudes toward the Freedmen's Bureau as accurately and
succinctly as possible. Asked whether the Freedmen's Bureau was a
good thing, he answered, "Yes, if the nigger is to be free, I reckon it is;
but it's a mighty bitter thing for us."[19]

Even more immediate than the matter of labor and contracts was the
precariousness of human life itself and the actions of the bureau to
preserve it. Although there was no provision in the act of March 1865 for
medical service, Howard interpreted his powers broadly so as to bring

the bureau into this essential work. At the time of the creation of the bureau, the army and the freedmen's aid societies had turned their attention to the needs of the physically and mentally ill, the maimed and the deformed, the orphaned and the aged. For this work Howard established a medical division which received supplies from the surgeon general and also detailed doctors to the bureau. Thus, even without direct appropriations, much could be done; by September 1866, more than 200,000 freedmen and 8,000 white refugees had been treated, bringing a substantial reduction in the death rate in each group.[20] The bureau also issued rations to the destitute. Despite Howard's determination not to feed those who could take care of themselves, in 1865 and 1866 nearly ten million rations were issued to freedmen and more than 5.5. million to refugees.[21] To enable refugees to return home and freedmen to reach places of employment, transportation was provided for more than ten thousand persons before the end of September, 1866.

With Oliver O. Howard as its chief it was all but inevitable that the bureau would undertake a program of education for the freedmen. Nearly a decade earlier Howard had expressed his faith in education for blacks as the only hope for the progress of a race "turned loose in the world, with all their simplicity and improvident habits." (It is manifest that even a humanitarian such as Howard accepted some of the racial stereotypes of his era.) In 1865, viewing the problem at closer range, he reiterated this conviction, adding that black education should also include moral and religious training. Only with such training would they be able to overcome the "fearful prejudice" against them and gain the "privileges and rights that we now have difficulty to guarantee."[22]

Owing to the refusal of Congress to appropriate money, it was impossible for the bureau to enter the educational field alone or unassisted. However, there were a number of freedmen's aid societies already active in the education of blacks. Among them were the National Freedmen's Relief Association, the Western Freedmen's Aid Commission, and the Northwestern Freedmen's Aid Commission. In addition to these secular societies were church supported organizations such as the American Missionary Association. At the time of the formation of the bureau, therefore, there were at least 750 teachers and 75,000 blacks receiving instruction from them in the South. Howard hoped to combine all these organizations into one agency with the bureau as superintendent and coordinator. Although he was unable to do this, the bureau did improve the organization of the educational work. In 1865 and 1866 the bureau served the benevolent societies primarily by providing buildings free of rent, transportation for teachers and supplies, and rations at cost. After 1866 it was able to make a more substantial contribution, so that when it ceased to exist in 1872 it had expended more than $3.5 million for construction and maintenance of schools.[23]

It soon became evident that if black education was to continue, institutions for the training of teachers would be necessary. Beginning in 1867, therefore, the bureau, again in cooperation with the benevolent societies, took the lead in establishing Negro colleges and normal schools. By 1871 eleven colleges and universities and sixty-one normal schools had been established, among them Hampton Institute, Stover College, Atlanta University, Fisk University, Lincoln Institute, and Howard University.[24] In the long run, these institutions may have been the bureau's most important legacy.

Before concluding this summary of the bureau's operations it is necessary to comment on its judicial functions, particularly because of their bearing on the legislation introduced by Senator Trumbull early in 1866. No part of the bureau's operation was more complicated or aroused more bitter resentment in the South. Courts were established within the bureau because of the absence of regular courts in the former Confederate states at the end of the war and the prevailing practice in the South of not permitting blacks to testify in cases involving whites. To assure blacks of their civil rights, Howard instructed the assistant commissioners to hear cases involving blacks and whites. Although most cases had to do with wages and contracts, there were times when the bureau had to handle criminal cases. The composition of the bureau courts was, as a rule, determined by circumstances. The most common arrangement was the one-man court, similar to an army summary court. Another type was the three-man court, consisting of a bureau agent, a representative of the planters, and a black representative of the freedmen.

An important effect of the bureau courts was to encourage local courts, as they became active, to admit testimony from blacks, with the purpose of bringing about the withdrawal of the bureau courts. Only infrequently, however, did blacks enjoy equal justice in the local courts because witnesses for the prosecution were likely to be white, the testimony of blacks was ignored, and the juries were all white. When cases were tried in the local courts agents were instructed to attend trials and to report instances of discrimination, to act as "next friend" of the freedmen.[25]

Of all the frustrations General Howard and his bureau had to endure, none was more galling than the attitude of Andrew Johnson toward the bureau and his policy of restoring land to ex-Confederates under his amnesty proclamation of May 29, 1865. We have noted that the president followed a program of political "restoration"; now he adopted a program of property "restoration" as well.

Except for a few radicals, not many men held out any hope at the end of the war for a general confiscation of land. There was some reason to expect, however, that the abandoned land placed under the control of the bureau might be transferred to the freedmen, not as a gift but by sale at a minimum price. Also, as we have seen, this land was the major source of income for the bureau. Whatever the intentions of Howard and the other bureau officials might have been, the bureau could not have effected a broad confiscation policy because it controlled only about one five-hundredth of the land of the former Confederate states.

Before the president's proclamation Howard had instructed bureau officials not to return land to "disloyal persons"; after the proclamation he awaited specific orders before changing this policy. He instructed his subordinates to set aside all land properly under their control, pointing out that the president's proclamation "did not extend to the surrender of abandoned or confiscated property, which by law [had] been set apart" for refugees and freedmen.[26] At this point Johnson took a firm hand with Howard. Through a series of executive orders he instructed the commissioner to restore to former rebels all property not already sold under court decree.[27]

At no place was the effect of Johnson's order felt more acutely than on the Sea Islands and in the coastal region under the command of General Saxton. Now scores of former landowners in this region applied for restoration of their property. Saxton, who served also as assistant commissioner for South Carolina, refused to return land to which freedmen had been granted "possessory titles" under Sherman's order. Saxton contended that these lands had been promised to the freedmen and thus did not fall under Johnson's order. To settle the matter, Johnson sent Howard to South Carolina to find a solution "mutually satisfactory to freedmen and landowners," which Howard interpreted, correctly, to mean the restoration of the lands to the original owners.

In mid-October Howard arrived in Charleston, where he conferred with Saxton and a representative of the planters and then arranged a meeting with the freedmen at Edisto Island. Throughout his administration of the Freedmen's Bureau it is doubtful that Howard ever had to perform a more painful duty than this one, forced as he was into the dilemma of violating his own convictions about freedmen's rights in the obedience of the orders of his commander in chief. Although commissioner of the bureau, Howard was still an army officer and was always sensitive to his subordinate position to his military superiors. Indeed, the dual role of army officer and bureau official made the administration of the bureau difficult and awkward, not only for the commissioner but for assistant commissioners and agents as well.

The Edisto Island meeting took place in a large hall that was filled to the rafters with freedmen. The rumor had already spread among them that Howard was coming to announce the restoration of the land to the former planters and the removal of the freedmen. In his *Autobiography* Howard described the scene:

> In the noise and confusion no progress was had till a sweet-voiced negro woman began the hymn "Nobody knows the trouble I feel—Nobody knows but Jesus," which, joined in by all, had a quieting effect on the audience. Then I endeavored as clearly and gently as I could to explain to them the wishes of the President, as they were made known to me in an interview had with him just before leaving Washington. Those wishes were also substantially embodied in my instructions. My address, however kind in manner I rendered it, met with no apparnt favor. They did not hiss, but their eyes flashed unpleasantly, and with one voice they cried, "No, no!" Speeches full of feeling and rough eloquence came back in response. One very black man, thick set and strong, cried out from the gallery: "Why, General Howard, why do you take away our lands? You take them from us who are true, always true to the Government! You give them to our all-time enemies! That is not right!"

He tried to explain to them that they had no "absolute title" to their homesteads and urged them to make the best terms possible with the legal owners. A committee of freedmen assured Howard that under no circumstances would they work again under overseers. Some were willing to work for wages, but most preferred to rent the lands.[28]

In the denouement of the Port Royal and Sea Island experiment one can see that the Freedmen's Bureau, well before the end of 1865, was caught up in the emerging executive-legislative conflict. There were other men involved in it, however, in addition to the president, General Saxton, General Howard, whose activities are revealing as they relate to the failure of the bureau and, indeed, to the ultimate abandonment of the Negro during Reconstruction. First among these men was Edward S. Philbrick, a handsome and impressive young man who had contributed money to the original Port Royal experiment and had accompanied Edward L. Pierce to South Carolina. After Pierce's departure, Philbrick remained as a superintendent under Saxton. From the beginning Philbrick was skeptical of the Gideonites, whom he described as "broken down schoolmasters and ministers" who would not contribute very much to the production of cotton. The plantations under Philbrick's charge were more productive than the others, but not without some cost to the black workers. Applying laissez faire concepts to the Sea Island situation, he resented the sale of land to the freedmen at less than the going market price, and he paid his workers less than he would have had to pay in the North. The better hands, he complained, had gone to the army, leaving him with an inferior labor force. He conceded that education and northern moral example might in time enable the black worker to command higher wages, but that time had not yet arrived. Philbrick claimed to be testing the capacity of free labor in the South in contrast with slave labor, and he concluded that the former was more productive. The question has been properly raised, however, whether these workers were "unequivocally *free*." Willie Lee Rose points out that, although "the legal status of slavery is absolute, freedom . . . admits of degrees. While Philbrick had, as he said, 'no paupers' on his places, it is arithmetically clear that Negroes had shared only a minute part of the wealth produced on [his] plantations."[29]

Other New Englanders who had connections with the Sea Islands were Edward Atkinson and John Murray Forbes, both successful businessmen, the former in textiles and the latter in railroading and the China trade. Forbes actually accompanied Pierce and his party to Port Royal—where he was more favorably impressed with Philbrick than with Pierce's schoolmarms—and became an investor in one of Philbrick's enterprises. Atkinson, a longtime advocate of a freedmen's bureau, had for some years contended that free labor would produce more cotton than slaves and at the same time liberate northern textile manufacturers from the grip of southern planters. The Port Royal experiment provided an opportunity to test his theory. Atkinson saw the bureau as an agency for aiding the freedmen and for helping the northern investor. The former slave-owning planter would also have a place in the scheme of things; by combining with northern investors he could regain his lands and help to promote "peace and good order and habits of industry" among his former slaves. The support of the bureau by such men was, therefore, hedged with qualifications. If the choice between Andrew Johnson and the bureau was to be one between traditional property rights or long-range federal planning and some paternalism toward blacks, it was clear that such men would choose the former and reject the latter.[30]

By December 1865, it was evident to General Howard that the Freedmen's Bureau, as constituted under existing legislation, could not withstand the offensive Andrew Johnson had launched against it. Although the most serious damage was done by the restoration of abandoned lands, the source of the bureau's revenue, that was not all—Johnson had now begun to dismiss bureau officials who opposed him. "Every report received from our agents bore evidence of trouble then existing and apprehended," Howard would recall. These were the circumstances that led Senator Trumbull to visit the commissioner in his Washington office where, together, the two men worked out the details of the Freedmen's Bureau Bill that was introduced to the Senate on January 5, 1866.[31]

The bill, presented as an act to amend the already existing law, extended the life of the bureau "until otherwise provided by law"; its authority was enlarged to cover refugees and freedmen in all parts of the United States, and a somewhat more formal organization was provided, with additional personnel. The secretary of war was authorized to issue "provisions, clothing, fuel, . . . medical stores, and transportation . . . as he may deem needful for . . . destitute and suffering freedmen and refugees, their wives and children." No person was to be deemed destitute, suffering, or dependent, however, who could find employment and by proper "industry and exertion" avoid such a condition. The president was authorized to set aside unoccupied public lands in five southern states which might be rented to loyal refugees and freedmen in plots not exceeding forty acres with the ultimate right of purchase. Occupants of lands under General Sherman's order were to be confirmed in their possession for a period of three years. Where former owners had had lands restored to them, the commissioner might resettle dispossessed freedmen on public lands. Land was also to be provided for the erection of buildings for asylums and schools for refugees and freedmen dependent on the government for support.

Where "civil rights belonging to white persons, including the right to make and enforce contracts, to sue, be parties, and give evidence, to inherit, purchase, lease, sell, hold and convey real and personal property, and to have full and equal benefit of all laws and proceedings for the security of person and estate, including the constitutional right of bearing arms" were refused on account of race, color, or previous condition of slavery or involuntary servitude, there was to be military protection and jurisdiction. Violation of the civil rights provisions of the act would constitute a misdemeanor punishable by a fine not exceeding $1,000 or imprisonment not exceeding one year, or both. Freedmen's Bureau officers were to "take jurisdiction" in such cases, except in states where the ordinary course of judicial proceedings had not been interrupted by the rebellion or in any state "fully restored in all its constitutional relation to the United States."[32]

There would, of course, be strenuous opposition to such a measure. The leading adversary in the Senate was Thomas A. Hendricks, a Democrat from Indiana and also a member of Trumbull's judiciary committee. His remarks are important not only because of his criticism of the Freedmen's Bureau Bill, per se, but because they embrace so much of what was to become the standard case of Democrats and Johnsonian Republicans against congressional reconstruction. Hendricks made the customary complaints about the operation of the bureau and its agents: there had been no uniform policy for bureau procedures; blacks had been led to excessive expectations and thus been discouraged from making contracts; the bureau had extended its jurisdiction into places where it had no legal authority to act, such as the District of Columbia and Kentucky. The bureau would be too expensive—it had requested an appropriation of nearly $12,000,000. At a time when the people were burdened with a huge national debt, would

THOMAS A. HENDRICKS
Reproduced from the collection of the Library of Congress

it not be wiser to abolish the bureau altogether? The time limitation established under the original bill was now abolished, and he feared that the bureau would become permanent. With its host of new officials, which Hendricks thought unnecessary, it might be a threat to states' rights: "It will be useless to speak any longer of limitations upon the power of the General Government, it will be idle to speak of the reserved power of the States; State rights and State power will have passed away if we can do what is proposed in . . . this bill." Such an agency would apply its illegal power in Indiana—a state "that provides for her own paupers, . . . that provides for the government of her own people, may . . . be placed under a government that our fathers never contemplated, a government that must be most distasteful to freemen." The intrusion of the bureau in Indiana might undermine the laws and the state constitution, under which blacks were not allowed "many civil rights and immunities . . . enjoyed by the white people" and were prohibited from migrating into the state.[33]

Hendricks challenged Trumbull's argument that the Freedmen's Bureau was valid under the Thirteenth Amendment. Slavery, said Hendricks, was a "domestic relation" only; the amendment had merely broken "asunder this relation between the master and his slave." The state laws which had "authorized this relation [are] abrogated and annulled . . . but no new rights are conferred upon the freedmen." Civil rights, including contracts, testifying in court, sitting on juries, marriage—all these were still within the province of the states.[34]

The only provision of the act with which the Indiana senator could concur was that pertaining to public lands. The application of the homestead principle to the problem of the freedman might well be acceptable to a western Democrat. "If we ever expect to do anything substantially for the colored people," he said, "to encourage them to obtain homes," it might be accomplished through a "reasonable appropriation of the public lands for that purpose."[35] As a matter of fact, however, the public land provision of the bill was not a homestead act for the freedmen. The Homestead Act of 1862 granted land in 160 acre plots to actual settlers who would cultivate the land and improve it. Under the Freedmen's Bureau Bill, freedmen would have to purchase the land.[36]

Trumbull replied immediately to Hendricks in a speech designed primarily to assuage the fears and uncertainties of the Indiana senator. The bureau, he said, was not to be a permanent institution, but merely an agency to aid "helpless, ignorant, and unprotected people" until they could care for themselves. The expense would not be so great as Hendricks feared, for the bureau was still to be under the War Department and many officers would still be paid by the army with no additional

compensation. The possibility that the bureau might extend its operation into Indiana, or any other northern state, was remote. True, if
freedmen should congregate in large numbers in places along the Ohio
River, such as Cairo, Illinois, or Evansville, Indiana, and become a
charge on these communities, the bureau "would have a right to extend
its jurisdiction over them, provide for their wants, secure for them
employment, and place them in a situation where they could provide for
themselves." But there would be no interference with the laws of
Indiana.

The civil rights provisions of the bill were not to provide any special
rights to blacks but rather equality between blacks and whites. The
Indiana law forbidding interracial marriages, of which Hendricks had
spoken, would not be affected because it applied to both the white and
the black party in any proposed marriage contract and was therefore
not discriminatory. Although Trumbull did not mention Negro suffrage, certainly he had it in mind when he assured his fellow senators
that the bill had nothing to do with "political rights." Here Trumbull
spoke for that large majority in the North, irrespective of party, who
believed that under the Constitution the determination of suffrage
qualifications was one of those powers reserved to the states. He also
expressed his faith in education as the least expensive and most effective way of elevating blacks and making them self-sustaining.

Doubtless, on many of these points, there was substantial agreement
between the two senators, for they were both apostles of the American
democratic faith in the nineteenth century, which had not been radically
changed by the Civil War. Also, Trumbull and Hendricks came from
neighboring states of the Old Northwest, and before the disruptions of
the 1850s both had belonged to the Democratic party. An awareness of
the areas of agreement—as well as disagreement—among men who
thought of themselves as adversaries is elucidating, if not vital, to an
understanding of the ultimate direction and end of Reconstruction.

The major point of disagreement between the two senators had to do
with what constituted slavery, the meaning and intent of the Thirteenth
Amendment, and the related question of how far restoration had
progressed. Hendricks was alarmed by those sections of the bill that
conferred judicial authority upon the bureau, and he rejected the Thirteenth Amendment as its proper source. Trumbull, on the other hand,
held that the amendment did, indeed, confer such authority. In his
view, the abolition of slavery was not merely a removal from the master
of his power to control the slave, leaving him adrift and at the mercy of
the states, to be deprived of his civil rights. If this was the condition of
the freedman, said Trumbull, "the trumpet of freedom that we have

been blowing . . . has given an 'uncertain sound,' and the promised freedom is a delusion." "With the destruction of slavery necessarily follows the destruction of the incidents of slavery. When slavery was abolished, slave codes in its support were abolished also."[37]

If the Thirteenth Amendment provided the constitutional authority for moving against the institution of slavery in the several southern states, the authority for implementing it with such an agency as the Freedmen's Bureau rested in the war power; for, as Trumbull stated it, "the powers of the Government do not cease with the dispersion of the rebel armies. They are to be continued and exercised until the civil authority of the Government can be established firmly and upon a sure foundation not again to be disturbed or interfered with." None of the government departments, said Trumbull, understood that the military authority had ceased to operate in the rebellious states, and the president had not restored the writ of habeas corpus in those states. Therefore, no restoration had, as yet, taken place, despite the contrary implications of the Indiana senator.

The Freedmen's Bureau Bill passed in the Senate on January 25 by a large majority and with the unanimous support of the Republicans; even the pro-Johnson senators, Dixon and Doolittle, voted for it. On February 6, the House approved it by an equally substantial majority.

It is a generally accepted notion that Senator Trumbull did not expect Johnson to veto the bill, indeed that he was amazed at the veto. He described two visits with the president to discuss both the Freedmen's Bureau Bill and the Civil Rights Bill, from which he took the impression that they met with his approval, and he submitted copies of both measures to the president before introducing them. In the debate on the measure Trumbull quoted passages from Johnson's annual message to show that it was not contrary to his program.

Senator Fessenden also participated in the debate in defense of the bill with a speech in which he complimented Johnson and expressed agreement with him on fundamental questions. No man, Fessenden said, had shown "a greater respect for the Constitution or a more profound respect for the rights and privileges of the coordinate branches of the Government than the President of the United States.[38]

There were rumors circulating in political circles of an impending break between Johnson and his party, but senators and congressmen who visited the White House concluded that they were groundless. The northern press was also conciliatory and sought to allay the effect of such rumors. The *New York Tribune* expressed its satisfaction that there need not be and probably would not be a break between Congress and the president. *Harper's Weekly* said that "the perpetual distrust of the President . . . [was] wholly unjustifiable. His purpose [was] certainly beyond suspicion."[39]

Despite these outward signs, there were some clues as to what the president's reaction might be; the failure to perceive them suggests some myopia on the part of moderate Republican leaders, especially Trumbull. Their very genuine desire to avoid a clash may have led them to indulge in some wishful thinking. Trumbull, let us recall, had been made aware of the need for new legislation by reports from the South of injustices to freedmen under presidential policies. Then, in framing the legislation, Trumbull had worked with General Howard, who had come to regard new legislation as mandatory because of the actions of "the President himself, who had . . . drifted into positive opposition to the Bureau law—a law that he was bound by his oath of office to execute, but one that his process of reconstruction had caused to be violated in the spirit, if not in the letter, so as to render it nugatory."[40] In his

GIDEON WELLES
Reproduced from the collection of the Library of Congress

defense of the Freedmen's Bureau Bill, Trumbull had claimed not to be concerned about reconstruction, per se, a neat device for avoiding conflict with the president. But, in fact, the bureau, its purpose and its justification, went to the heart of the matter—protection of persons by federal authority, the use of the military to guarantee civil rights, and the crucial question of whether the policy for the former Confederate states would be one of "reconstruction" or "restoration." It appears that moderates, such as Trumbull and Fessenden, were not yet willing, at the beginning of 1866, to weigh all the evidence in making their estimate of the president.

The explanation of the president's veto of the Freedmen's Bureau is partly that he believed it to be a threat to his kind of restoration. But for a more complete explanation we must go beyond that to the man himself, his way of conducting his office, and to the influence of his immediate and trusted advisors. Nearly two weeks elapsed between the passage of the bill and the president's veto. Did Johnson arrive at his decision through thoughts and actions during these crucial days? Or must we search more widely, beyond the specific provisions of the bill, to an earlier time and to matters with a more indirect and subtle bearing on it? There are several factors that must be considered. One was the pressure from the border states, to which Johnson was very sensitive. These states insisted that the bureau and the military jurisdiction that went along with it must be ended. The most strident demand came from Kentucky, whose governor threatened that unless the bureau was removed he would convene the state assembly and take the lead in adopting legislation that would make it difficult, if not impossible, for blacks to live in the state.

Then there was the political question, and the constant concern of the president about the sources of his political following. He had not yet moved, as he would before the end of the year, to form a new party of Republicans and Democrats who favored his policies, but he was keenly aware of the support he was receiving from northern Democrats and could ill afford to ignore or neglect them. A veto would be reassuring to these Democrats, none of whom had voted for the bill in Congress. James Gordon Bennett's *New York Herald,* the most influential independent newspaper, had denounced the bill and called for a veto. When the veto was finally decided on, Bennett was one of the first to be informed, by telegraph from the White House.[41]

These factors are clearly related to a more significant one, the growing conviction of the president that there was a radical conspiracy against him, and his inability to distinguish between radicals and moderates. The relationship between Johnson and Secretary of the Navy

Gideon Welles, his closest adviser and one on whom he could always count for reinforcement of his views, has an important bearing on the president's attitudes. It was perhaps unfortunate that Welles's chief informant of affairs in Congress was Charles Sumner—a personal friend despite their political differences—with whom Welles carried on regular Saturday evening conversations. In Welles's diary we can follow Sumner's caveats and chastisements, beginning at the time of the assembling of the Thirty-ninth Congress in early December and continuing to mid-February. On December 8, Sumner "denounced the policy of the President . . . as the greatest and most criminal error ever committed by any government," for which Welles, McCulloch, and Seward must bear some responsibility. A few days later Sumner sent Welles a copy of a newspaper containing a memorial calling for Johnson's impeachment. On December 16, Sumner, "almost beside himself," criticized the president for moving "without the consent and direction of Congress." On January 13, he branded Johnson as "the greatest enemy of the South that she had ever had, worse than Jeff Davis," and he warned that Congress was "becoming more firm and united every day" in its insistence on a change in executive policy.[42]

Welles, of course, reported all this faithfully to Johnson, as evidence that "a deep and extensive intrigue was going on against him," and suggested that the use of presidential patronage and "a summary removal of one or two mischievous men . . . would be effective and salutary." Even Senator Trumbull, the secretary suspected, had become a part of these "dark, revolutionary, reckless intrigues." Welles's animosity toward the Freedmen's Bureau Bill and its framers was already evident before he had read it, because of his opposition "to that system of legislation, and to the Government's taking upon itself the care and support of communities." After examining the bill he was even more adamant: The "Freedmen's Bureau scheme [was] a governmental enormity"; there was a disposition in Congress "to promote these notions of freedom by despotic and tyrannical means."[43] He did not see how the president could sign such a measure, and he certainly would not advise it.

Yet, despite his indignation, one can detect in Welles a note of ambivalence toward the freedmen. "Something is necessary," he admitted, "for the wretched people who have been emancipated, and who have neither intelligence nor means to provide for themselves." All he had to propose, though, was that in time, "if let alone, society would [adapt] itself to circumstances and make circumstances conform to existing necessities." Meanwhile, there would be "suffering, misery, wretchedness," not "entirely confined to the blacks."[44] If one finds confusion and contradiction in these passages, it was of a sort common to men of the post–Civil War era resting, so to speak, in a state of limbo between the age of romantic reform and the age of social Darwinism.

It is evident that, during the weeks preceding the veto, Andrew Johnson did not seek advice from both sides in order to arrive at a reasoned and objective decision. Rather he was a lonely figure in the White House, in contact only with those who agreed with him and were ready to reinforce him in his convictions, and in a frame of mind where the presumed, and largely mythical, conspiracy against him might seem very real indeed. "Shut up in the White House," as W. R. Brock has so aptly stated it, "taking little or no exercise, working with extraordinary and commendable industry, cut off from those who wished to work with him and seeing only those who agreed with him or had favors to ask, he came to live in a world which had less and less contact with political reality."[45]

On the morning of February 19, Johnson held a special cabinet meeting, where he presented his veto message. Welles, Seward, McCulloch, and Dennison supported the veto. Stanton did not make a strong argument against it, but was disappointed, as were Harlan and Speed. Welles, ignoring the fact that the author of the bill was a moderate and that Republicans had voted unanimously for it, believed that the veto would lead to a rupture between Johnson and "a portion of the Republican members of Congress." Now the "master spirits," who were "active as well as cunning," would "intrigue with the Members."[46] If Welles was predicting that the veto would isolate the radicals and thus weaken them in their difficulties with the president he could not have been more wrong. On the contrary, the veto was an early step in the transformation of the contest between executive and radicals into an executive-congressional conflict. It set the stage for the election of 1866 and ultimately for impeachment.

The message Johnson sent to the Senate on February 19 may be seen as consisting of two separate but related parts—first, his objections to the bill itself and his concerns about its effects and, second, the question of representation in Congress of the former Confederate states, in other words, "restoration" or "reconstruction." He began by asserting that, since the original act had not yet expired, there was no need for new legislation. Taking a somewhat different tack, he pointed out that the original bureau had been established to cope with wartime conditions and to aid in the transition from slavery to freedom. But "the institution of slavery [he said] has been already effectively and finally abrogated throughout the whole country" by a constitutional amendment, "and practically its eradication has received the assent and concurrence of most of the States in which it at any time had an existence."[47] Because of its provisions for the use of military power in peacetime and its "invasion of civil and judicial functions" the law was unconstitutional. The authors of the Constitution had never contemplated such a "system of support for indigent persons." Congress had never before "thought itself impowered to establish asylums beyond the limits of the District of Columbia, except for the benefit of . . . disabled soldiers and sailors." Nor had it ever "founded schools for any class of our people, not even for the orphans of those who [had] fallen in defense of the Union, but [had] left the care of education to the much more competent and efficient control of the States, of communities, of private associations, and of individuals."[48] Moreover, by taking away land from former owners without prior legal proceedings the bill violated constitutional "due process of law."

Raising the bugaboo of the bad effect of the bureau on the attitudes and expectations of freedmen, the message read, "It will tend to keep the mind of the freedman in a state of uncertain expectation and restlessness, while to those among whom he lives it will be a source of constant and vague apprehension." In one remarkable passage Johnson, oblivious to the restraints already placed on freedmen under the laws and practices of his own regime of presidential restoration, applied to the freedmen the prevailing concepts of self-help, individualism, and laissez faire:

> Undoubtedly the freedman should be protected, but he should be protected by the civil authorities, especially by the exercise of all the constitutional powers of the courts of the United States and of the States. His condition is not so exposed as may at first be imagined. He is in a portion of the country where his labor can not well be spared. Competition for his services from planters, from those who are constructing or repairing railroads, and from capitalists in his vicinage or from other States will enable him to command almost his own terms. He also possesses a perfect right to change his place of abode, and if, therefore, he does not find in one community or State a mode of life suited to his desires or proper remuneration for his labor, he can move to another where that labor is more esteemed and better rewarded. In truth, however, each State, induced by its own wants and interests, will do what is necessary and proper to retain within its borders all the labor that is needed for the development of its resources. The laws that regulate supply and demand will maintain their force, and the wages of the laborer will be regulated thereby. There is no danger

that the exceedingly great demand for labor will not operate in favor of the laborer.

Neither is sufficient consideration given to the ability of the freedmen to protect and take care of themselves. It is no more than justice to them to believe that as they have received their freedom with moderation and forbearance, so they will distinguish themselves by their industry and thrift, and soon show the world that in a condition of freedom they are self-sustaining, capable of selecting their own employment and their own places of abode, of insisting for themselves on a proper remuneration, and of establishing and maintaining their own asylums and schools. It is earnestly hoped that instead of wasting away they will by their own efforts establish for themselves a condition of respectability and prosperity. It is certain that they can attain to that condition only through their own merits and exertions.[49]

In the second part of the message Johnson placed the argument for the unconstitutionality of the act on a different base, the absence of representatives from "the eleven States which are to be mainly affected by its provisions." This led him into the question of the "right of Congress to judge . . . 'of election returns, and qualifications of its own members.' " Such authority, he asserted, could "not be construed as including the right to shut out in time of peace any State from the representation to which it is entitled by the Constitution." In Johnson's judgment, most of the seceded states had been fully restored and were "to be deemed as entitled to enjoy their constitutional rights as members of the Union."[50]

The message contains at least three references to the power and function of the president that seem contradictory, if not confused. One of the president's arguments against the bill is that the system of justice under the Freedmen's Bureau, with its "countless number of agents established in every parish or county in nearly a third of the States," with "no supervision or control by the Federal courts," would place a power in the hands of the president that "ought never to be entrusted to any one man." Further on he voiced his fears that the "care, support, and control of 4,000,000 emancipated slaves" by the bureau "would inevitably tend to a concentration of power in the Executive which would enable him, if so disposed, to control the actions of this numerous class and use them for the attainment of his own political ends."[51] There may, indeed, have been some merit to these arguments, based on possible dangers. But conveniently the president overlooked the power he was already wielding. Without consulting Congress he had estab-

lished his own system of restoration, under which governments had
been reestablished and representatives sent back to Congress expecting to be seated. Now he all but dictated that Congress accept his policy,
with the caveat that to act otherwise would be to violate the Constitution.

Toward the end of the message, the argument took another curious
turn. Having warned against the dangers of excessive executive power,
Johnson now invested the office with peculiar prerogatives vis-á-vis the
legislature. From this exalted position he lectured Congress on its
duties:

> The President of the United States stands toward the country
> in a somewhat different attitude from that of any member of Con-
> gress. Each member of Congress is chosen from a single district or
> State; *the President is chosen by the people of all the States. As
> eleven States are not at this time represented in either branch of
> Congress, it would seem to be his duty on all proper occasions to
> present their just claims to Congress.* There always will be differ-
> ences of opinion in the community, and individuals may be guilty of
> transgressions of the law, but these do not constitute valid objec-
> tions against the right of a State to representation. I would in no
> wise interfere with the discretion of Congress with regard to the
> qualifications of members; but I hold it my duty to recommend to
> you, in the interests of peace and the interests of union, the admis-
> sion of every State to its share in public legislation when, however
> insubordinate, insurgent, or rebllious its people may have been, it
> presents itself, not only in an attitude of loyalty and harmony, but
> in the persons of representatives whose loyalty can not be ques-
> tioned under any existing constitutional or legal test.[52]

The injection into his argument that the president has a particular
obligation to protect the states—to protect democracy as it was then
generally understood—harks back to Andrew Jackson, whose veto of
the bill to recharter the Bank of the United States bears some resemblance to it. The model of Abraham Lincoln skillfully wielding
executive power was also before him. Actually, Johnson went beyond
both Jackson and Lincoln. Jackson had been concerned to establish the
presidency as an equal coordinate branch of government. Lincoln, with
the war power to fall back on, enlarged the executive power while
taking scrupulous care not to affront Congress or challenge it unduly.
Johnson, by presenting the president as the only true representative of
the whole nation, came closer than any other nineteenth-century president to the assertion of imperial power. Nothing else that he said, no

other posture he assumed, aroused more bitter resentment of Republicans in Congress.

The growth of executive power in America has come about, to a considerable extent, by the governance of determined and adroit presidents during times of crisis. Johnson's inauspicious effort to enlarge and then to exploit the executive power had the opposite effect; it led to his impeachment and nearly to his removal from office and to the ascendancy of Congress. Even so, Johnson's effort, in the long run, should not be ignored or minimized, since it lay midway between Andrew Jackson and Theodore Roosevelt, whose "Stewardship Theory" would set the tone for the rise of an "imperial presidency" in the twentieth century.

Northern Republicans of all persuasions were shocked, and sometimes saddened, by the veto. *Harper's Weekly*, which had been consistently friendly to Johnson, said that the message was "a sore disappointment to the truest friends of the President." Of his sincerity there was still no doubt, but "he seems to us not entirely master of his own positions."

> If the President believes that the word of the nation sacredly pledged to the freedmen will be kept by the black codes of South Carolina and Mississippi, his faith would remove mountains. And if he proposes to abandon the freedmen to civil authorities created exclusively by those who think that the colored race should be eternally enslaved, who deny the constitutionality of emancipation, and who have now a peculiarly envenomed hostility to the whole class, we can only pray God that the result may be what we have no doubt he honestly wishes it to be. We believe that he is faithful to what he conceives to be the best interests of the whole country. And while upon this question we wholly differ from him, we differ with no aspersion or suspicion.[53]

Other reactions were harsher. "When he appeals, nay demands," said the *Washington Chronicle*, "that the States, now almost as rebellious as they were a year ago—certainly as filled with hate of the great Congressional majorities and the loyal masses of the American people—shall be at once rehabilitated, he will send a thrill of dismay to every loyal heart throughout the wide domanin."[54] A Maine Congressman, writing to his governor, was shocked by "the monstrous and arrogant assumption, that the Members of Congress represent only localities (as though the aggregate did not completely represent the whole) while the President is the representative of the whole people, and the peculiar guardian of the rights, and interests of the unrepresented States. This is modest for a man chosen to preside over the Senate, and made President by an assassin."[55]

On the day of the veto the Joint Committee on Reconstruction was working on a compromise proposal to seat the representatives from Tennessee in Congress. The veto gave Stevens an opportunity to stop any such restoration of the rebel states. He accomplished it with a resolution in the House that was adopted by a unanimous Republican vote:

> Be it resolved by the House of Representatives, the Senate concurring, that in order to close agitation upon a question which seems likely to disturb the action of the government, as well as to quiet the uncertainty which is agitating the minds of the people of the eleven states which have been declared to be in insurrection, no senator or representative shall be admitted into either branch of Congress from any of said states until Congress shall have declared such state entitled to such representation.[56]

The day after the veto Trumbull, in a long speech in the Senate, presented a detailed and learned refutation of it. It was an eloquent effort, perhaps the best of Trumbull's political career. The nation, Trumbull assured his colleagues, would not be flooded with bureau agents unless the president himself saw fit to appoint them, for under the provisions of the bill he was authorized to appoint only "so many as may be needed." It had "never entered the mind . . . of a single advocate of this bill that the President . . . would so abuse the authority entrusted to him as to station an agent in every county of these States."[57]

If the rebellion had ended, as the president contended, by what authority had he suspended the writ of habeas corpus? If it had ended it was only "so far as the conflict of arms is concerned; . . . the consequences of the rebellion is not ended; peace is not restored; the safety of the citizens where the rebellion existed is not yet established, and till it is, till the courts can be reestablished, [and] . . . can administer justice peaceably . . . the military authority may properly be continued." As Trumbull explained it, the bureau was simply an agency for the application of proper and constitutional military power.

In answering Johnson's objections to those provisions setting aside land for freedmen and for schools and asylums, Trumbull, speaking of the unprecedented nature of the current crisis, approached what might have been the heart of the problem of reconstruction:

> I have read that whole paragraph in order to do no injustice to the views of the President. The objection which the President makes is

that it has never heretofore been thought that Congress was empowered to pass provisions of this character. The answer to that is this: we never before were in such a state as now; never before in the history of this Government did eleven States of the Union combine together to overthrow and destroy the Union; never before in the history of this Government have we had a four years' civil war; never before in the history of this Government have nearly four million people been emancipated from the most abject and degrading slavery ever imposed upon human beings; never before has the occasion arisen when it was necessary to provide for such large numbers of people thrown upon the bounty of the Government, unprotected and unprovided for.

As a matter of fact, however, said Trumbull, the government *had* voted money for those who could not care for themselves—for Indians and for Africans brought to American shores by slave traders. Could it not, therefore, "provide for those among us who have been held in bondage all their lives?" His description of the plight of the freedmen belies his reputation as a cold and calculating man lacking warmth and sentiment: "Here are hundreds and thousands of these poor, ignorant, degraded human beings who never went off the plantation where they were born in their lives. They do not know how to travel. They do not know where to go; they have no means to pay for subsistence by the way; they do not know whither the railroads lead; the railroads would not carry them if they did, and were able to pay. As a friend suggests, they cannot read the finger-boards by the wayside; and where are they to go, and what is to be done with them?"

That passage in the veto message stating the presumptive power of the executive as the only elected official "chosen by the people of all the States" and thus the spokesman for the eleven unrepresented states elicited from Trumbull a sharp rejoinder. How many votes, the senator inquired, had Johnson got in the eleven states for which he appointed himself the representative? "Sir, he is no more the representative of those . . . States than I am, except as he holds a higher position. I come here as a representative chosen by the State of Illinois, but I come here to legislate, not simply for the State of Illinois but for the United States of America, and for South Carolina as well as Illinois."[58]

In concluding, Trumbull trenchantly summarized the considerations that compelled him to oppose the veto:

> The President believes it unconstitutional; I believe it constitutional. He believes that it will involve great expense; I believe it will save expense. He believes that the freedman will be protected

without it; I believe he will be tyrannized over, abused, and virtually reenslaved without some legislation by the nation for his protection. He believes it unwise; I believe it to be politic. I thought, in
advocating it, that I was acting in harmony with the views of the
President. I regret exceedingly the antagonism which his message
presents to the expressed views of Congress, not only as to the
proper mode to be pursued in reference to protecting the refugees
and freedmen, but as to the present condition of the rebellious
States. I shall rejoice as much as any one to have those States
restored in all their constitutional relations at the earliest period
consistent with the safety and welfare of the whole people. I shall
rejoice when those States shall abolish all civil distinction between
their inhabitants on account of race or color; and when that is done
one great object of the Freedmen's Bureau will have been accomplished.[59]

Trumbull's stirring appeal did not result in the repassage of the
Freedmen's Bureau Bill over the veto. This time five Republicans,
including Cowan, Dixon, and Doolittle, voted against it and thus prevented the necessary two-thirds majority. The bureau continued to
operate under the existing law until July, when an amended bill was
adopted and passed over a presidential veto.

On Washington's Birthday, just three days after the veto, Andrew
Johnson, spurred on by a crowd of serenaders that had gathered outside
the White House, made a speech that revealed more about his character
and personality than anything he had said or done before. It astonished
and angered his enemies and embarrassed his friends. Placing himself in
the tradition of Washington and Jackson and asserting that he was
carrying on the policies of Abraham Lincoln, Johnson likened himself to
Jesus Christ: "The founder of our holy religion . . . came into the world
and saw men condemned under the law, and the sentence was death.
What was His example? Instead of putting the world or a nation to
death, He went forth on the cross and testified with His wounds that He
would die and let the world live."

One rebellion having been put down, Johnson said, another rebellion
now threatened, led by "an irresponsible central directory" which had
assumed nearly all the powers of Congress "without even consulting the
legislative and executive departments of the Government." Having
fought the "Davises, the Toombses, the Slidells, and a long list of such,"
he would now fight northern traitors who would threaten the Union.
Somebody in the crowd called out, "Give us their names," and Johnson
obliged:

The gentleman calls for [their] names. I am talking to my friends and fellow-citizens here. Suppose I should name to you those whom I look upon as being opposed to the fundamental principles of this Government, and as now laboring to destroy them. I say Thaddeus Stevens, of Pennsylvania; I say Charles Sumner, of Massachusetts; I say Wendell Phillips, of Massachusetts. [A voice, "Forney!"]

I do not waste my fire on dead ducks. I stand for the country, and though my enemies may traduce, slander, and vituperate, I may say, that has no force.

Again, as in the veto message, Johnson presented himself as the tribune of the people and their protector against "those who want to destroy our institutions and change the character of the Government. Are they not satisfied with one martyr? Does not the blood of Lincoln appease the vengeance and wrath of the opponents of this Government? Is their thirst still unslaked? Do they want more blood?" If Johnson's fate was to be assassination, "if my blood is to be shed because I vindicate the Union and the preservation of this Government in its original purity and character, let it be so; but when it is done, let the altar of the Union be erected, and then, . . . lay me upon it."[60]

A number of historians have seen this speech, and similar ones during the campaign of 1866, as a reversion to the crude and uninhibited politics of eastern Tennessee, the locale of Johnson's early struggles. Some contemporaries explained it in the same way. Welles, for example, wrote in his diary that it was "the manner and custom in the Southwest, and especially in Tennessee, to do this on the stump."[61] We cannot discount the influence of Johnson's early political conditioning, but it hardly suffices as an explanation of his erratic public behavior after he became president. If an answer to this enigma is to be found, it is in the character and psyche of the man, in some combination of his strengths and weaknesses—courage, tenacity, self-righteousness, an acute sensitivity to his lowly origins, and a tendency to view public differences as personal vendettas. In certain settings, this potent combination could lead to flights of fancy or incoherence.

Johnson's closest cabinet advisors regretted that he had made the speech. Hugh McCulloch had advised him not to speak to the serenaders, and the president assured him that he had no intention of doing so. But with the large crowd urging him on "his wise resolution was forgotten—his combativeness was aroused—and he made such a speech as no President can make without suffering in the estimation of thoughtful men." All his "offhand public addresses," said McCulloch, were of this type. They were "bad in substance, bad in language, bad in style;

the very opposite of his messages and other communications to Congress, which are scarcely inferior in any respect to the best that have been issued from the Executive Mansion."[62] Welles was "sorry that he had permitted himself to be drawn into answering impertinent questions to a promiscuous crowd and that he should have given names of those whose course he disapproved. Not that his remarks were not true, but the President should not be catechized into declarations."[63]

In Congress moderates kept their poise and refrained from public statements that might further damage their relationship with the president. Privately, they were distressed and uncertain about the future. In the Senate, for example, Fessenden still spoke "respectfully and kindly" of Johnson, but in a letter to a favorite cousin he said:

> As certainty is preferable to surprise, the President's recent exhibitions of folly and wickedness are also a relief. The long agony is over. He has broken faith, betrayed his trust, and must sink from detestation into contempt. The consequences I cannot foresee, but they must be terribly disastrous. I see nothing ahead but a long indecisive struggle for three years, and, in the meantime great domestic convulsions, and an entire cessation of the work of reform—perhaps a return to power of the Country's worst enemies—Northern Copperheads. For these calamities we are indebted in great measure to such miserable toadies as Doolittle and Dixon, who have made it their business to flatter our weak President, and make a party for him against the views and wishes of the great body of their political friends.[64]

It was all but inevitable that Thaddeus Stevens would respond to the president. In doing it, he showed how varied his weapons could be by using a stiletto rather than a bludgeon. The speech reported to have taken place in front of the White House, said Stevens, never happened. "That speech . . . was one of the grandest hoaxes ever perpetrated. . . . I am glad to have at this time opportunity . . . to exonerate the President from ever having made that speech. It is a part of the cunning contrivance of the copperhead party, who have been pestering our President since the 4th of March last."[65]

The Freedmen's Bureau veto and the Washington's Birthday speech mark an important turning point in the executive-legislative conflict. From that time on it was an open affair for all to see. Granted, the unrelieved truculence of radicals such as Sumner and Stevens was aggravating, but in retaliating as he did Johnson made his own party more vulnerable to attack and gave the radicals more publicity and more importance than they could have gained in any other way.[66]

Chapter 4

Trumbull and Civil Rights

THE CIVIL RIGHTS BILL, which Senator Trumbull had introduced along with the Freedmen's Bureau Bill, passed in the Senate on February 2 by a majority of 32 to 12 and in the House on March 13 by 111 to 38. Johnson vetoed it on March 27, but within two weeks both houses had passed it over the veto, and it became law. Although the two measures are properly linked together, in that they were both designed to protect loyal whites and freedmen in the southern states, there were some fundamental differences between them; the first veto was not the equivalent of the second. True, there was one central core of support for the measures and another in opposition, but around the periphery were people who changed their minds, not merely owing to political pressure, of which there was much, but also owing to differences between the two bills. Both measures rested on the premise that freedmen were entitled to traditional American civil rights. The Freedmen's Bureau Bill was intended to provide the means, through the application of the war power, to protect the freedmen temporarily in the hope, if not the expectation, that the states would ultimately awaken to their responsibilities and assure equal protection to all persons. The question of citizenship was left in abeyance.

The Civil Rights Bill was more fundamental, in that it conferred national citizenship on blacks and sought to bring the federal government permanently to their protection. The citizenship conferred upon them carried with it "the same right in every State and Territory . . . to make and enforce contracts; to sue, be parties, and give evidence; to inherit, purchase, lease, sell, hold, and convey real and personal property; and to full and equal benefit of all laws and proceedings for the security of persons and property as is enjoyed by white citizens." The remainder of the law provided punishments for its violation and the means for its enforcement. Violation of the act by depriving protected persons of their rights was a misdemeanor punishable by a fine "not exceeding one thousand dollars or imprisonment not exceeding one year, or both." Federal district and circuit courts would have cognizance of violations of the act and of civil and criminal cases affecting persons denied rights guaranteed to them under it. District attorneys, marshals, commissioners appointed by circuit and territorial courts, and agents of the Freedmen's Bureau would constitute the enforcement personnel. The president, when he had reason to believe that a violation had been or might be committed, was authorized to employ the naval or land forces of the United States or the militia. Questions of law arising under the provisions of the act might be appealed to the Supreme Court.[1]

In explicating and defending the Civil Rights Bill Trumbull again fell back on the Thirteenth Amendment. The southern "black codes," he admitted, did not "make a man an absolute slave," but they deprived him of "the rights of a freeman." It was "perhaps difficult to draw a

LYMAN TRUMBULL
Reproduced from the collection of the Library of Congress

precise line, to say where freedom ceases and slavery begins, but a law that does not allow a colored person to go from one county to another is certainly a law in derogation of the rights of a freeman. A law that does not allow a colored person to hold property, does not allow him to teach, does not allow him to preach, is certainly a law in violation of the rights of a freeman, and being so may properly be declared void." What were the means, and where was the authority for the abolition of slavery and the assurance of freedom? It was to be found, said Trumbull, in the second section of the amendment, which "vests Congress with the discretion of selecting [the] 'appropriate legislation.' " Did it follow that, to secure their freedom and their civil rights, blacks should be made citizens? Trumbull argued that this was the basis of the whole bill. In addressing himself to the question, he quoted Blackstone on the distinction between natural and civil liberty: "every man who enters society gives up a part of his natural liberty, which is the liberty of the savage, . . . for the advantages he obtains in the protection which civil government gives him." For a clarification of civil liberty he turned again to Blackstone, who had defined it as "natural liberty, so far restrained by human laws and no further, as is necessary and expedient for the general advantage of the public." Under such a definition of civil liberty, Trumbull thought it ought to be understood that "the restraints introduced by law should be equal to all, or as much so as the nature of things will permit." And how would such equality be assured? Through the granting of citizenship, together with the constitutional guarantee that "The Citizens of each State shall be entitled to all Privileges and Immunities of Citizens of the several States."[2]

The enforcement provisions were similar to those of the Fugitive Slave Law of 1850, especially the appointment of commissioners and the payment of fees for their services. Trumbull admitted that they were copied from that act, and then added, "Surely we have the authority to enact a law as efficient in the interests of freedom, now that freedom prevails throughout the country, as we had in the interest of slavery when it prevailed in a portion of the country." Whatever logic there might have been in using the Fugitive Slave Law as a model for the enforcement provisions of the Civil Rights Act, it left Trumbull vulnerable to his traducers and the bill open to some effective criticism. Senator Willard Saulsbury of Delaware asked, "What did the honorable Senator say, and what did other honorable Senators say, when the Fugitive Slave Law gave the power to marshals to summon persons to make arrests? They were horrified. What was their language? 'Is thy servant a dog that he would do this thing?' "

Although the Civil Rights Bill applied federal power to the protection of blacks, Trumbull did not see it as an encroachment on states' rights, for, he said, "It will have no operation in any State where the laws are equal, where all persons have the same civil rights without regard to color or race." Whether or not there was federal intervention, then, would be determined by the states themselves; they could avoid it by enacting and enforcing laws that assured uniformity among blacks and whites.[3]

Many radicals who voted for the Civil Rights Bill and worked for its passage over the veto believed that Negro suffrage was a civil right and that the bill ought to have provided for it. Some of the conservative opponents of the bill feared that it would eventually lead to Negro suffrage. Their attitudes manifested the almost universal absence of Negro suffrage in the northern states and the opposition to it by the majority of both major parties. Trumbull received from a Chicago friend, Dr. Charles A. Ray, a caveat on the subject that expressed the view of a large segment of the Republican party. If the president should agree with the Civil Rights Bill and "war is made upon him because he will not go to the extent of negro suffrage," Ray warned, "he will beat all who assail him."

> The party may be split, the Government may go out of Republican hands; but Andy Johnson will be cock-of-the-walk. The people, so far as I understand, are of the opinion that the war for the Union is over. . . . And as for the negro, they think that when he has the rights which your bill will give him, he must be contented to look upon the elective franchise as a something to be earned by giving evidence of his fitness therefore.[4]

Republican senators and congressmen could not, with impunity, ignore such messages from their constituents. In Trumbull's case, however, the warning was unnecessary, because he did not believe national citizenship automatically conferred suffrage on anybody. The conclusion of his Senate speech on the bill was a reassurance to his colleagues and to the nation on this point: "This bill has nothing to do with the political rights or *status* of parties. It is confined exclusively to their civil rights, such right as should appertain to every free man."[5]

In the Senate the most vigorous challenge to the bill came from Willard Saulsbury, a Delaware Democrat. It was a caustic attack, less moderate than Senator Hendricks's speech against the Freedmen's Bureau Bill, and less conciliatory even than the president's veto message. At some points it barely missed being a personal vendetta against Trumbull. It was the sort of speech congressmen might expect from border state Democrats in the atmosphere of 1866. The Civil Rights

Bill, Saulsbury charged, was a flagrant betrayal of the Union instituted by the founding fathers, a Union intended "simply as a contract and agreement of union and government" among the states. Surely they could not have supposed that "in the short term of eighty years their children would be subjected to the absolute control and the omnipotent will of the Federal Congress." The Thirteenth Amendment, properly interpreted, meant simply that "a person heretofore a slave of another shall be no longer his slave, and it operates no further." If it had been intended to bestow upon the freed slave all the rights of a free citizen, the amendment should have been specific on this point.

Although he did not question Trumbull's honesty in avowing that the bill did not confer political rights, Saulsbury did not have the least doubt that, should it become law, "it will receive very generally, if not universally, the construction that it does confer a right of voting in the States." This was so because the term *civil rights* was a generic one, "which in its comprehensive significance includes every species of right that man can enjoy" other than that emanating from a state of nature.[6] In its enforcement provisions, Saulsbury continued, the bill was an unconstitutional assault upon the policy and judicial powers of the states. As he quaintly stated it, "There cannot be a case of chicken-stealing in any State of this Union where freed negroes are not allowed to testify that can, if this bill is to be operative and in force, be determined in the State courts."

An important premise of Saulsbury's thought was that America was and ought to remain a white man's country. If former slaves were now free, their freedom was the equivalent of that of the antebellum free Negroes, whose liberty was so precarious and so circumscribed as to make their lot little better than that of slaves. For Saulsbury, the "time for shedding tears over poor slaves [had] well nigh passed. . . ."

> The tears which the honest white people of this country
> have been made to shed from the oppressive acts of this
> Government in its various departments during the last four years
> call more loudly for my sympathies than those tears which have
> been shedding and dropping and dropping for the last twenty years
> in reference to the poor, oppressed slave—dropping from the eyes
> of strong-minded women and weak-minded men, until, becoming a
> mighty flood, they have swept away, in their resistless force, every
> trace of constitutional liberty in this country.

The Delaware senator, it seems, had an obsession about larceny among blacks; he boastfully proclaimed how his state dealt with the problem:

Do you know what our law does with them? It provides for whipping his bare back. We have a whipping-post in our State, and I think it is the most efficient means I ever knew for the prevention of thieving. For five years it was my duty as the law-officer of the State to prosecute in my State, and we never were troubled with those fellows from Philadelphia and Baltimore who would slip over and steal a horse or anything else after once the lash was applied to them. How the humane feelings of all New England would be shocked—even the honorable Senator opposite me would have to come before the Senate of the United States and talk of the inhumanity to one of these pets of congressional legislation because his back had been made to feel the lash.[7]

It would be a mistake to conclude from this summary of the Delaware senator's speech that racism or a lack of concern for civil rights was peculiar to the former slave states. It is even possible that, because of the institutional background from which such men came, they were freer of cant than some of their northern colleagues. The history of race relations in America makes it abundantly clear that these have not been exclusively southern problems.[8] Even so, the blatant and crude Negrophobia, the parochial view of the Constitution, the inability or unwillingness to perceive the changes resulting from the war, the absence of a sense of history were manifestations of the condition of the Democratic party as it descended to its nadir in the early months of Reconstruction. As Andrew Johnson reassessed his political position, rejected the overtures and proposals of such men as Trumbull and Fessenden, and even considered the formation of a new party, men such as Saulsbury would be inevitably drawn to him, and he in turn would depend increasingly on them.

Andrew Johnson did not contemplate for very long what action to take on the Civil Rights Bill. He was determined not to deviate from his established policy; thus the veto was the only alternative open to him. He was losing touch with some important realities of party politics. Two instances are especially illustrative of Johnson's dilemma and his way of coping with it. The first was the gubernatorial election in Connecticut between the Democrat James E. English and the Republican Gen. James R. Hawley. Both candidates sought an endorsement from President Johnson, English on the grounds that he and his party championed the presidential program of restoration, Hawley as the nominee of the Union-Republican party. Hawley, a strong Union man with antislavery sympathies and an excellent war record, leaned toward the congressional position. He recognized the validity of some of Johnson's objections to the Freedmen's Bureau Bill, but stated forthrightly that he would have voted for it if he had been a member of Congress. He favored civil rights for blacks under a new constitutional amendment. He opposed federal legislation for Negro suffrage but hoped that Connecticut would provide for it under its own laws. He felt that Johnson had been provocative and too severe in his remarks about Sumner and Stevens in the Washington's Birthday speech. A distorted account of these views, picturing Hawley as a pro-Negro, anti-Johnson candidate, was published in the Connecticut Democratic press.

Actually, Hawley agreed with resolutions adopted by the Connecticut Republican convention supporting both Johnson and Congress and expressing confidence that they could cooperate in bringing about "the extinction of the doctrine of Secession; the repudiation of all pecuniary obligations incurred in support of the Rebellion; the sacred inviolability of the national debt; the complete destruction of slavery in fact as well as in name; and the enactment of appropriate laws to assure to every class of citizens the full enjoyment of the rights and immunities accorded to all by the Constitution of the United States."[9] But this was not enough for the President, who preferred the Democratic platform, which saluted him for his stand against Negro suffrage and new amendments to the Constitution and for his restoration policy.

Hawley turned to his friend from Connecticut, Secretary of the Navy Gideon Welles, in search of an endorsement from the Johnson administration. His appearance in Washington embarrassed Welles, who admitted that he did not know what to do, and Hawley went away empty-handed. Welles would have liked to make the endorsement but pleaded that he could not do so "without accompanying it with qualifications which would destroy its effect." Aside from personal considerations, the decision was for Welles a simple one. Hawley did not unequivocally favor the administration policy or unequivocally oppose "the schemes of the Radicals who would defeat it." Hawley's direct appeal to the president for an endorsement was also rejected.[10]

Candidate English also came down to Washington for a visit with the president. Johnson was favorably impressed and admitted privately that he hoped for his election, but he would make no public statement for him. Actually, Johnson, without using English's name, did in effect endorse him. Toward the end of the campaign he sent a telegram that was read at an "English and Johnson" rally. Its meaning and the intention of its author could not have been misunderstood: "In reference to the elections in Connecticut or elsewhere, . . . I am for the candidate, who is for the general policy, and the specific measures promulgated, of my administration in my regular message, veto message, speech on 22nd February, and the veto message sent in this day. There can be no mistake in this, I presume it is known, or can be ascertained, what candidates favor or oppose my policy, or measures as promulgated to the country." The Republican ticket won the election in spite of Johnson's endorsement of the Democrat. But a Democratic functionary wrote to Welles that if the president's message had come two weeks earlier the Democrats would have won.[11]

The second case in point had to do with the role of Governor Oliver P. Morton of Indiana, an influential Republican leader in a crucial state. In a state with more than its share of Peace Democrats, Morton, to carry on the war and to keep his party intact, had made himself a kind of dictator. On the other extreme of the Hoosier political spectrum Morton was threatened by George W. Julian, a congressman from Indiana's most thoroughly antislavery district and a dedicated and doctrinaire radical, one who outdid even Thaddeus Stevens in his demand not only for confiscation of rebel lands but for the trial and execution of rebel leaders.

The Morton-Julian feud had been going on since the inception of the Republican party in the mid-1850s; if anything, it became more intense with the end of the war and the coming of reconstruction when Morton, a party man to the core, stood firmly behind Andrew Johnson. At the end of September 1865, Morton invaded Julian territory, with a powerful speech at Richmond, Indiana, in which he denounced the conquered province concept and defended the Lincoln-Johnson position that a state could not secede from the Union. The major emphasis of the speech was its opposition to Negro suffrage, at least until after a period of preparation of blacks through education and the acquisition of land. Morton reminded the radicals that they had not included Negro suffrage in their own Wade-Davis Bill, and he asked his fellow Hoosiers how they could demand Negro suffrage in the South while maintaining their own legal and constitutional restraints on black people. Morton's defense of Johnson's restoration exacerbated the radical-conservative schism in Indiana, but Johnson was grateful to the governor and said that his speech was the ablest public defense of his policy.[12]

What Johnson did not know about Morton was that his argument on Negro suffrage, or other policy questions, at a given moment was not a matter of primary importance for him. In concentrating on his first priority, the preservation and strengthening of his party, the *volte-face* had become a characteristic of the governor's political style. Any idea that Morton might have followed Johnson into the Democratic party or agreed to any combination with Democrats was wishful thinking. Had the president shared his political objectives, Morton was just the sort of leader whose support would have made Johnson's presidency more vital and more durable.

In December 1865, Morton was en route to Paris in search of expert medical treatment for a stroke of paralysis. He went by way of Washington, where he had a conference with Johnson, who entrusted him with a secret mission to Napoleon III. Arriving back in New York on March 7, 1866, Morton was apprised of the Civil Rights Bill and the prospect of a presidential veto. He hurried on to Washington for another meeting with Johnson. The conversation was a long one, in which the governor urged the president to sign the bill, warning that his failure to do so would be "the rock upon which the President and the Republican party would separate." Johnson was "laboring under great emotion," wrote Morton's biographer.

> Large beads of perspiration stood on his forehead. He was stubborn and seemed to think he was strong enough to build up a new party. Morton argued that new parties could only be organized on great questions, that the pending issues must be fought out by the organizations then existing, that "all roads out of the Republican party led into the Democratic party," and that if the President did not sign the bill, Morton would feel, when he left him, that they could not meet again in political fellowship. When Morton left the President he believed that the latter was lost to the Republicans, and he so informed several members of Congress whom he met later in the day.[13]

Upon his return to Indiana Morton discovered that the state Republican convention, in an attempt to placate both factions of the party, had adopted a weak and amorphous program from which the Democrats, now praising Johnson for his stand against Congress, took hope. Morton entered the contest with an attack on the Democrats that was one of the most vitriolic ever made by a party leader against the opposition. "Every unregenerate rebel lately in arms against his government calls himself a Democrat," proclaimed the governor.

> Every bounty jumper, every deserter, every sneak who ran away from the draft calls himself a Democrat. Bowles, Milligan, Walker, Dodd, Horsey and Humphreys call themselves Democrats. Every "Son of Liberty" who conspired to murder, burn, rob arsenals and release rebel prisoners calls himself a Democrat. John Morgan, Champ Ferguson, Wirtz, Payne and Booth proclaimed themselves Democrats. . . .
> Beware how you connect your fortunes with a decayed and dishonored party, indelibly stained with treason, upon whose tombstone the historian will write, "false to liberty, false to its country, and false to the age in which it lived." The Democratic

party has committed a crime for which history has no pardon, and the memories of men no forgetfulness; whose colors grow darker from age to age, and for which the execrations of mankind become more bitter from generation to generation. It committed treason against liberty in behalf of slavery; against civilization in behalf of barbarism, and its chronicles will be written in the volume which records the deeds of the most dangerous and malignant factions that have ever afflicted government and retarded the progress of mankind.[14]

Clearly, such a harsh political metamorphosis cannot be attributed simply to an unfriendly interview with Andrew Johnson. But Morton's discovery of Johnson's stubborn refusal to play the game of party politics according to the rules, especially his suggestion of a new party including Democrats, apparently set off the delicate psychic mechanism that pointed Morton in a new direction. Oliver P. Morton, soon to be senator from Indiana, was destined to be, par excellence, a "Stalwart" Republican leader.

Other less strident appeals came to the president from his followers to sign the Civil Rights Bill. Governor Jacob D. Cox of Ohio, whose opposition to Negro suffrage and advocacy of a colonization policy for blacks made him anathema to radicals in the Western Reserve, wrote Johnson that "if you can find it in accordance with your sense of duty to sign the bill, it will with our Western people make you fully master of the situation, and remove the possibility of any such opposition in the Union ranks on other measures as would prove at all embarrassing to your administration." It would assist in "holding together our State organization."[15]

Of all the possible conciliators among Republican leaders Senator John Sherman of Ohio was in the best position to effect a rapprochement between the two factions. Like Morton, he was a committed party man, but he was more temperate than Morton, and he was in Washington, where the important work of conciliation would have to be done. He was the younger brother of Gen. William T. Sherman, who took Johnson's side. As the son-in-law of Thomas Ewing, the general provided a family connection with one of the most eminent Ohio statesmen in the mid-nineteenth century and now also in the Johnson camp.

In a Senate speech at the end of February Sherman made a strong appeal in defense of the president. Johnson had faithfully executed the Freedmen's Bureau Bill (of 1865), he said, and had "continued Lincoln's policy as well as the main features of the Wade-Davis bill." It was unreasonable to condemn him for his opposition to Negro suffrage while it was denied in all except six northern states. Although Sherman deeply regretted the Washington's Birthday speech, he felt that "no true friend of Andrew Johnson . . . would not be willing to wipe out that speech from the pages of history." "Now is no time," he concluded, "to quarrel with the Chief Magistrate. . . . I will not denounce him for hasty words uttered in repelling personal affronts. I see him yet surrounded by the Cabinet of Abraham Lincoln pursuing his policy. No word from me shall drive him into political fellowship with those who, when he was one of the moral heroes of this war denounced him."[16]

Although Sherman had voted for the Freedmen's Bureau Bill, and would do so again, he conceded that some of Johnson's reasons for vetoing it may have been reasonable. Nor was there any question about his constitutional right to do so. The president had agreed to the necessity of protecting the rights of freedmen; the senator would not "quarrel with him about the means." If conciliation was to take place, however, there would have to be a quid pro quo on the part of the president. Logically, this would be his approval of the Civil Rights Bill, which had received the almost unanimous support of Republican-Union men in and out of Congress.

In the middle of March Sherman went up to Connecticut to campaign for the Republican ticket. In a speech at Bridgeport he again tried to allay any fears of an impending break between the president and Congress. There were some disagreements, to be sure, he said, for it was "the established nature of the human mind to disagree. . . . Only by discussion and comparison of views [might] the highest human wisdom [he] elicited." But "no Union man need feel anxious or uneasy because of the differences between the President and Congress." It was Sherman's "solemn conviction . . . that Andrew Johnson never [would] throw the power we have given him into the hands of the Copperhead party of the United States." The Civil Rights Bill had passed Congress and was in the hands of the president. "If he signs it," Sherman concluded, "it will be a solemn pledge of the lawmaking power of the nation that the negroes shall have secured to them all their natural and inalienable rights. I believe the President will sign it." The veto shattered Sherman's confidence in Johnson. At this point the senator accepted the radical argument that the president had abandoned his party.[17]

In the light of repeated words of praise and the appeals of men who clearly wished to sustain him and considering their willingness to overlook his incredible gaffes, what was it that led Johnson to veto the Civil Rights Bill? Is it possible that, with all the advice from and consultation with men in a position to know the mood of the party, Johnson could have been unaware of the effect of a veto? The only reasonable conclusion seems to be that he did know what he was doing and that he took action without the usual doubt or hesitancy common to leaders making vital decisions. Because his support now came almost wholly from northern Democrats and southern secessionists, Johnson was about ready to abandon the party under whose banner he had been elected vice-president and ascended to the presidency.

The day before submitting the veto Johnson had presented the matter to the cabinet. This time, in contrast to cabinet attitudes on the Freedmen's Bureau Bill, only Welles unreservedly approved of the president's decision. Welles was convinced that "what is called the Civil Rights bill . . . must lead to the overthrow of [the] Administration as well as that of [the] mischievous Congress which had passed it. The principles of that bill, if carried into effect, must subvert the government. . . . The Alien and Sedition Laws were not so objectionable." Seward agreed to the section providing for Negro citizenship, but expressed some doubts about the other sections. Stanton could not fully approve the enforcement provisions but strongly recommended approving the law. McCulloch had not studied the bill carefully but, apparently persuaded by Stanton's argument, said that he would be "gratified if the President could see his way clear to sign" it.[18] The state of mind of the president as he faced his decision can be seen in a sententious remark he made to his personal secretary, Col. William G. Moore. The two men were in Johnson's bedroom having a glass of wine. Johnson pacing the floor, suddenly turned to Moore and said, "Sir, I am right. I know I am right, and I am damned if I do not adhere to it."[19]

On March 27, Johnson sent his veto message to the Senate. Although his tone was gentler than that of the Freedmen's Bureau veto, he was just as intransigent in adhering to his views. He was still defending the Constitution, standing firm against federal centralization, and preventing the Africanization of America. In effect, the president said that the federal government had neither the authority nor the obligation to guarantee civil rights through legislation. The message was simply a restatement, with more detail in respect to the specific question to civil rights, of his first annual message. Just as Chief Justice Taney had done in the Dred Scott case, Johnson drew a distinction between federal and state citizenship: "The power to confer the right of State citizenship is just as exclusively with the several States as the power to confer the right of Federal citizenship is with Congress." He posed the question whether blacks "possess the reguisite qualifications to entitle them to all the privileges and immunities of citizens of the United States." Was it necessary to make them citizens in order to secure their civil rights? He answered the question by comparing native-born blacks to foreigners, who were required to give evidence of their fitness for citizenship. Thus the bill discriminated against many "intelligent, worthy, and patriotic foreigners in favor of the Negro." In its provisions for the "security of the colored race," he said, the bill went "infinitely beyond any that the General Government had ever provided for the white race. . . . The distinction of race and color is . . . made to operate in favor of the colored against the white race." A "perfect equality of the white and colored races is attempted" under federal law, even though "in the exercise of State policy over matters exclusively affecting the people of each State it had frequently been thought expedient to discriminate between the two races." Here Johnson raised the specter of interracial marriage, a ubiquitous fear of the opponents of both the Freedmen's Bureau Bill and the Civil Rights Bill, which everybody knew was not among the enumerated civil rights included in the measure.[20]

Finally, Johnson went beyond states' rights, the Constitution, and civil rights, per se, to social and economic theory, as he understood it. In his view, the relationship of whites to blacks was basically that of capital to labor. Before the war it had been one of master and slave, with "capital owning labor." Now there was a new relationship requiring a "new adjustment, which both are interested in making harmonious. Each has equal power of settling the terms, and if left to the laws that regulate capital and labor it is confidently believed that they will satisfactorily work out the problem." True, capital had "more intelligence," but labor understood its own interests and its value; capital would have to pay that value. The Civil Rights Bill, Johnson charged, frustrated the adjustment of capital and labor. "It intervenes [between them] and attempts to settle questions of political economy through the agency of numerous officials whose interest it will be to foment discord between the two races, for as the breach widens their employment will continue, and when it is closed their occupation will terminate."[21]

Having taken issue with every feature and every provision of the act, Johnson nevertheless assured Congress that he fully recognized "the obligation to protect and defend [former slaves] wherever and whenever it shall become necessary, and to the full extent compatible with the Constitution of the United States." Just when and under what conditions Johnson might see fit to act in fulfillment of the obligation was something of a mystery to his contemporaries; it has remained so for historians. It appears, however, that there was virtually no point, short of another effort at secession to reestablish slavery, at which Johnson would have been willing to see the federal government define and protect the civil rights of black people.

Although the basic argument of the veto message was Johnson's own, he was not without advice in framing it. The writings of Lawanda and John Cox are informative not only with respect to Johnson's intentions; they are also suggestive as to other courses of action he might have followed. In preparing his message, Johnson had before him drafts from three of his advisers, Welles, Seward, and Henry Stanbery. The Welles draft was brief and unequivocal in its support of the veto. Stanbery, a reputable Ohio lawyer of conservative persuasion and connections, had just entered the circle of presidential advisers. Johnson had tried without success to place him on the Supreme Court and later, upon the resignation of James Speed, would make him attorney general, from which post he would resign in 1868 to become a counselor to Johnson in the impeachment trial. Johnson incorporated more of Stanbery's draft in the final message than of Welles's or Seward's.

More significant was the role of Seward in the preparation of the message. Had Johnson seen fit to follow Seward the message might have been conciliatory and served as a starting point for a combined legislative-executive effort. Seward approved of the objectives of the bill "to secure all persons their civil rights without regard to race or color" and agreed that all native-born Americans ought to be citizens. In a note among Johnson's papers Seward suggests what the president's approach might have been: "If you can find a way to intimate that *you are not opposed to the policy of the bill* but *only to its detailed provisions,* it will be a great improvement and make the support of the veto easier to our friends in Congress. I think a passage to this effect can be found in my notes heretofore sent." Undoubtedly one of the reasons why Johnson found Seward's suggestions unacceptable was that he and Seward did not agree on who were "our friends." The veto, say the Coxes, "was not a consistent argument against the bill. It was a contradictory composite designed to attract political support among both Republicans and Democrats." "It is just possible," they conclude, "that a greater deference to Seward's political acumen and his sensitivity to Republican racial attitudes might have spared the President . . . and the country a tragic experience."[22]

In his rejoinder to the veto Trumbull again related his efforts to act in harmony with the president: he had given Johnson copies of both the Freedmen's Bureau Bill and the Civil Rights Bill, and was amazed over the veto. He concluded with a brief statement on the meaning of the Thirteenth Amendment: "If the bill now before us, which goes no further than to secure civil rights to the freedmen, cannot be passed, then the constitutional amendment proclaiming freedom to all the inhabitants of the land is a cheat and a delusion."[23]

A generation later the constitutional historian John W. Burgess, who was no defender of radical Reconstruction, restated Trumbull's argument in his comments on the Civil Rights veto. "Real civil liberty is always national," said Burgess. "Its concepts and principles spring out of the national consciousness of rights and wrongs. And civil equality is the first principle of modern justice, the most pressing behest of the public morality of the age. Moreover, this measure did not militate against the President's plan of Reconstruction. He could have accepted it without compromising that plan in the slightest, and it was a monumental blunder on his part that he did not do so."[24]

Johnson apparently intended the two vetoes to be a coup de grâce that would bring down the Congressional opposition. Their effect was just the opposite, for now there was a growing cooperation between moderates and radicals. Old enmities were, temporarily at least, put aside in the consolidation of Republican ranks. In order to assure that the Civil Rights veto would not be sustained the Senate drove one of its members from his office.

The dismissal of John P. Stockton from the Senate on the eve of the Civil Rights veto was not an act motivated by a concern for governmental or political ethics. It would not have happened except for the expected veto and the determination of the Republicans to assure the necessary two-thirds majority to override it. It may have been an act of injustice to Senator Stockton and to the legislature of the state of New Jersey. For these reasons traditional historians of the Dunning persuasion have made much of it, purporting to show to what lengths Johnson's enemies would go to defeat him. James G. Randall said simply: "The Senate unseated . . . Stockton . . . ostensibly on the ground that the State legislature had chosen him by a plurality instead of a majority vote of the two houses; but the motive seems to have been the elimination of a member who did not support the Radical program."[25]

Howard K. Beale pointed to the constant efforts of the radicals to convert to their cause senators of doubtful conservatism. "But they employed a more certain weapon than persuasion. Through skillful use of an unmerciful party whip, and the breaking of a pair by Senator Morrill of Maine, they unseated one of the Johnson Senators, Stockton of New Jersey." In this vein Beale reported the maneuverings in the Senate leading up to the final vote on Stockton's dismissal.[26]

David M. Dewitt, in his *Impeachment and Trial of Andrew Johnson* (1903), presented the episode in great detail. His presentation of the facts of the case is accurate enough; his distortions derive from his assumptions, his charged words, and his omissions. "By great good fortune," Dewitt said, "the facts lying at the bottom of the almost incredible piece of injustice about to be narrated are matters of record and drawn to the minutest detail never for a moment subject to dispute." The Civil Rights veto, the occasion for the whole episode, said Dewitt, was "Brief, calm, courteous and dignified in its tone, cogent in its logic and invulnerable in the points it made—in these particulars the message furnished a refreshing contrast to the unseemly struggle . . . in the Senate, as well as to the indecorous exhibition in the House. . . . The unconstitutionality of the main provisions . . . was expounded with a master's stroke."[27] In Dewitt's account those who voted against Stockton were moved by malicious forces and a determination to undermine the Constitution. Those who wavered and then voted for dismissal were the most suspect of all.

A curious omission in the Dewitt account is the role of William Pitt Fessenden, one of Dewitt's heroes for his vote against Johnson's conviction in 1868 but a prime mover in the Stockton ouster. "The Senator from Maine," said Dewitt later in his narrative, "was a statesman rather than a politician. . . . Distinguished in bearing, cautious in judgment, experienced in public affairs, . . . he was a character that would cut no grotesque capers in the seat of Lincoln."[28] Yet the forceful argument of such a man was omitted from Dewitt's account of the stockton affair.

The revisionists have done better than this. W. R. Brock, in his brief treatment of the matter, says that the means for unseating a Democratic senator to secure the two-thirds majority against the veto was "not very creditable."[29] McKitrick, who treats the matter in more detail, describes it as "a very questionable transaction," one with a "shaky legitimacy." But he assesses the forces that came into play and the roles of all the major participants without pejorative terms and without resort to a devil theory of history.[30]

The Stockton affair actually began in the legislature of New Jersey early in 1865, when the term of Senator John C. Ten Eyck was about to expire and the legislature was obliged to elect a successor. In the lower house Democrats and Republicans each had thirty members, but in the upper house there was a Democratic majority of thirteen to eight. Under New Jersey law a senator was elected by a joint meeting of the two houses, but a majority of each house was required to convene such a meeting. Republicans hoped that they could prevent the convening of the joint session and thus postpone the election of a senator until after the fall elections of 1865, in which they expected a Republican victory. Public clamor against leaving one of New Jersey's Senate seats vacant made the Republican plan unworkable. Yet there was still a possibility of denying the post to the unpopular Stockton by appealing to dissident Democrats to prevent a majority vote of the joint session. The Democrats, seeing their dilemma, forestalled by one vote a Republican move to adjourn sine die, adopted a resolution for the election of a senator by a plurality, and hastily elected Stockton under this ruling. The Republicans had been outmaneuvered.

When the Thirty-ninth Congress convened in December, Stockton was allowed to take his seat in the Senate and was sworn in, but a protest from the Republican members of the New Jersey legislature challenged the legality of the election. The matter was then referred to the Judiciary Committee, from which Trumbull reported that Stockton had been legally elected and was entitled to his seat. In the committee there was only one dissenting vote. Between the report of the committee on January 30 and March 22 no action was taken on the Stockton case. Except for rumors that a veto was forthcoming, it is highly improbable that the Senate would have touched it. As we have seen, it was Fessenden who most effectively challenged the validity of Stockton's election. Fessenden's argument was that the election of Stockton under the plurality rule was not carried out under legislative authority. It was a convention, he argued, constituted of the same members as the legislature to be sure, but still an extralegal body and in violation of "acknowledged parliamentary and common law," that had presumed to have elected him.

The first vote in the Senate, on March 23, favored Stockton's retention of his seat by a vote of twenty-one to twenty, whereupon Lot M. Morrill of Maine, who had made a pair with the ailing William Wright of New Jersey, broke the pair and voted against Stockton, making it a tie vote, twenty-one to twenty-one, still insufficient to oust him. At this point Stockton made a tactical error by asserting his right to vote and casting his vote in his own behalf. The question was reopened on the twenty-seventh, the day of Johnson's veto message, when Stockton was dismissed by a vote of twenty-three to twenty. For the radicals and most moderates the two-thirds majority had become a vital necessity.[31]

On April 2, the Senate overrode the veto by the exact two-thirds majority required under the Constitution. Three days later the House passed it by a more substantial majority. Actually, more than the ejection of Stockton was necessary to the victory in the Senate. Soloman Foot of Vermont had died and had been succeeded by the Republican George F. Edmunds. Dixon of Connecticut and Wright of New Jersey were ill. When Johnson men requested a postponement of the vote until Dixon's return Benjamin Wade replied, "If God Almighty has stricken one member so that he cannot be here to uphold the dictation of a despot, I thank Him for His interposition, and I will take advantage of it if I can."[32] Dixon was carried into the Senate chamber on a stretcher, but his presence did not alter the final result. William M. Stewart of Nevada and Edwin D. Morgan of New York, whose votes Johnson had counted on, both voted against the president. Administration men were bitter about Morgan, whom they considered to be committed to them. But the New York senator, in an effort to keep peace between the president and Congress, had recommended a compromise bill which Johnson rejected. Convinced that legislation was necessary, he voted for the Civil Rights Bill, bringing cheers from the Senate galleries and the contempt of Gideon Welles and the handful of Johnson men in the Senate.

The Civil Rights conflict in the Senate had its personal tragedy as well. For James H. Lane of Kansas whether to vote for or against the veto was an anguished question. After voting to sustain the veto, it appears that the old leader of the Free State party in the Kansas war regretted his decision, but there was no road back. Criticized by his constituents and feeling alienated from former friends, in July he committed suicide.

The Civil Rights Bill was the first major legislative enactment ever passed over a presidential veto. The narrow margin by which it passed and the conviction of moderates and radicals that there was no possibility of working with the president brought a new unity among Republicans. Even Sumner and Fessenden patched up their ancient feud for a time.

Senator John Sherman, writing to his brother, expressed the despair of moderate Republicans with Johnson's leadership:

> As to the President, he is becoming Tylerized. He was elected by the Union party for his openly expressed radical sentiments, and now he seeks to rend to pieces this party. There is a sentiment among the people that this is dishonor. It looks so to me. What Johnson is, is from and by the Union party. He now deserts it and betrays it. He may varnish it up, but, after all, he must admit that he disappoints the reasonable expectations of those who entrusted him with power. He may, by a coalition with Copperheads and rebels, succeed, but the simple fact that nine tenths of them who voted for him do not agree with him, and that he only controls the other tenth by power entrusted to him by the Union party will damn him forever. Besides, he is insincere; he has deceived and misled his best friends.[33]

Young Ignatius Donnelly, congressman from Minnesota, exulted in the victory of the Thirty-ninth Congress in overriding the veto. He was convinced that "a purer, more patient, and at the same time abler and more patriotic body of men never convened in any age or country."[34]

If this account emphasizes the responsibility of Andrew Johnson for the break between executive and Congress, it is important not to overlook the abominable behavior of some radicals. The bitter invective of a Thad Stevens, the arrogant self-righteousness of a Charles Sumner, and the vulgarity of a Ben Wade would have sorely tried the patience of any president. Even a man more confident than Johnson would have been tempted to retaliate in kind. Although such conduct is a luxury presidents can ill afford, it would not have been so harmful had Johnson not made a more damaging error in his failure to discriminate between men and factions. Those who opposed him in any way he perceived as in league with the enemy, and he thereby eventually alientated the moderates, who could have been of inestimable help to him in formulating and implementing a restoration program. His assertion of executive power in a system of coordinate branches of government was not tempered with an awareness that negotiation between the executive and the legislative must take place in order for the government to function at all. Johnson, for all his scruples about the Constitution, was not very knowledgeable about how the constitutional system actually worked.

To some extent, also, Andrew Johnson was a victim of the American presidential system, under which it is too easy for a chief executive to become isolated. The temptation to surround themselves with sycophants who tell them what they want to hear is too great for many presidents to resist. Keeping the lines of communication open to all shades of opinion, especially to the opposition, requires a conscious effort that many presidents, for all their assertions to the contrary, are unable or unwilling to make. As we have seen, there was almost nothing in the personality or character of Andrew Johnson that might have made his conduct of the office different from what it was.[35]

Johnson's conduct of the executive office suggests that the American presidency, and the nation, might well be served if the chief executive were compelled from time to time to face the opposition, as is the British prime minister. The ensuing dialogue might lead to a better discrimination between historionics and genuine threats, between matters that must be dealt with and those that ought to be ignored. It might keep the president more fit to practice the political art. One of the saddest things about Andrew Johnson was that under the pressures of the office, his political capacities did not grow; they declined.[36]

Chapter 5

Struggle for an Amendment—First Phase

ALTHOUGH THE CONTEST over the Freedmen's Bureau Bill and the Civil Rights Bill was important in the growing antagonism between the president and Congress and enters significantly into the history of Reconstruction, it was somewhat peripheral to the really vital accomplishment of Congress in 1866, the adoption of the Fourteenth Amendment, which in the long run may be the most important of all the constitutional amendments. It defines citizenship in such a way as to make blacks citizens of the nation and the states in which they live; it protects the civil rights of all persons through the "due process" and "equal protection" clauses; and it calls for the reduction of representation of states that deny the vote to any of its male citizens, namely blacks. It also denies the right to hold federal and state offices to certain persons who had participated in the rebellion; it upholds the validity of the public debt of the United States and forbids the payment of debts incurred in aid of the rebellion. It gives Congress the power to enforce the provisions of the amendment.

In tracing the events leading to the adoption of the amendment on June 13, we return to the proceedings of the Joint Committee on Reconstruction, which on April 30 reported an amendment to Congress. The amendment that was finally adopted, however, was not simply the product of the committee. It emerged, rather, from proposals made by individual members of both houses, modifications of the committee's proposal, and a secret caucus of Republican senators. Perhaps the most important proposal of all, one which provided the committee with a vitally necessary starting point, came from Robert Dale Owen, who was not even a member of Congress.

There are other questions, too, that demand consideration in any account of the formulation and adoption of the amendment. Why did it not provide for Negro suffrage? Was it a partisan device to assure continued Republican control? How could the rebel states, which some radicals claimed had committed "state suicide" or had been reduced to territorial status, ratify an amendment? Why was Tennessee restored upon ratification, two years before any other state? Were there members of the committee or of Congress who intended that the word "person" in Section 1 should be interpreted in such a way as to protect corporations against state laws? Why did Andrew Johnson advise southern states not to ratify the amendment? These questions provide a backdrop that may reduce some of the ambiguities in the history of the amendment from its formulation to its adoption by Congress during the first six months of 1866.

Some months before the end of 1865 Republicans were making proposals and stating beliefs that would have an effect on or find their way into the Fourteenth Amendment. At first they revolved around the question of Negro suffrage. Before leaving on his mission to the South, Carl Schurz had appealed to the president to establish it under presidential fiat. Early in the summer, Senator Howard of Michigan wrote to Sumner that Negro suffrage was "our *only* security and the only means of making emancipation effectual." Blacks, he said, were as worthy of the vote as "Irish Copperheads." Congress had the power to confer the ballot and ought to use it "at the *earliest possible day* so as to put an end to this executive reconstruction, which seems likely to restore slavery and bring rebels into [C]ongress." James A. Garfield favored it with some qualifications, such as "intelligence" and "cultural standards," but until there was in the South "a voting population that [could] be entrusted with power" the rebel states should remain unrepresented in Congress. Ben Wade saw Negro suffrage as a weapon that might be effective in preventing the president from leading the Republican party to destruction. Some men who favored it doubted the authority of Congress to institute it. Others, like Oliver P. Morton of Indiana, were reluctant to push it in the face of political and civil rights restrictions in their own states. Even so, the *Chicago Tribune* came out late in July for a constitutional amendment to establish a national uniform suffrage.[1]

These early expressions of opinion about Negro suffrage constituted something less than a commitment to assure blacks of their civil or political rights through congressional action. There were continued warnings to Republican leaders not to allow Negro suffrage to become a major issue, above all not to use it against Andrew Johnson in a contest between him and Congress. We have noted the advice to Lyman Trumbull on this point and his assurances that the franchise was not a civil right that Congress could guarantee or protect. Men close to the president who still sought party harmony and the continuing Republican ascendancy advised their radical friends not to be precipitate in pushing Negro suffrage. Toward the end of August McCulloch predicted, in a letter to Charles Sumner, that if the Republicans went into any election on the suffrage issue they would lose three-fourths of the northern states.

Despite these admonitions, some radicals in Congress, such as Sumner and Julian, and the old antislavery faction out of Congress led by Wendell Phillips, clung to Negro suffrage as a sine qua non of reconstruction policy. Radicals of a more practical stripe heeded the warnings and, while not abandoning suffrage outright, adjusted their arguments to the prevailing exigencies. By the time Congress assembled in December, therefore, the debate had taken a different tack and the major emphasis was on the question of representation. It was the end of slavery and the consequent end of the three-fifths provision in the Constitution that now made representation paramount. As Roscoe Conkling would soon demonstrate in Congress, the fifteen former slave states would have ninety-four representatives based on total population but only sixty-five based on white population alone.[2] These statistics were ominous to congressional Republicans confronted by a president who insisted that the rebel states were already restored and that Congress could not enact legislation pertaining to them in the absence of their representatives. Negro suffrage was a weak reed not only because of the antipathy to it in the North but because, even if it could have been adopted, it would have to be made effective, an unlikely prospect while the president still controlled affairs in the South. It was not strange, then, that Congress would attempt to meet the problem by placing some limitations on southern representation. And because the three-fifths clause was a constitutional provision the only sure remedy would be through the amending process.

Civil rights, as differentiated from suffrage, was uppermost in the minds of some men. We have seen this with Lyman Trumbull, the author of the Civil Rights Bill. Even more conversant with the subject was Congressman John A. Bingham of Ohio, the member of the Joint Committee on Reconstruction who would be responsible for the "due process" and "equal rights" clauses of the amendment. By 1860 there was in existence a body of abolitionist scholarship on the subject flowing from debates on slavery over the past thirty years. Even before the war Bingham had drawn on these arguments in addressing himself to "natural and inalienable rights," the rights of national citizens under the Fifth Amendment and the privileges and immunities of citizens under the comity clause.[3]

In his reminiscences James G. Blaine wrote of another "public ap-

prehension" that was promptly brought to the attention of the Thirty-
ninth Congress—the possibility of a combination of secessionists and
Democrats who would compensate slaveholders for their losses, stop
payments of bounties and pensions to soldiers and their families, and
impair the public credit.

Men of financial skill and experience saw that if such a contingent
liability should overhang the National Treasury the public credit
might be fatally impaired. The acknowledged and imperative
indebtedness of the Government was already enormous;
contingencies yet to be encountered would undoubtedly increase it,
and its weight would press heavily upon the people until a firmly
re-established credit should enable the Government to lower the
rate of interest upon its bonds. So long as the Government was
compelled to pay its interest in coin, while the business of the
country was conducted upon the basis of suspended paper, the
burden upon the people would be great. It would be vastly
increased in imagination (and imagination is rapidly transformed to
reality in the tremulous balance which decides the standard of
public credit) if the Nation should not be able to define with
absolute precision the metes and bounds of its aggregate
obligation. Hence the imperious necessity of excluding all
possibility of the payment of from two to three thousand millions of
dollars to the slave-holders of the South. If that were not
accomplished, the burden would be so great that the Nation which
had survived the shock of arms might be engulfed in the manifold
calamities of bankruptcy.[4]

Men from every faction of the Republican party, from Johnson's
cabinet to the most ardent radicals, shared some, if not all, of these
apprehensions. Charles Sumner, we may recall, had made the point
dramatically at the Massachusetts Republican Convention, when he
waved a Treasury note before his audience with the admonition not to
allow it to become worthless by giving in to rebel demands. In his
Atlantic article he returned to the theme again: "Our foremost duties
now," he wrote, "are to pay our debts, and they are twofold: first, to the
national freedman; and, secondly, to the national creditor."[5]

These concerns and aspirations, together with the inability to cooperate with the president and the knowledge that he had a plan of restoration where they did not, provided the atmosphere in which Congress
struggled to create and adopt a new constitutional amendment.

How to present an intelligible account of the framing of the amendment has long been a conundrum for historians, for it is one of the most

complex chapters in American political and constitutional history. Although the Joint Committee on Reconstruction finally reported a resolution that was debated and modified so as to emerge as the Fourteenth Amendment, the committee was by no means the sole architect or engineer. Proposals were made by members of both houses as well as by men who were not in the government at all. Congress felt the sting of critics whose demands could not be ignored with impunity. The task was an exacting one, which called for an amendment that would serve as a basis for a congressional reconstruction program and at the same time attract the necessary two-thirds majority to pass. In making our way through the labyrinth we shall follow the chronology of events from early December 1865 to the passage of the amendment in mid-June 1866, noting the essential points of debate. Then, with some insight perhaps, we may consider each section of the amendment and some of the more important interpretations.

JAMES G. BLAINE
Reproduced from the collection of the Library of Congress

The debate in Congress on representation was opened by Thaddeus Stevens on December 5, a month before the first meeting of the joint committee. Stevens proposed to amend the Constitution by providing that "representation shall be apportioned among the States which may be within the Union according to their respective legal voters, and for this purpose none shall be named legal voters who are not either natural born citizens . . . or naturalized foreigners." For some weeks this proposal was discussed, not so much in public debate as in private conferences, until early in January James G. Blaine of Maine came out against it. Blaine's purpose was the protection of New England, where there were fewer voters relative to the population than in other regions. This was so because of the extensive migration out of the region by young men as well as educational qualifications on voting. Blaine pointed out that California and Vermont had almost equal populations but that the voting population of California was more than twice that of Vermont. His proposed amendment, therefore, would apportion representation by "respective numbers, which shall be determined by taking the whole number of persons, except those whose political rights or privileges are denied or abridged by the constitution of any state on account of race or color."[6]

Roscoe Conkling, taking the side of Stevens, presented his statistics to demonstrate that no region of the country would be disadvantaged by making voters the basis of representation. He then made two proposals, either of which might serve as a constitutional amendment. The first provided that "whenever in any . . . State the political rights or privileges of any shall be denied or abridged on account of race or color, *all persons* of such race or color shall be excluded from the basis of representation." The second excluded only those persons so denied their rights and privileges.[7] Although the early opposition to New England came from representatives of Pennsylvania and New York, most of the subsequent opposition was to come from the western states. Both Democrats and Republicans entered into this regional quarrel and thereby introduced a theme into the debate over the amendment that would persist throughout the session.

While Congress was still deeply involved in the debate over representation, Congressman Samuel Shellabarger of Ohio carried the argument back into the realm of theory, to the condition and status of the Confederate states after secession. Although his line of argument was similar to that of Stevens, the conclusions were closer to Sumner's "state suicide" theory. Commonly known as the "forfeited rights" theory, John W. Burgess called it the "Sumner-Shellabarger" theory. Shellabarger sought a middle ground, legally and constitutionally, on

which reconstruction might proceed. Like Stevens, he found in the law
of nations (Grotius and Burlamanqui) and in the *Prize Cases* authority
for the United States to carry on the war as if it had been one against an
enemy nation. But he did not go all the way with Stevens to the concept
of conquered provinces. "I shall not consider," he said, "whether by the
rebellion, any State lost its territorial character or defined boundaries
or subdivisions, for I know of no one who would obliterate these geo-
graphical qualities of the States." This "most momentous Constitutional
question" he would "condense and affirm in a single sentence."

> It is under our Constitution possible to, and the late rebellion did
> in fact so, overthrow and usurp in the insurrectionary States the
> loyal State governments as that, during such usurpation, such
> States and their people ceased to have any of the rights or powers of
> government as States of this Union: and this loss of the rights and
> powers of government was such that the United States may and
> ought to assume and exercise local powers of the lost State
> governments, and may control the readmission of such States to
> their powers of government in this Union, subject to and in
> accordance with the obligation to "guaranty to each State a
> republican form of government."

If the territorial character of the states had not changed, their political character had; they had forfeited their political rights. In invoking
the constitutional guarantee of a republican form of government as a
basis of the power of Congress, Shellabarger cited the decision in
Luther v. *Borden*, a case relating to the Dorr Rebellion in Rhode Island
in 1842. The words, ironically, are those of Chief Justice Roger B.
Taney: "as the United States guarantees to each State a republican
government, Congress must necessarily determine what government is
established in a State before it can decide whether it is republican or
not. When the Senators and Representatives of a State are admitted
into the councils of the Union the authority of the government under
which they are appointed is recognized by the proper constitutional
authority. And its decision is binding on every other department of the
Government."[8] Shellabarger did not at this time offer any suggestions
as to the details of congressional action; he proposed no constitutional
amendments. But he came closer than anybody else to defining the
theoretical and constitutional base upon which congressional reconstruction would rest.

All these proposals were made in December and early January,
before the joint committee had begun its work. At its first business
meeting, on January 9, Stevens submitted the same amendment he had

proposed in the House a month earlier, that "Representation shall be apportioned . . . according to the number of . . . respective legal voters." Conkling moved to amend it by inserting the word "male," so that only "legal voters . . . either natural born or naturalized male citizens" would be counted. This was done over the vigorous protests of Susan B. Anthony and Elizabeth Cady Stanton, leaders of the women's rights movement who hoped that women as well as blacks might benefit from the movement for civil and political rights of the Reconstruction era. They were particularly annoyed with Conkling's proposal because it would add a provision limiting the rights of women that had not heretofore been included in the Constitution. Morrill tried without success to insert an educational clause, limiting the number of voters to those males who could read and write. It is apparent that the committee, while abandoning Negro suffrage as a prerequisite for restoration, was exploring ways in which it might influence such suffrage regulations as the states might enact.

At the next meeting of the committee a number of proposals were made. Morrill now would base representation on respective numbers of *persons*, not voters, in each state but "deducting therefrom all of any race or color, whose members or any of them are denied any of the civil or political rights or privileges." Boutwell favored compulsory Negro suffrage. Bingham proposed an amendment giving Congress the "power to secure all persons in every state . . . equal protection in their rights of life, liberty, and property." Finally, a subcommittee consisting of Fessenden, Stevens, Howard, Conkling, and Bingham, was appointed to consider all these proposals and to make a recommendation to the Committee on the matter of the "apportionment of representatives in Congress."[9]

On January 20, the subcommittee reported two alternative proposals to be presented as amendments to the Constitution. The first was a federal guarantee of "political or civil rights or privileges," irrespective of color, race, or creed. The second, on representation, was with some modification adopted by the Committee: "Representatives and direct taxes shall be apportioned among the several States which may be included within this Union, according to their respective numbers, counting the whole number of persons in each State, excluding Indians not taxed; provided that whenever the elective franchise shall be denied or abridged in any State on account of race or color, all persons of such race or color shall be excluded from the basis of representation."[10]

Stevens reported the resolution to the House on January 22, with the intention of having it passed "before the sun goes down." But it was not that easy. Opposition came from radicals who demanded an explanation of the meaning of the amendment or who were not satisfied with the absence of a provision for Negro suffrage and from Democrats who were opposed to any amendment. Finally Conkling came to the defense of the amendment, pointing out that to defeat it would be advantageous to the South. The former slave states, he said, would have "twenty-eight votes . . . here and in the electoral college for those held not fit to testify in court, not fit to be plaintiffs in a suit, not fit to approach the ballot box." "Shall the death of slavery add two-fifths to the . . . power which slavery had when [it] was living?" Conkling conceded that suffrage was a "right reserved to the States . . . to which they will long cling before they surrender it." Could it be expected, then, that northern states that had denied suffrage to Negroes—"some of them have repeatedly and lately pronounced against it"—would approve an amendment providing for it?[11]

Shellabarger, attracting much attention from both sides of the House, warned the House that the amendment might make disfranchisement based on race in the states constitutional, and therefore opposed it. James Brooks of New York, a Democrat not known to be an advocate of women's rights, proposed that white women should be given the vote and introduced a petition of Susan B. Anthony that women be protected by the amendment. John M. Broomal of Pennsylvania would alter the amendment so that "whenever the elective franchise shall be denied by the Constitution or laws of any state to any portion of its male citizens over the age of twenty-one years, the same proportion of its population shall be excluded from the basis of representation." His avowed purpose was to bring about universal manhood suffrage in all the states, not just Negro suffrage in the South. The Republican Henry J. Raymond of New York and the Democrat Aaron Harding of Kentucky condemned the majority for trying to amend the Constitution in the absence of representatives from eleven southern states.[12]

Meanwhile, an Ohio congressman had moved that the resolution be sent back to the committee with instructions to make male voters the basis of representation and to apportion direct taxes according to property. Over the objections of Stevens and Conkling, it was recommitted on January 31. The committee did delete the words "and direct taxes" but otherwise left the resolution in its original form. On the same day Stevens brought the resolution back into the House where, after everybody had had an opportunity to have his say, the resolution passed by a vote of 120 to 46.[13]

Despite his annoyance with the House for its dilatoriness, Stevens had succeeded in getting the resolution through in only ten days. Fessenden, who had charge of it in the Senate, was not so fortunate, for he had Charles Sumner to contend with. Shortly before he introduced the resolution Fessenden had written in a personal letter of Sumner's announced intention to "put his foot on it and crush it." "Well," Fessenden wrote, "the amendment is the Committee's and not mine. I shall make a half hour's speech on it, and be followed by Sumner with a printed oration which he says will take two days. He is waiting for this opportunity to show the country the difference between a great orator and a mere talker. We shall see how it ends." The amendment was, indeed, the committee's and not Fessenden's, for he preferred one that would make inoperative and void "all civil and political distinctions on account of race or color." He would have held the rebel states under military rule until a majority of whites, by their own voluntary action, accepted the amendment and adopted equal laws for blacks.[14] Yet here he was, responsible for the passage of the amendment in the Senate.

Sumner's promised oration—"Equal Rights for All"—came on February 5 and 6, lasting five hours in all. As was his wont, Sumner had prepared diligently; he claimed to have read "everything on the subject from Plato to the last French pamphlet." He probably had, and he crammed it all into this monumental effort. James G. Blaine thought it hardly proper to call it a speech. Rather, "It was a great historic review of the foundation of the Republics of the world, an exhaustive analysis of what constituted a true republic, closing with an eloquent plea for the ballot for the freedmen." For Sumner the ballot was "the great guarantee," "a peacemaker, a schoolmaster, a protector." "Show me," he said,

> a creature with erect countenance and looking to heaven, made in the image of God, and I show you a man who, of whatever country or race—whether darkened by equatorial sun or blanched with northern cold—is an equal with you before the heavenly Father, and equally with you entitled to all the rights of human nature. . . .
> You cannot deny these rights without impiety. God has so linked the National welfare with National duty that you cannot deny these rights without peril to the Republic. It is not enough that you have given liberty. By the same title that we claim liberty do we claim equality also. . . . The Roman Cato, after declaring his belief in the immortality of the soul, added, that if this were an error it was an error that he loved; and now, declaring my belief in liberty and equality as the God-given birthright of all men, let me say in the same spirit, if this be an error it is an error which I love; if this be a fault it is a fault which I shall be slow to renounce; if this be an illusion it is an illusion which I pray may wrap the world in its angelic form.

To be assured that every state would be protected under the constitutional guarantee of a republican form of government, Sumner proposed as a joint resolution that

> there shall be no oligarchy, aristocracy, caste or monopoly invested with peculiar privileges or powers, and there shall be no denial of rights, civil or political, on account of race or color within the limits of the United States or the jurisdiction thereof, but all persons therein shall be equal before the law, whether in the court-room or at the ballot-box, and this statute, made in pursuance of the Constitution, shall be the supreme law of the land, any thing in the constitution or laws of any State to the contrary notwithstanding.[15]

During the early months of 1866 Senator Fessenden was so ill that he wondered whether he could make it through the session. Anxious to have laws enacted and constitutional amendments accepted, Sumner's ponderous oratory made him irascible; but an opportunity to strike back raised his spirits. Fessenden's reply to Sumner's February 5–6 speech was one of those occasions. Attempting to expose Sumner's ineptness as a legislator, Fessenden asked, "Does the Constitution authorize oligarchy, aristocracy, caste or monopoly?"

> Not at all. Are you not as safe under the Constitution as you are under an Act of Congress? Why re-enact the Constitution merely to put it in a bill? What do you accomplish by it? What remedy does it afford? It is merely as if it read in this way: "Whereas it is provided in the Constitution that the United States shall guarantee to every State of the Union a republican form of government, therefore we declare that there shall be a republican form of government, and nothing else." That is all there is of it. Of what particular use it is as a bill, practically, is more than I can tell. I presume the Honorable Senator from Massachusetts will very easily explain it, but it reminds me (I say it with all due respect to him) of a poetical travesty of a law argument by an eminent lawyer of his own State, running somewhat in this way:—
>
> > "Let my opponents do their worst,
> > Still my first point is point the first,
> > Which fully proves my case, because
> > All statute laws are statute laws."

One of Sumner's arguments in defense of universal suffrage, Fessenden pointed out, had been "that taxation and representation should go together." Why, then, should not every female who was taxed also have the right of suffrage? "I notice," said Fessenden, "that the Honorable

Senator carefully and skillfully evaded that part of the proposition." A
more effective challenge was Fessenden's reminder that in December
1865 "Sumner had proposed an amendment providing for representation based on the number of voters. Did not such an amendment leave to
the states the same powers that existed under the Committee proposal?" Fessenden asked.[16]

It would be unfair to conclude that, because Sumner's speech of
February was not consistent with his proposal of December, he was not
a genuine reformer committed to Negro suffrage as a necessary condition for restoration. The growing intensity of the executive-legislative
conflict and the failure of the southern states under Johnson's regime to
ensure political and civil rights for blacks might logically explain a
change of mind such as he had apparently undergone. Also, Sumner had
become the chief spokesman in Congress of such antislavery reformers
as Wendell Phillips, Theodore Tilton, and George L. Stearns.

Even so, Sumner's perceptive biographer, David Donald, makes a
convincing argument that there were matters of Massachusetts politics
that provide part of the explanation of Sumner's more radical stance.
John A. Andrew, retiring from the governorship of Massachusetts after
five successive terms, says Donald, posed a threat to Sumner's leadership of the Republican party in the state. Formerly of a radical bent, by
1866 Andrew had developed a more conciliatory attitude toward the
South. He favored Negro suffrage but felt it should come only when it
could be secured by the approval of southern whites. In his famous
valedictory address in early January Andrew had described Sumner's
scheme of representation based on voters as a "delusion and a snare."
Without alluding to the opposition in New England to such a plan, but
certainly aware of it, Andrew argued his case on altruistic grounds.
Southern love for the Union, he reasoned, would not be increased by
reducing representation from the southern states. "Nor, while Connecticut and Wisconsin refuse the suffrage to men of color, will you be able to
convince the South that your amendment was dictated by political
principles, and not by political cupidity." By accepting the representation amendment of the joint committee, Sumner would appear to be
abandoning Negro suffrage while agreeing to an unworkable compromise. Some members of the Massachusetts press were also skeptical
of the senator's motives: he appeared to be dodging Negro suffrage
while resorting to "a politician's trick to get rid of the question," in
contrast to Andrew's more forthright position. "To keep from being
outflanked by Andrew," Donald writes, "Sumner had no choice but to
oppose the amendment when it reached the Senate, and to oppose it in
such vehement language that everybody would forget that he had

sponsored an almost identical proposal." After the "Equal Rights for All" speech, Donald adds, "there was little possibility that Andrew or anybody else could accuse Sumner of bartering away principle."[17]

Debate in the Senate dragged on until March 9, by which time many speeches had been made. Among those who spoke was John B. Henderson of Missouri, who moved a substitute for the committee's amendment providing that "no State, in prescribing the qualifications requisite for electors therein, shall discriminate against any person on account of color or race." In his vigorous defense of his proposal Henderson said, "I am aware that the Senate will vote it down now. Let them vote it down. It will not be five years from today, before this body will vote for it. You cannot get along without it. You may adopt the other proposition, but the States will not accept it." He saw the pending amendment as a compromise "that the whites may govern the blacks in the State governments of the South and wring from them sweat and tears, provided the northern and eastern States are permitted to control the national Government." Its purpose, Henderson said, was to give New England the same undue power in the House it already had in the Senate, but "let it be done in another name than mercy to the black man." Hendricks of Indiana also branded the measure as an attempt by the Northeast to control the West. If the federal nature of the government was to be destroyed for the benefit of the manufacturing interests of the Northeast, he asked, why not also alter the composition of the Senate in accordance with the conception of representation expressed in the amendment? Hendricks concluded his speech amidst a burst of applause from the galleries.[18]

Henderson and Hendricks, a radical Republican and a states' rights Democrat, were in substantial agreement that their region, the old West, was drifting into a disadvantageous position vis-à-vis the Northeast. With them the theme, frequently obscured beneath the rhetoric on the Negro and the South, now briefly surfaced. It was a theme that persisted and had its effects throughout the critical year and beyond.

Finally, on March 9, after another exchange between Sumner and Fessenden, the amendment came to a vote (yeas twenty-five to nays twenty-two), short of the necessary two-thirds majority. Democrats, administration Republicans, and radical followers of Sumner combined to defeat it.[19] "I regret exceedingly that the amendment was lost," Fessenden wrote the following day, "for we can get nothing so good. If we carry any other through Congress it will not be adopted by the States, and the blacks are left without hope. This is owing to [Sumner's] folly and wickedness."[20]

To be sure, Sumner had been instrumental in defeating the amendment; if all the radicals who followed his lead in opposing it had voted for it the amendment would have passed. But the role of Sumner can be exaggerated, because the amendment was wholly satisfactory to almost nobody. Even its most ardent advocates, Stevens and Fessenden, had simply done their duty as chairmen of the joint committee by presenting it in the most favorable light. It was satisfactory to no faction of the Republican party, and of course the Democrats voted against it.

The northern press was also decidedly cool toward the amendment. The antislavery press, including Theodore Tilton.'s *Independent* and Phillips's *National Anti-Slavery Standard,* stood solidly behind Sumner and egged him on. Sumner, said the *Standard,* had probably damaged his standing in his party by his gallant fight. But that was of "little consequence, for the doom of a party capable of such legislation is sealed. Let the graves of the old Federal and Whig and the Democratic parties be once more opened, for the feet of those who shall carry the Republican party out also, are already at the door. God," the apocalyptic message concluded, "has not bought the freedom of four millions of His children at the cost of a million human lives, to be defrauded in the purchase by such compromise, cowardice, and criminality even, as generally lie at the base of legislation like this."[21]

The *New York Times* presented the standard administration argument that no reconstruction measures should be taken until the southern states had been restored. Both *Harper's Weekly* and the *New York Tribune,* after some hesitation, supported the amendment. The *Nation,* recently established as the organ of liberal opinion, was gratified that the amendment did not punish the older eastern states for "sending large drafts of their young men to the West," as representation based on legal voters would have done, and that "it did not cheapen the suffrage" by tempting the states to compete for votes. But it did not "secure any human being in any of the revolted states in the possession of his rights. It [did] not provide for freedom of speech, of the person, or of instruction," nor did it do anything for "the restoration of industry. No Southerner would find in it any reason for laying aside his fear or old hatred for the Union or for desiring to be in feeling, as well as in fact, and in law, one of its citizens." And if the amendment should pass, *"we should* be morally responsible for it." The *Nation* believed, however, that "an amendment forbidding any man's exclusion from political rights on the ground of race or color [was] still possible." Before long, it argued, such an amendment could be carried in the northern states and it would therefore become evident that the rejection of Negro suffrage in those states, such as Connecticut and Wisconsin, did not "express the feeling of the people in its highest and noblest moods."[22]

Any proposed amendment to the Constitution would have had to serve as a compromise satisfactory to a large Republican majority. In addition, it would have had to be the nucleus of a congressional plan of reconstruction or restoration. The representation amendment was too narrow to serve these purposes. Thus Charles Sumner and the others who brought about its defeat were probably, wittingly or unwittingly, rendering a service to their party and to the nation. The next amendment reported by the committee would contain five sections that were informed by the major issues demanding recognition in the process of reconstruction. But in mid-March the committee was back where it had started in January, with no amendment and no plan of reconstruction.

The defeat of the amendment left the Republican party in a quandary, grasping at straws to find a solution to the reconstruction enigma. For a time it appeared that the answer might be found in a return to representation based on the number of legal voters. Doolittle had made such a suggestion in February without attracting much attention, but now the press gave it some credence. Grimes and Sumner each introduced resolutions for the reduction of representation in proportion to the number of male citizens denied the vote. One might wonder what had happened to Sumner, the champion of universal suffrage. Had he been humiliated by the barbs of Fessenden and others? Had he had second thoughts about combining with Democrats to defeat his party's program? His biographer says that, despite his tendency to cling to abstract principles, he was not above compromise when it suited him. Also, because his proposal did not contain the words "race or color," he could still claim that he had not abandoned Negro suffrage.[23]

The most important proposal of this time of uncertainty was that of Senator William M. Stewart of Nevada. Born in New York state in 1827, Stewart had enrolled in Yale College in 1848 with the intention of studying law. But in 1850, lured by the discovery of gold, he migrated to California and entered mining, only to leave it as soon as he had accumulated enough capital to study law in Nevada City, California, where he was admitted to practice in 1852. By 1854 he was acting attorney general of the state and a partner in San Francisco of Henry S. Foote, an ex-governor and ex-senator from Mississippi, whose daughter Stewart soon married. The discovery of silver attracted him in 1859 to Virginia City and Carson City in Nevada Territory, where he became an authority on mining law. For successfully defending the original claimants of the Comstock Lode he received a fee of $500,000. He played an important part in the territorial government of Nevada and was elected to the Senate when the territory became a state in 1864. For a time Stewart supported Johnson's restoration program, but later became one of the president's most caustic critics, one who favored impeachment. He also was to be the author of the Fifteenth Amendment. This leonine man, standing over six feet tall, wearing a long, flowing silver beard, possessed of enormous energy and confidence, was a truly impressive figure in Washington during the Reconstruction era.[24]

Stewart's plan, which he presented as several resolutions on March 10, was not a proposed constitutional amendment but a compromise plan for the restoration of the rebel states. It provided that the former Confederate states would be "recognized as having resumed [their] former relations" with the federal government and that representatives would be admitted to Congress when the states had amended their constitutions so as to give equal civil rights to blacks, to repudiate war debts, to agree that there would be no further claims with respect to former slaves, and to guarantee equal suffrage with no discrimination based on race, color, or previous condition. Those persons qualified to

WILLIAM M. STEWART
Reproduced from the collection of the Library of Congress

vote in 1860 were not to be "disfranchised by reason of any new tests or conditions." When these provisions had been ratified by a majority of the voting population there was to be a general amnesty. Loyal states were requested to amend their constitutions in the same way. There was to be nothing compulsory about these conditions; states might accept or reject them, for Stewart did not intend to "assert a coercive power on the part of Congress . . . but only to make an appeal to their own good sense and love of country, with a view to the prevention of serious evils now threatened." Commonly known as the plan of "universal amnesty and universal suffrage," its advantages were that there was something in it to appeal to every segment of opinion and that it would have obviated the long and uncertain process of adopting a constitutional amendment.

At the conclusion of the speech, some radicals gathered around Stewart to welcome him as a new convert to their cause. Some assumed, mistakenly, that he had proposed universal suffrage, but not many were as yet prepared to accept universal amnesty. The proposal received a great deal of favorable comment from the northern press and some support from the South. With this groundswell of public opinion in its favor, even Andrew Johnson could ill afford to move precipitately against it. It is doubtful that, given the opportunity, the southern states or the radicals would have accepted it. They were not given the opportunity, however, because Johnson's veto of the Civil Rights Bill doomed any such compromise proposal. A month later, Stewart presented his plan to the joint committee, too late for it to receive serious consideration.[25]

After its bitter experience with the representation amendment the joint committee turned back briefly to civil rights. On February 3 the committee, by a vote of seven to six, adopted a resolution that "the Congress shall have power to make all laws which shall be necessary and proper to secure to the citizens of each state all privileges and immunities of citizens in the several states (Art. 4, Sec. 2); and to all persons in the several states equal protection in the rights of life, liberty, and property (5th amendment)." When on February 13 Bingham reported the resolution to the House, there was so little enthusiasm for it that he consented, on the advice of Stevens, to have it recommitted so that it could be reported again at a more favorable time. On the twenty-sixth Bingham did report it again and defended it during the three days of debate that followed. When it became clear that the proposal had no chance of receiving the required two-thirds majority, he agreed to defer it until early April. It was not introduced to the House again as a separate measure or in the form in which Bingham had

presented it, but considerably altered it would appear as Section 1 of the
amendment later proposed by the committee.

In defending the amendment, Bingham said that it was "simply a
proposition to arm Congress . . . with power to enforce the bill of rights,
as it stands in the Constitution today." What did Bingham mean by the
Bill of Rights? Did he mean simply the first eight amendments to the
Constitution? Clearly he did not, since he cited Article 4, Section 2, the
comity clause, which declares that "Citizens of each State shall be
entitled to all the Privileges and Immunities of Citizens of the several
States," along with the "due process" clause of the fifth amendment.
This bill of rights, according to Jacobus ten Broek, was the "immortal
Bill of Rights" that Bingham had come to know and to cherish as a
representative of the "abolitionized Western Reserve of Ohio."[26]

Robert S. Hale of New York, the most effective critic of the amendment, argued that it would undermine the existing federal system by
interfering with the reserved rights of the states. In effect, he asserted,
it was "a provision under which all State legislation, in its codes of civil
and criminal jurisprudence and procedure, affecting the individual citizen, may be overridden, may be repealed or abolished, and the law of
Congress established instead." Thus it was "an utter departure from
every principle ever dreamed of by the men who framed our Constitution." In "meddling with matters of State jurisdiction" it "proposes an
entire departure from the theory of the Federal Government." For the
Bill of Rights, including the Fifth Amendment, "do not contain . . . a
grant of power anywhere. On the contrary, they are all restrictions of
power." The existing Constitution, Hale continued, had been tested
"through peace, through foreign war, through civil war, having found
its strength, its elasticity, its sufficiency for all circumstances and all
trials." Was it then wise to "alter it thus rashly, to alter it in its most
vital and essential principle, to amend it by substituting a new principle
for the very same that animated the system created by it?"

Bingham replied by posing a question of his own.

> The gentleman says that the sufficiency of the Constitution has
> been tested and found in the past. I ask him now if he knows of a
> single decision in which the sufficiency of the Constitution to secure
> to a party aggrieved in his person within a State the right to
> protection by the prosecution of a suit, which by the organic law of
> the State was denied to him, has ever been affirmed, either by
> Federal statute or Federal decision, or whether the nation has not
> been dumb in the presence of the organic act of a State which
> declares that eight hundred thousand natural-born citizens of the

United States shall be denied the right to prosecute a suit in their courts, either for the vindication of a right or the redress of a wrong?[27]

Even though the proposal did not find its way into the Fourteenth Amendment in the form presented by Bingham, the debate on the subject is important for at least two reasons. First, it is another example of how persistent northern men could be in clinging to states' rights, indicating that, in the realm of government and politics, the Civil War was not the centralizing force some historians and pundits have assumed. Second, it bears on the meaning of the first section of the amendment that was ultimately adopted and on the intention of its framers, to which we shall return in examining the interpretations of the amendment.

Having reported two proposed amendments to Congress, the joint committee was ready to do the work for which it was created—to "inquire into the condition of the States which formed the so-called Confederate States of America, and report whether they, or any of them, are entitled to be represented in either House of Congress, with leave to report at any time, by bill or otherwise." If any southern state had met the conditions for restoration, that state was Tennessee. In the eastern part of the state some 40,000 men had voted against secession. Many of them had continued to resist the Confederacy by fleeing southern conscription and joining the Union army. In January 1865, Andrew Johnson, the military governor, assembled a convention of loyal people which proposed an amendment for the abolition of slavery to the state constitution and a declaration that secession, an "act of treason and usurpation," was null and void and that debts incurred in aid of the rebellion were not to be paid. These measures were then adopted by a large majority of the loyal people of the state. On March 4, "Parson" Brownlow was elected governor along with a legislature of "unconditional" Unionists. This new government then proceeded to ratify the Thirteenth Amendment, to disfranchise former Confederate officials, and to enact civil rights for freedmen.

The importance of Tennessee went beyond the restoration of one southern state. The readmission of the president's state might serve as a basis for a rapprochement between the president and Congress, or Johnson might view the failure of Congress to readmit his state as further evidence of congressional intransigence and hostility toward him. Also, the way in which Tennessee was restored might influence relations between Congress and the president. To restore her without any conditions would appear to be a congressional corroboration of

Johnson's restoration program and would be interpreted by him as a victory. But to demand conditions beyond those already established under presidential restoration would constitute another challenge to Johnson. Whatever Congress might think about the readiness of Tennessee for restoration, to maintain its asserted right to a coordinate, or dominant, role in reconstruction would dictate that it establish some conditions.

There were still other questions that members of the joint committee had to ponder as they searched for a solution to the problem of Tennessee: Would the admission of the state become a precedent that would lead to the restoration of other states without Tennessee's credentials? And what would the restoration of even one state do to the precarious Republican majority necessary to override presidential vetoes?

On February 15 Bingham reported from the subcommittee on Tennessee a bill for the readmission of the state of the Union.

> Whereas, The people of Tennessee have presented a Constitution and asked admission into the Union, and which on due examination is found to be republican in its form of Government.
>
> Be it enacted, by the Senate and House of Representatives of the United States of America in Congress assembled, that the State of Tennessee shall be one, and is hereby declared to be one of the United States of America, on an equal footing with the other states in all respects whatever.

To have restored Tennessee on these terms without additional demands from Congress would have been nearly to accept presidential reconstruction, for such conditions as were required had already been met. The committee did not vote on Bingham's proposal, but postponed it until the next meeting. Two days later the committee met and discussed the proposal at length and finally voted favorably on a slightly modified version of it. However, at this point, Williams of Oregon moved that the whole subject of Tennessee be referred to a select committee of three members, to be appointed by the chairman. In a very crucial eight to seven vote the committee approved this motion. Most important of all was Fessenden's vote in favor of the motion and his appointment of the select committee. By appointing three radicals—Williams, Conkling, and Boutwell—he removed the Tennessee question from the hands of the more moderate original committee. On the nineteenth Conkling reported a resolution from the select committee that senators and representatives would be seated when certain conditions had been agreed to. Tennessee was "never [to] assume or pay any debt or obligation contracted or incurred in aid of the late rebellion, nor [to] ever repudiate any debt or obligation . . . in aid of the Federal government against said rebellion," and she was "forever [to] maintain in [her] constitution the provision . . . disavowing the doctrine of secession." All persons who had voluntarily given aid and comfort to the rebellion were to be excluded from the franchise for five years and from offices of "honor, trust, and profit." These conditions were to be ratified by a majority of the qualified voters of the state. Boutwell tried, without success, to have another condition included—that "said state shall make no distinction in the exercise of the elective franchise on account of race or color."

On the same day that Conkling introduced his resolution Andrew Johnson vetoed the Freedmen's Bureau Bill, and thereby gave Thaddeus Stevens an opportunity to defer the whole Tennessee matter. When the committee met on the following day—the twentieth—Stevens said that, in his opinion, "the expediency and propriety" of action on Tennessee had "materially changed since yesterday." Now, he said, "the first duty of the committee was to declare the power of Congress over the subject of reconstruction." He succeeded in having all other business postponed so that he might offer a concurrent resolution.

> Be it resolved by the House of Representatives, the Senate concurring, that in order to close agitation upon a question which seems likely to disturb the action of the government, as well as to quiet the uncertainty which is agitating the minds of the people of the eleven states which have been declared to be in insurrection, no senator or representative shall be admitted into either branch of Congress from any of said states until Congress shall have declared such state entitled to such representation.

It passed in the House immediately and a few days later in the Senate, where its adoption was made easier by Johnson's Washington's Birthday speech.

During the first week of March the committee returned again to the Tennessee question and on the fifth adopted a resolution to admit her with conditions similar to those of the Conkling resolution. On the same day Bingham reported this resolution to the House, with the request that it be recommitted. His intention was to report it again in two weeks, but he did not do so for four months. By that time Congress had adopted the Fourteenth Amendment and Tennessee had ratified it, clearing the way for its restoration two years before any other ex-Confederate state.[28]

During the period of eighteen days from February 15 to March 5, the crucial actions of the committee were the establishment of the new subcommittee on Tennessee, the vote of Fessenden in favor of that action, and his appointment of three radicals to it. If Fessenden had voted the other way the original Bingham resolution undoubtedly would have been restored in such a way that it could have been interpreted as a compromise with the president. Considering Fessenden's reputation as a moderate and his keen awareness of his role as conciliator between Johnson and the radicals, his actions in this instance seem to be out of character. How, then, can his decision be accounted for? Although the effect of the Freedmen's Bureau veto should not be underestimated, Fessenden's move toward a more radical stance took place two days before the veto. Undoubtedly he was influenced, as were many Republicans, by the Black Codes and Johnson's indulgence of Southerners in the issuance of pardons. The testimony of blacks and loyal southern whites before the committee made its members wary about compromising away the power of Congress in the formulation of a reconstruction policy. Also, Johnson had publicly stated his opposition to any further constitutional amendments—at a time when the committee had two amendments before Congress—and to Negro suffrage in the District of Columbia.

W. R. Brock, in his analysis of Fessenden's actions, attaches great importance to a conversation between the senator and the president on January 28. "It has often been surmised," Brock writes, "that the two men simply failed to communicate with each other, but it is equally plausible to suppose that they came to understand each other only too well." Brock goes on to speculate as to what was probably said at that meeting: Fessenden knew on the day of the interview "that the Committee's proposal for tying apportionment to negro suffrage would shortly be before Congress, and . . . could hardly have concealed this from the president in what was intended to be a full and exploratory discussion." He also knew that "some version of the civil rights amendment would probably be presented to Congress and again he could hardly have concealed this from the President." And how would Johnson react? He would find in these actions the " 'centralism' which he believed would destroy the American system of government." It is also possible, Brock continues, "that Johnson found confirmation, in his talk with Fessenden, for his belief that Stevens controlled the committee." The president might also have been left with a mistaken notion about the role of Bingham. Since Tennessee had not yet been discussed in the committee, how would Johnson have known that Bingham, the author of the civil rights amendment, "was also the spokesman for the immediate admission of that state." The interview, Brock concludes, could hardly have done anything "to correct the President's erroneous understanding of moderate Republican opinion."[29]

It is also possible—Brock does not suggest this—that Johnson went even further, that he told Fessenden of his opposition to any more amendments and of his refusal to accept Negro suffrage in the District of Columbia, the same things he said to Senator Dixon later the same day. Brock's speculations about the Johnson-Fessenden conversation are interesting and perceptive and may, indeed, be a clue to Fessenden's decision to act with the radicals. However, considering Fessenden's actions and attitudes from the formation of the committee on through to the issuance of its report six months later, one might wonder whether Brock's explanation is not overly complex, whether the senator's course of action had not already been determined before the end of January. At the first business meeting of the committee, nearly three weeks before his conversation with the president, Fessenden proposed a resolution that "the insurgent states cannot, with safety to the rights of the people of the United States, be allowed to participate in the Government until the basis of representation has been modified, and the rights of all persons secured, either by new provisions, or the necessary changes in the existing provisions, in the Constitution of the United States, or otherwise." Thus at the outset the senator had established his course of action in the committee. There is no evidence indicating that he ever changed it. Francis Fessenden, the senator's son and biographer, said of his father at this time: "The idea of many of the members of Congress was to hurry and get the Southern States back, but for himself he was in no hurry to have them come back. They went out by their own motion; he would offer them a fair proposition, and if they did not choose to accept it they might remain outside the Union until they did. Though Mr. Fessenden was called a conservative, he was radical in his ideas of what the constitutional amendment should be."[30]

If the foregoing is an accurate assessment of Fessenden's position, it would have been unthinkable of him to barter away the powers of Congress by admitting any state without conditions established by the legislature, and his decision to go with the radicals was the expected, if not the inevitable, one. On the same day that he supported the radicals in the matter of the subcommittee (February 17), Fessenden, in a letter to a favorite cousin, wrote: "I . . . have just come from a four hours' session of the reconstruction committee, in which nothing was concluded, though progress was made. I think we shall conclude to admit Tennessee in some shape. I hope so as to make a valuable precedent.

Whether the President will be easy there I cannot tell; but *though I will do something to keep peace, I will not vote away one inch of the safeguards necessary in this terrible condition of affairs.*"[31]

If there is some uncertainty about the place of Fessenden in the Republican spectrum, it probably results from his dual role as chairman of the joint committee and legislative leader. Once the committee had decided on a proposal to submit to Congress, Fessenden felt responsible to present it in its most favorable light, whether or not he fully agreed with it. His refusal to resort to the tactics of Thaddeus Stevens and his dislike of Sumner should not obscure the fact that he was closer to both of them than to conservative Republicans, the political scions of Andrew Johnson. He may even have been closer to them than to the moderate Lyman Trumbull. By not publicly aligning himself with any congressional faction Fessenden, more than anybody else, strengthened the legislature in withstanding the challenge from the executive. This, more than anything else, made him the most important Senate leader of 1866. But there is still another reason for observing him with some care, one relating to the persistent problem of the historian in categorizing or classifying his characters, specifically the ambiguity in using such words as *radical, moderate,* and *conservative.* To avoid the atomization of history and to make sense of it, some effort at classification is necessary. We cannot dissect every character who makes his appearance; yet the case of Fessenden shows us how tentative such classification should be. We cannot simply label Fessenden as a moderate and leave the matter there. He was an amalgam of conservative, moderate, and radical—conservative in his concern for the preservation of traditions and institutions, moderate in his methods, despite some impatience with obstreperous colleagues, and radical in his concern for human rights.

Chapter 6

Congress Adopts the Amendment

DURING THE early part of its existence the Joint Committee on Reconstruction was anything but a resounding success. The withdrawal of the resolution on Tennessee was its third failure in less than two months. And the meeting of March 5 was to be its last until April 16. (The subcommittees continued to meet and to take testimony.) It was a time, indeed, of no little turmoil in and out of Congress. Near the middle of this period of six weeks came the Civil Rights veto, dashing the hopes of many who still sought a compromise with the president. Even before the veto there was growing concern over the absence of a congressional policy; now its need was all the more evident, and the committee bore the brunt of the criticism for the failure. One senator made his point by submitting a proposal with the request that it be referred to the judiciary committee. A correspondent of the *Cincinnati Commercial* wrote from Washington: "It is a Babel of opinion here—a political chaos. No two prominent men think alike. Congress is very weak and powerless because there is no unity of purpose or action in that body."[1] There were renewed fears that the federal government would assume the rebel debt while permitting repudiation of the federal debt. The Finance Committee of the Union Congressional Committee responded by publishing a circular warning that "A division in our councils at the present time would be fruitful of untold evils tending to the destruction of our financial system and the repudiation of our public debt."[2]

Negro suffrage advocates continued to make their demands. Phillips wrote to Sumner of the elements of strength in the radical cause: "We radicals have all the *elements* of national education in our hands—pressure of vast debt—uncertainty of it—capital unwillingness to risk itself in the South but longing to do so—vigilant masses—every returned soldier a witness—every defeated emigrant to the South a witness." He urged Sumner not to lower himself to "raw whiggery (Fessenden), cowardly Republicanism (Wilson), disquieted cop-

perheads (Doolittle), unadulterated treason (Raymond), solid ignorance of this epoch at least (Trumbull)."[3] The *Chicago Tribune* reas-
serted the necessity of universal suffrage to protect northern immigrants to the South and laborers against "Negro competition at existing
low rates."[4]

In two long editorials the *Nation* joined in the chorus of discontent: It
had become evident that Congress, "which is from its very nature in
closer contact with the country and better informed of its thoughts and
feelings . . . than the Executive can possibly be, is the branch which has
and ought to have most to do with such a work of reorganization as is
now before us." But having sat for four months, Congress still had no
policy. "We hear a great deal of the President's policy; it is something
definite, determined, capable of being set down in black and white and
discussed in all its bearings; but we never hear of the policy of Congress,
because there is no such thing. The people are ready to keep the South
out until it complies with certain conditions, but they want to know what
these conditions are." The reconstruction committee had produced several "valuable measures" but no "well-defined plan." If the committee
did not soon get down to more serious work "we greatly fear the coming
fall will find the public thoroughly out of patience with Congress and
quite ready to let the president and his friends have their own way. He
would be a bold man who should venture to predict what would then
happen, or to calculate how much of the fruits of our victories would be
left to us." A few days later the *Nation* returned even more urgently to
the same theme: let Congress come up with a plan; even if it could not be
passed over a veto, but "let it be something upon which we can go to the
country with firmness and confidence."[5]

The entreaties of the *Nation* and others were to be answered not by
the committee or Congress but by an outsider, Robert Dale Owen, the
son of the great British reformer and founder of New Harmony and a
reformer of reputation in his own right. Owen, as we have seen, had
been chairman of the American Freedmen's Inquiry Commission,
whose work had culminated in the establishment of the Freedmen's
Bureau. Then in late 1865, in a public letter to Andrew Johnson, Owen
had proposed a constitutional amendment to prohibit discrimination in
the suffrage because of color and requiring a literacy test to determine
the qualifications of all voters in presidential and congressional elections.[6] Toward the end of March 1866, he appeared in Washington with
a proposed amendment to the Constitution and a plan for the restoration
of the southern states. Having already presented his plan to Governor
Morton, who warmly approved of it, Owen now sought out members of
the committee and others in Congress. The first committee member he

contacted was Thaddeus Stevens, to whom he read his proposed
amendment.

SECTION 1. No discrimination shall be made by any State, nor by
the United States, as to the civil rights of persons, because of race,
color, or previous condition of servitude.

SECTION 2. From and after the fourth day of July, eighteen
hundred and seventy-six, no discrimination shall be made by any
State nor by the United States, as to the enjoyment, by classes of
persons, of the right of suffrage, because of race, color, or previous
condition of servitude.

SECTION 3. Until the fourth day of July, eighteen hundred and
seventy-six, no class of persons, as to the right of any of whom to
suffrage discrimination shall be made by any State, because of race,
color, or previous condition of servitude, shall be included in the
basis of representation.

SECTION 4. Debts incurred in aid of insurrection, or of war
against the Union, and claims of compensation for loss of
involuntary service or labor, shall not be paid by any State nor by
the United States.

SECTION 5. Congress shall have power to enforce, by
appropriate legislation, the provisions of this article.

Owen had also drawn up an enabling act which, together with the
amendment, constituted his plan of restoration. The act provided that
when the amendment should become a part of the Constitution and
when the insurrectionary states had ratified it and modified their constitutions to bring them into accordance with Section 1, their senators
and representatives should be admitted to Congress, "Provided, That
no person who, having been an officer in the army or navy of the United
States, or having been a member of the Thirty-sixth Congress, or of the
Cabinet in the year one thousand eight hundred and sixty, took part in
the late insurrection, shall be eligible to either branch of the National
legislature until after the fourth day of July, one thousand eight
hundred and seventy-six."

As Owen related it,[7] as soon as he had finished reading the amendment Stevens said, "Read that to me again." He read it again and asked
Stevens if he had an hour or so to spare. "I have nothing half so
important to do as to attend to this," Stevens replied. "Take your own
time." In the conversation that followed the two men agreed that the
freedmen "ought to be regarded as the wards of the Federal government," and that the nation's first duty was to them. "Let the cursed
rebels lie on the bed they have made," said Stevens. But Owen believed

that "the interests and fate of the negro" could not be separated "from those of the planter. If we chafe and sour the whites of the South, the blacks must necessarily suffer." Because the Negro was not yet prepared to use the right of suffrage or to legislate, we "must think and act for him as he is, and not as, but for life-long servitude, he would have been. We seclude minors from political rights, not because they are unworthy, but because, for the time, they are incapable. So of foreigners; we grant them the privileges of citizenship only after five years probation." Stevens answered, "I hate to delay full justice so long." There was a danger, Owen continued, that if the Negro were made a legislator he might become "a nuisance and a laughing stock." But, said Stevens, "if the negroes don't rule impertinent traitors will. Isn't that as bad?"

Despite the differences between them, Stevens was enthusiastic about the amendment. "I'll be plain with you, Owen," he said: "We've had nothing before us that comes anywhere near being as good as this, or as complete. It would be likely to pass, too; that's the best of it. We haven't a majority, either in our committee or in Congress, for immediate suffrage; and I don't believe the States have yet advanced so far that they would be willing to ratify it. I'll lay that amendment of yours before our committee tomorrow, if you say so; and I'll do my best to put it through." The discussion then turned from the amendment to the enabling act. Stevens "flared up" at this, Owen recalled, and said, "That will never do! Far too lenient. It would be dangerous to let these fellows off on such easy terms." Owen pointed out that the rebel states would probably postpone Negro suffrage until 1876, so that under the third section they would be entitled to only forty-two representatives instead of sixty-six. "Surely," he said, "you can manage that number, even if they should happen to be ultra secessionists." Perhaps so, Stevens agreed, "But you forget the Senate. The eleven insurrectionary States would be entitled to their twenty-two Senators, suffrage or no suffrage."

In Fessenden, whom Owen visited next, he found a very different personality—"Cold, deliberate, dispassionate, cautious." "He heard me patiently," Owen wrote, "but with scarcely a remark." He promised to give careful attention to Owen's plan and to see him again. When they met again two days later Fessenden said, "in guarded and general terms, that he thought well of the proposal, as the best that had yet been presented to [the] committee." All the Republican members "received the proposal more or less favorably," Owen recalled, but Bingham had some reservations about the first section, which he thought ought to be more specific on civil rights. "The Democrats," said Owen, "held back."

Charles Sumner was one of the persons outside the committee with whom Owen talked. "I cannot vote for this amendment," Sumner told him. "It contains a tacit recognition that the ex-slaveholders have a right to withhold suffrage from the freedmen for ten years longer." It was "a question of abstract principle, . . . not of expediency." Owen asked if he believed an amendment for immediate suffrage could pass during the current session or the next. "Probably not . . . ," answered Sumner, "and it may be several years before it does. If so, let the responsibility rest on those who reject it." To Owen's suggestion that the Negro would then be left without "the protection even of a prospective right" Sumner replied, "I shall be sorry if that prove so. . . . I think no one feels the wrongs of the negro more strongly that I do. But not even to mitigate his sufferings for the time can I consent to palter with the right, or to violate a great principle. I must do my whole duty, without looking to consequences."

Owen's conversations with Stevens and Sumner, the two great radical leaders in Congress, illustrate anew the fundamental differences between them. Each was dedicated in his own way to equality for blacks; yet one, while not giving an inch unnecessarily to the power of the planter class, would never lose sight of the legislative function and the importance of the dominance of his party in the determination and application of long-range measures. The other, holding to his abstract principles above party considerations, would see his duty in a different way, one that did not take account of consequences.

When the committee finally met on April 16, for the first time in six weeks, it did not discuss the Owen plan. Instead, it heard William Stewart give a long report on the plan he had presented in the Senate; but despite the acclaim for this plan the committee took no action on it. At the next meeting, on April 21, Stevens presented the Owen amendment, and it was discussed in detail, section by section. The only important change was the insertion of Bingham's civil rights section, that "No state shall make or enforce any law which shall abridge the privileges or immunities of citizens of the United States; nor shall any state deprive any person of life, liberty or property without due process of law, nor deny to any person within its jurisdiction the equal protection of the laws," which would reappear in Section 1 of the Fourteenth Amendment. With this change the amendment was adopted and ordered to be reported to Congress. On that day, however, Fessenden was ill with a mild case of the varioloid, and as the members were about to leave the room somebody suggested that "it would seem a lack of courtesy if the most important report of the session" should be made in his absence. The committee decided, therefore, to postpone the matter for a few days, until the chairman's expected return. Another week passed before Fessenden recovered. By that time the committee had emasculated the Owen amendment, so that the resolution reported from the committee at the end of April bore little resemblance to it.

Why was the Owen plan, which the committee had received so favorably, abandoned? One indirect factor was the "leakiness of the Committee . . . by which publicity is given to everything said and done under lock and key."[8] On April 24 both the *Chicago Tribune* and the *New York Times* announced the rumor that the committee had agreed to the plan. "Our actions on your amendment had . . . got noised abroad," Stevens later told Owen, and knowledge that Negro suffrage, even of a prospective nature, was included aroused fears for the forthcoming election. Caucuses of members of Congress from several states, including New York, Illinois, and Indiana, agreed that the issue should be avoided. "They were afraid," said Stevens, "that if there was a 'nigger in the wood pile,' . . . it would be used against them as an electioneering handle." They decided that "negro suffrage, in any shape, ought to be excluded from the platform, and they communicated these decisions to us."[9] The *New York Times*, reporting on the actions of the New York delegation, said that "the question of a negro-suffrage condition, either immediate or remote, was received with very little favor."[10]

At least one other inducement from outside the committee might have led the radicals to be more conciliatory on the suffrage question. On April 19 the report of Benjamin C. Truman had been submitted to Congress. In contrast to the earlier report of Carl Schurz, it did not contain very much on which radicals could make their case, but there was one statement that undoubtedly caught their eye: "If the politicians of the South have the absolute certainty laid before them that in 1870 their representation in Congress will be diminished largely in consequence of the non-enfranchisement of the negro, they will see to it before that time that the proper reform is introduced." Such an eventuality, Truman believed, would be more desirable for whites and Negroes than enforced Negro suffrage imposed from Washington.[11]

Although the demand for a compromise political platform, without Negro suffrage, for the 1866 campaign had its effect on the committee's rejection of the Owen plan, one might wonder whether this was the only determinant, whether the Republican members' acceptance of the plan was as unqualified as Owen thought. Was the committee's decision not to send the plan to Congress on April 21 actually taken out of consideration for Fessenden, the indisposed chairman? Or was this a convenient pretext for withholding it in order to change it substantially or block it? A review of the original reaction of the committee members to Owen's plan and a perusal of the committee journal for the latter half of April suggest that the real explanation was not to be found in the "Political Results from the Varioloid," as the dispirited Owen believed.

Let us recall how Stevens, in his first conversation with Owen, had reacted to the plan. He had been enthusiastic about the amendment, as the best proposal he had seen up to that time, but had considered the enabling act far too lenient. Bingham was not very enthusiastic about the Owen amendment because of its inadequacy in regard to civil rights; indeed, he had already proposed a section of his own on that subject,[12] and on the day the Owen plan was introduced Bingham succeeded in having his "due process" and "equal protection" provisions inserted into the amendment. Then, in presenting the plan to the committee, Stevens held that it would be necessary to submit the amendment and the enabling act separately to Congress. Apparently he would support the former and not the latter, which is to say that he really did not favor the Owen *plan* of reconstruction. When the committee met two days later Stevens withdrew the Owen enabling act and submitted one of his own, whose list of persons made ineligible for service in the national legislature was greatly extended, so as to include diplomatic officers of the "so-called confederate government, or officers of the army or navy of said government above the rank of colonel in the army or lieutenant in the navy," persons "in regard to whom it shall appear to have treated officers or soldiers or sailors of the army or navy of the United States, of whatever race, or color, captured during the Civil War, otherwise than lawfully as prisoners of war," and persons "in regard to whom it shall appear that they are disloyal." After a long discussion the committee accepted Stevens's bill with only minor modification.

At the important April 28 meeting Stevens, having rewritten Owen's enabling act, moved against his amendment and persuaded the committee to eliminate all of Section 2, the section that postponed Negro suffrage for ten years. The committee went on from there to write its own amendment, which it would present to Congress on April 30. "Greatly vexed" and disappointed, Owen called upon Stevens for an explanation of what had happened. All his labor had been lost, Owen lamented. "Yes," said Stevens, "but not by my vote. Don't imagine that I sanction the shilly-shally, bungling thing that I shall have to report to the House tomorrow." After explaining the matter of Fessenden's absence, Stevens said, "So I let it pass, thinking that a few days would make no difference. God forgive me for my folly." "Damn the varioloid!" he said to Owen in parting. *"It changed the whole policy of the country."*[13] Clearly, Stevens was dissembling.

Even though the committee rejected it, the Owen plan occupies an important place in the evolution of the Fourteenth Amendment. Containing an omnibus amendment and an enabling act, it provided a good working model for the committee, whose plan, in form if not in substance, was similar to it. Even more important, it spurred the lackluster committee into activity again. On the afternoon of April 28 Orville H. Borwning happened to meet Senator Reverdy Johnson in the Capitol. Johnson told him that he had been with the committee all day and that the majority had agreed upon "a proposition to keep all the Southern states out till amendments to the Constitution were adopted, which would not be adopted and would produce a revolution if they were."[14] Two days later Senator James Grimes wrote to his wife of that last committee meeting: "We have just agreed upon a plan of reconstruction, which will be reported tomorrow, and which, so far as I can learn, is quite acceptable to our friends. It is not exactly what any of us wanted; but we were each compelled to surrender some of our individual preferences in order to secure anything, and by doing so became unexpectedly harmonious."[15] These contrasting statements of a Maryland Democrat and an Iowa Republican, each containing an element of truth, are indicative of the perplexities affecting well-intentioned men as they struggled in the spring of 1866 to formulate a workable program of reconstruction.

The resolution that Stevens and Fessenden reported to the House and the Senate consisted of an amendment and two bills setting forth conditions for the restoration of the southern states. The amendment read:

SECTION 1. No state shall make or enforce any law which shall abridge the privileges or immunities of citizens of the United States; nor shall any State deprive any person of life, liberty, or property without due process of law; nor deny to any person within its jurisdiction the equal protection of the laws.

SECTION 2. Representatives shall be apportioned among the several States which may be included within this Union according to their respective numbers, counting the whole number of persons in each State, excluding Indians not taxed. But whenever in any State the elective franchise shall be denied to any portion of its male citizens not less than twenty-one years of age, or in any way abridged, except for participation in rebellion or other crime, the basis of representation in such State shall be reduced in the proportion which the number of male citizens shall bear to the whole number of such male citizens not less than twenty-one years of age.

SECTION 3. Until the 4th day of July, in the year 1870, all persons who voluntarily adhered to the late insurrection, giving it aid and comfort, shall be excluded from the right to vote for Representatives in Congress and for electors for President and Vice-President of the United States.

SECTION 4. Neither the United States nor any State shall assume or pay any debt or obligation already incurred, or which may hereafter be incurred, in aid of insurrection or of war against the United States, or any claim for compensation for the loss of involuntary service or labor.

SECTION 5. The Congress shall have power to enforce by appropriate legislation the provisions of this article.

The first of the two bills provided that whenever the amendment "shall have become a part of the Constitution . . . and any State lately in insurrection shall have modified its constitution and laws in conformity therewith, the Senators and Representatives from such State, if found duly elected and qualified, may, after having taken the required oath of office, be admitted into Congress as such." The second bill listed a number of persons ineligible to hold federal office.

1. The President and Vice-President of the Confederate States of America, so-called, and the heads of departments thereof.

2. Those who in other countries acted as agents of the Confederate States of America, so-called.

3. Heads of Departments of the United States, officers of the Army and Navy of the United States, and all persons educated at the Military and Naval Academy of the United States, judges of the courts of the United States, and members of either House of the Thirty-Sixth Congress of the United States who gave aid or comfort to the late rebellion.

4. Those who acted as officers of the Confederate States of America, so-called, above the grade of colonel in the army or master in the navy, and any one who, as Governor of either of the so-called Confederate States, gave aid or comfort to the rebellion.

5. Those who have treated officers or soldiers or sailors of the Army or Navy of the United States, captured during the late war, otherwise than lawfully as prisoners of war.

With the presentation of this plan of restoration the committee, as such, completed its part in the framing of the Fourteenth Amendment. Although its members would participate significantly in the congressional debates on the amendment, the committee met only once more during the first session of the Thirty-ninth Congress, on June 6, when Fessenden called it into a brief meeting to approve his report.

The press and the public were generally not favorably impressed with the committee's plan. Joseph Medill, editor of the *Chicago Tribune*, wrote to Trumbull that it was an "offspring of cowardice" showing a "want of faith in the people." He would have preferred either Owen's or Stewart's plan. "Even the Conservatives do not throw up their hats over it." The *Nation* was surprised that no provision had been made for Negro suffrage, "which, considering who the majority of the committee are, must be due to sheer want of confidence in the public." Although pleased that the committee had finally brought forth a plan, the *Nation* had little hope of having any plan adopted before the fall elections. The committee could not have believed, said the *Cincinnati Commercial*, that there was any possibility of restoring the Union under its plan.[16] The *New York Tribune* would have preferred a much stronger and simpler plan embracing universal amnesty and impartial suffrage; but because it was not possible "that all individual views and prejudices shall be gratified" it urged "every Unionist in Congress to adopt the . . . report as a basis, amending wherever that may be practicable, but resolved to accept and vote for it when it should have been perfected by the action of the two Houses."[17]

The *National Anti-Slavery Standard* branded the plan a fraud, "the blighted harvest of the bloodiest sowing the fields of the world ever saw." Phillips wrote to Stevens that the committee had been guilty of "a fatal and total surrender," which would enable the South to "control the Nation, mold its policy and shape its legislation for a dozen years to come."[18] But the *New York Times* thought the plan was "sweeping enough to satisfy the most exacting Radical," and denounced it as an effort "to prolong indefinitely the exclusion of the South from Congress, by imposing conditions to which the Southern people would never submit."[19]

Andrew Johnson commented that the committee had practically abandoned Negro suffrage and had recognized the unconstitutionality of the Civil Rights Bill. One correspondent found in this statement some hope that the president might now seek a compromise with Congress, especially if Tennessee was restored.[20] Instead, Johnson called a meeting of his cabinet, where he denounced the plan and insisted that each cabinet member declare himself for or against it. He then released to the press an official account of the meeting.

> The President was earnest in his opposition to the report of the committee, and declared himself against all conditions

precedent to the admission of loyal representatives from the Southern States in the shape of amendments to the constitution, or by the passage of laws. He insisted that under the constitution no State could be deprived of its equal suffrage in the Senate, and that Senators and Representatives ought to be at once admitted into the respective houses as presented by law and the constitution. . . . He remarked, in general terms, that if the organic law is to be changed at all, it should be at a time when all the States and all the people can participate in the alteration.[21]

Having introduced the committee's amendment and bills on April 30, Stevens opened the debate in the House on May 8. He admitted that the amendment was not all the committee desired: "It falls far short of my wishes, but it fulfils my hopes. I believe it is all that can be obtained in the present state of public opinion. . . . We did not believe that nineteen of the loyal States could be induced to ratify any proposition more stringent than this. I say nineteen, for I utterly repudiate and scorn the idea that any state not acting in the Union is to be counted on the question of ratification." It was "absurd," he said, to suppose that more states than those which proposed the amendment should participate in making it valid, "that states not here should be counted as present." He would take all he could get "in the cause of humanity, and leave it to be perfected by better men in better times."

He proceeded then to a discussion of the amendment section by section. The provisions of the first section, he said, had all been asserted in one form or another in the Declaration of Independence. But the Constitution was deficient on civil rights by limiting only the actions of Congress and not those of the states. The amendment was designed to correct that defect by allowing "Congress to correct the unjust legislation of the States, so far that the law which operates upon one man shall operate equally upon all."[22]

Stevens considered Section 2, fixing the basis of representation, to be the most important one. Its effect, he said, would be "either to compel the States to grant universal suffrage or so to shear them of their power as to keep them in a hopeless minority in the national Government, both legislative and executive." This article, he said, was not so good as the earlier one rejected by the Senate; for that article, providing that "if *one* of the injured race was excluded the State should forfeit the right to have any of them represented," would have hastened black enfranchisement. But the earlier proposal, said Stevens, striking out at Sumner, "was slaughtered by a puerile and pedantic criticism, by a perversion of philological definition which, if when I had taught school a lad who had studied Lindley Murray had assumed, I would have expelled him from the institution as unfit to waste an education upon." Departing briefly from the content of the amendment, Stevens commented on the freedmen's imperative need for land: "Forty acres of land and a hut would be more valuable to him than the immediate right to vote. Unless we give him this we shall receive the censure of mankind and the curse of Heaven."

Stevens anticipated that Section 3, prohibiting rebels from voting for members of Congress or presidential electors until 1870, would "encounter more difference of opinion," but *his* only objection to it was that it was too lenient. "I know," he said, "that there is a morbid sensibility, sometimes called mercy, which affects a few of all classes, from the priest to the clown, which has more sympathy for the murderer on the gallows than for his victim." He hoped that he was as capable of humane feelings as others—he had long wished for the abolition of capital punishment—but he "never dreamed that all punishment could be dispensed with in human society," allowing "anarchy, *treason,* and violence [to] reign triumphant." Section 3 provided the "mildest of all punishments ever inflicted on traitors. I might not consent to the extreme severity denounced upon them by a provisional governor of Tennessee—I mean the late lamented Andrew Johnson of blessed memory—but I would have increased the severity of this section." Even so, Stevens would not move or vote for any modification "lest the whole fabric should tumble to pieces." On Section 4, forbidding the assumption of the Confederate debt or compensation for former slaves, he found it unnecessary to comment, "for none dare object to it who is not himself a rebel."

He concluded the speech with an appeal to congressmen to approve the amendment: "sacrifice as we [the committee] have done your peculiar views, and instead of vainly insisting on the instantaneous operation of all that is right accept what is possible, and 'all these things shall be added unto you.' "[23] The speech was one of Stevens's best, one in which he demonstrated the diversity of his leadership. He had turned his invective on both Charles Sumner and Andrew Johnson, while expressing his own humanitarianism. Above all, he was the parliamentary leader who never lost sight of his first objective, the adoption of the amendment.

Most of the debate that followed related to Section 3. James G. Blaine began it with a query. Under a law of July 17, 1862, both Lincoln and Johnson had issued a number of pardons, with the recipients fully restored to all the rights and privileges of citizenship. "Do we not," Blaine asked, "place ourselves in the attitude of taking back by constitutional amendment that which has been given by act of Congress and by presidential proclamation issued in pursuance of law? And will not this course be justly subject to the charge of bad faith on the part of the Federal Government?" Stevens replied that a pardon "extinguishes the crime" and that "none of those who have been fully pardoned are affected by this provision." Blaine thought this was "a very strange construction" which "effectively nullifies what has been understood as the intent and purpose of the section." He believed that it would lead to "infinite mischief and complication" and, at the proper time, he would move to strike it out. (Subsequently the Senate did strike it out.)

Somewhat later the matter of pardons came up again; this time Stevens was better prepared to discuss it. His new explanation was that, while a pardon removed all liability to punishment for a crime it did not apply in the same way to the withholding of a privilege. It followed from this interpretation that persons who had "voluntarily adhered to the . . . insurrection, giving it aid and comfort," would be denied the right to vote.

James A. Garfield regretted unspeakably the omission of a Negro suffrage provision. If the right to vote was "not indeed one of the natural rights of all men," he said, it was necessary for their protection. He believed, with John Stuart Mill, "that the ballot is put into the hands of men, not so much to enable them to govern others as that [they] may not be misgoverned by others." Nor was Garfield wholly satisfied with Section 3. But he praised the work of the committee and was "delighted that we have at least reached the firm earth, and planted our feet upon solid granite, on enduring and indubitable principle."

Henry J. Raymond criticized the committee for the long delay in presenting its plan to Congress. He could see "nothing in the report which required any such delay, nothing which depends for its validity or force upon the evidence which, with such protracted pain, the committee had spent five months in collecting." He was adamant in his opposition to Section 3, which would exclude the great body of the people of the southern states from voting for federal officers. He accused the committee of including that section "for the express purpose of preventing the adoption" of the amendment, because the state legislatures were being asked to ratify a provision which denied them the vote. "We offer them," said Raymond, "in exchange for all these renunciations of political power and material advantage, the privilege of being misrepresented in Congress by men in whose election they had no voice or vote, and with whose past political action they have no sympathy whatever."[24]

Andrew J. Rogers led the attack from the Democratic side. In a casuistic argument in which he resorted to hyperbole and Negrophobia, he condemned his colleagues of the committee who had prepared the amendment. With encomiums for Andrew Johnson, he welcomed the president into the Democratic party. Together Johnson and the Democrats would put the "glorious flag" upon the "dome of the State Capitol of South Carolina . . . as it is over the dome of the Capitol of the United States, representing a union of love and equal representation." The first section of the amendment, said Rogers, was an attempt to "embody in the Constitution that outrageous and miserable civil rights bill which . . . was vetoed by the President . . . upon the ground that it was a direct attempt to consolidate the power of the States and to take away from them the elementary principles which lie at their foundation . . . , one of the most dangerous, most wicked, most intolerant, and most odious propositions ever introduced into this House." Section 2, said Rogers, was "unparalleled in ferocity . . . sapp[ing] the foundation of the rights of the States." As for the blacks, Rogers had "not the slightest antipathy to them," but the "American people believe[d] that this Government was made for white men and white women."

As Andrew Johnson had done in his Washington's Birthday speech, Rogers turned finally to the Scriptures to clinch his argument.

> Why, sir, the Scriptures tell me that when Christ came upon the earth the fallen world had been doomed to punishment for the commission of sin and had been assigned to eternal damnation. And I am informed by the same Scriptures that Christ gave His body, His blood, and His soul as a propitiation for the sins of mankind. Now, I ask you to emulate the noble example of the Saviour of the world. Let us treat our southern brethren like men, like freemen, like fellow-citizens. And we will have a laurel crown placed upon our brows, if not here, then in heaven, and we shall receive the plaudit, "Well done, good and faithful servants of the Republic."[25]

One senses in reading Rogers's speech that he was trying to imitate the tactics and style of Thaddeus Stevens, to turn Stevens's own weapons against him. But without the wit, the incisiveness, and the quickness of repartee of the "Old Commoner" the effort became ludicrous.

John A. Bingham was one of the last to speak on May 10, the final day of debate. The first section was necessary, he said, because it supplied a serious "want" in the Constitution for Congress "to protect by . . . law the privileges and immunities of all citizens . . . and the inborn rights of every person within its jurisdiction whenever the same shall be abridged or denied by the unconstitutional acts of any State." But, he assured his skeptical colleagues, the amendment did not take from the state "any right that ever pertained to it," for no state "ever had the right . . . to deny to any freeman the equal protection of the laws or to abridge the privileges and immunities of any citizen." The third (or punitive) section, he believed, brought no strength to the amendment. The real question relating to that section, he said, was one of policy rather than power, for "the sovereignty of the nation can unquestionably disfranchise the persons referred to, not only until 1870, but until seventy times seventy" through legislative enactment. Finally, turning from the amendment to restoration, Bingham appealed for the enactment of the enabling legislation and the speedy restoration of Tennessee: "Let that great example be set by Tennessee and it will be worth a hundred thousand votes to the loyal people in the free North. Let this be done and it will be hailed as the harbinger of that day for which all good men pray, when the fallen pillars of the Republic shall be restored without violence or the noise of words or the sound of the hammer, each

JOHN A. BINGHAM
Reproduced from the collection of the Library of Congress

to its original place in the sacred temple of our national liberties."[26]

Stevens concluded the debate with an appeal to the members to adopt the amendment with Section 3, "the most vital proposition of them all." Without that, he said, "It amounts to nothing. I do not care the snap of my finger whether it be passed or not if that be stricken out." If it was not retained "that side of the House [the Democratic] will be filled with yelling secessionists and hissing Copperheads. Give us the third section or give us nothing. Do not balk us with the pretense of an amendment which throws the Union into hands of the enemy before it becomes consolidated." To those who accused him of being unduly concerned for his party Stevens answered: "Gentlemen say I speak of party. Whenever party is necessary to sustain the Union I say rally to your party and save the Union. I do not hesitate to say at once, that section is there to save or destroy the Union party, is there to save or destroy the Union by the salvation or destruction of the Union party."

And finally Stevens the Calvinist demanded that rebels atone for their sins.

> Gentlemen tell us it is too strong—too strong for what? Too strong for their stomachs, but not for the people. Some say it is too lenient. It is too lenient for my hard heart. Not only to 1870, but to 18070, every rebel who shed the blood of loyal men should be prevented from exercising any power in this Government. That, even, would be too mild a punishment for them.
>
> Gentlemen here have said you must not humble these people. Why not? Do not they deserve humiliation? Do not they deserve degradation? If they do not, who does? What criminal, what felon deserves it more, sir? They have not yet confessed their sins; and He who administers mercy and justice never forgives until the sinner confesses his sins and humbles himself at His footstool. Why should we forgive any more than He?[27]

Beating down a last minute effort to alter Section 3, Stevens succeeded in bringing the amendment to a vote. Its passage by a vote of 128 to 37 was a victory for party discipline. Even Raymond voted for it, bringing applause from the floor and the galleries.[28]

The passage of the amendment in the House did not elicit much enthusiasm for it or much expectation that its passage in the Senate would be easy. Grimes, who earlier had been optimistic about its adoption, now predicted a long debate in the Senate with alterations in the amendment before its final passage.[29] A Chicago constituent wrote to Trumbull, "Republicans don't like it, Democrats don't like it, the North don't like it, the South don't like it." But he was hopeful the Senate would "make it satisfactory to somebody, Black or White, South or North."[30] Chief Justice Salmon P. Chase feared the amendment might be defeated owing to the number of sections in it, "points of attack that need not have been exposed."[31] The *Chicago Tribune,* taking a more practical political view, said that although the radicals might not like it, its opponents would find it difficult to attack effectively: "We would like to see them advocate the proposition that rebel legislatures shall have the authority to abridge the rights of the citizen, or to deprive any person of life, liberty, or property without due process of law." Il-linoisans would not be persuaded to oppose the reduction of rebel representation, and the provision on the debt was "extremely popular with capitalists and tax payers," who would "take care of the Cop-perhead demagogues who oppose the adoption of this great safe-guard against future trouble or national bank-ruptcy."[32]

After its adoption of the amendment, the House turned its attention to the bill for the restoration of the southern states. When it came up for discussion on May 15, Stevens moved immediately to postpone for two more weeks. He had learned, he said, that the Senate would not con-sider the amendment for another week and thought it would be awk-ward for the House to proceed until the Senate had acted on it. Bingham rose to challenge him. If the House considered the bill of any impor-tance, he said, it should not be postponed. "If it is necessary to pass the entire scheme for the reconstruction of the States lately in insurrection, as reported by the joint committee on reconstruction, then let the House do its duty, its whole duty, and leave the responsibility with the Senate, where it belongs." Suppose the Senate should not act on the amendment for some weeks or even months, Bingham continued, should the House stand idle and not "act upon the other measures necessary to the restoration of the insurrectionary States?" Stevens replied sharply: "I must say that I do not understand what the gentle-man from Ohio [Bingham] means. I thought it was understood that this bill should take the course I have indicated, but it so happens that my friend from Ohio never agrees long to what he and the rest of the committee may agree to at any time upon any particular point." Bin-gham was confused, said Stevens, if he supposed it was necessary to proceed with the bill to enable the states to ratify the amendment.[33]

As Joseph James suggests, the exchange between the two men brought to the surface "resentment that must have smouldered" during the secret meetings of the committee.[34] Whatever their understanding of the committee's recommendations might have been, their intentions were almost diametrically opposed. Bingham would use the committee report as a program of restoration, to bring the rebel states back into the Union as soon as possible. Stevens by separating the amendment from the enabling legislation, would delay it in the hope of getting harsher terms and eventually reconstruction. On the immediate issue, the consideration of the bill, Stevens won, when the House voted down Bingham's motion not to postpone.

If Stevens had been confident that the Senate would pass the amendment intact, as it had been received from the House, he probably would not have been so insistent on awaiting the action of the upper body. The presence of the third section in the amendment would have served as a guarantee that the southern states would not ratify the amendment. But he had heard the attacks on that section in the House and knew of the strong opposition to it in the Senate. Thus his hopes that the crucial section could be preserved must have faded, placing the whole matter in a different light. With the growing prospect that the southern states might indeed ratify the amendment, it became imperative for Stevens to delay or materially alter the enabling legislation.

Toward the end of May, therefore, when it was evident that the Senate would not accept Section 3, Stevens introduced into the House a plan of *reconstruction*, as distinguished from the plan of restoration recommended by moderates such as Bingham and embraced in the report of the Joint Committee on Reconstruction. Stevens's bill recognized the existing governments of the rebel states as de facto and valid for municipal purposes, "though irregular and not entitled to representation in Congress." It declared that all persons who had held office under or taken an oath of loyalty to the "so-called Confederate States" had forfeited their citizenship and required that they should be naturalized, as foreigners, before being allowed to vote. Constitutions and laws of the reorganized states were to "put all citizens upon an equal footing." The existing legislatures were to call for conventions, with male citizens of at least twenty-one years of age eligible to vote and to serve as members. Presumably the conventions would implement the restoration of the states in accordance with the provisions of the bill. (Stevens did not present the bill in its entirety, and it is not known to have been printed in full, but on June 5 the *Nation* published a version of it, which is the source of this account.) Although the bill is not known to have contained a specific provision for Negro suffrage or Negro participation in government, he intended that blacks and probably a minority of whites should share in the process of restoration. The House took no action on Stevens's plan at the time, but it was a harbinger of things to come after the election of 1866.[35]

The Senate was much more deliberate than the House in acting on the amendment. Fessenden reported it and the two bills on April 30, the same day Stevens reported it in the House. Two days later Dixon offered a substitute for the whole plan which, he said, was along the lines of the president's argument in his veto of the Freedmen's Bureau Bill. His resolution emphasized the need to admit every state "to its share in public legislation whenever it presents itself in an attitude of loyalty and harmony." Two weeks later Stewart moved to strike out Section 3, but no action was taken.

It was not until May 23 that the Senate began serious debate on the amendment. Because Fessenden was too ill to take charge of the measure, the duty of guiding it through fell to Howard of Michigan. Amidst some lethargy on the floor but with a large audience, including many blacks, in the galleries, Howard opened the debate with a speech of two hours. After praising the committee for its assiduous effort and its impartiality and fairness, he proceeded to discuss each section of the amendment. The first section, he said, was a "general prohibition upon all the States . . . from abridging the privileges and immunities of citizens . . . [or] depriving any person . . . of life, liberty, or property without due process of law . . . or denying him the equal protection of the laws." He was "sorry to be obliged to acknowledge" that the second section did "not recognize the authority of the United States over questions of suffrage in the several States." If he could have had his way he would have provided Negro suffrage "to some extent at least." But "the committee were of the opinion that the States are not yet ready to sanction so fundamental a change. . . . We may as well state it plainly. . . . It was our opinion that three-fourths of the States . . . could not be induced to . . . grant the right of suffrage, even in any degree or under any restriction, to the colored race."

He had opposed Section 3 in the committee because he did not believe that it would be of any practical benefit to the country, and he all but invited the Senate to reject it and replace it with a clause "prohibiting all persons who [had] participated in the rebellion, and who were twenty-five years of age at the breaking out of the rebellion, from all participation in offices, either Federal or State, throughout the United States." He took it for granted that no person would oppose Section 4, because the "assumption of the rebel debt would be the last and final signal" for the destruction of the nation. That section was a "necessity of such magnitude as . . . to demand our action and the action of the States . . . without delay." Section 5, giving Congress the power to enforce the provisions of the amendment by appropriate legislation, Howard looked upon as "indispensable."[36]

Following Howard's speech, several senators proposed amendments to the resolution. Wade proposed to strike out the word *citizen* in the first section and to substitute the word *person*. There had been a good deal of uncertainty, he said, about the word *citizen*. Even though the question seemed to be settled by the Civil Rights Bill, court decisions had thrown some doubt on the subject. Also, because the government might "fall into the hands of those who are opposed to the view that some of us maintain," the question should be placed "beyond all cavil for the present and the future." He would replace Section 2 with a provision similar to the original proposal of the committee on representation, that no class of persons should be counted when there had been discrimination in suffrage against any member of that class. Although he did not propose any substitute for Section 3, Wade agreed with Howard that it would have no effect. He preferred to exclude "those who [had taken] any leading part in the rebellion from exercising any political power here or elsewhere now and forever."

Wade, of course, endorsed the provision nullifying the rebel debt, but he would go a step further by guaranteeing the federal debt and making it "inviolable." This, he said, would place the debt incurred in the Civil War "under the guardianship of the Constitution . . . so that a Congress cannot repudiate it," would thus "give great confidence to capitalists and [would] be of incalculable pecuniary benefit to the United States." "I have no doubt," he said, "that every man who has property in the public funds will feel safer when he sees that the national debt is withdrawn from the power of a Congress to repudiate it and placed under the guardianship of the Constitution than he would feel if it were left at loose ends and subject to the varying majorities which may arise in Congress."[37]

Sherman proposed to strike out Sections 2 and 3 and to substitute for them one section which would base representation on the number of qualified voters in each state. Because this proposal was similar to one Johnson had recommended, one might infer that Sherman was still hopeful of a compromise with the president.[38] But considering Sherman's estrangement from Johnson at the time of the Civil Rights veto, a more reasonable conclusion would be that Sherman was speaking for western interests as opposed to those of New England.[39]

On the same day William Stewart, perhaps still smarting from the committee's rejection of his plan, delivered a long speech which the historian Benjamin B. Kendrick has said was "by far the most interesting and statesmanlike speech . . . made on the general subject of reconstruction at any time during the session."[40] It was indeed a *tour de force* in defense of Stewart's program of impartial suffrage and universal amnesty as well as a discourse on the nature of republican governments. He was convinced that Congress could not fully agree "as to what is expedient to be done to harmonize factions and to restore peace to our distracted country." Upon questions of expediency there was, he said, an "irreconcilable conflict of opinions," but there was very little difference among Union men as to what ought to be done. The solution to this dilemma was to follow the principle that "all men are entitled to life, liberty, and the pursuit of happiness," to let principle be the guide to expediency. Stewart had heard no proposal, he said, which "promised security for the future and protection for the friends of Government, and at the same time extended mercy to its enemies. Mercy pleaded generous amnesty; justice demanded impartial suffrage." He therefore proposed "pardon for the rebels and the ballot for the blacks."

The Freedmen's Bureau and the Civil Rights Act, Stewart believed, were "all very well in their way," but they were expensive to operate and ineffectual in "protecting or governing four million people." He admitted that he had been slow to commit himself to Negro suffrage, but he had come to see that "it alone would protect the Negro and redeem the pledge of the Government that he should be free." It followed from this line of reasoning that the second section of the proposed amendment would not do: "Why license the South to outrage equal rights for the small compensation of reduced representation?" If he could attract the votes of those who had "changed with the progress of events during the last six years," he said in appealing for the adoption of his plan, the rest might vote as they pleased: "Those who, in the language of Mr. Lincoln, 'adopt new views whenever they appear to be true views,' are the only persons wise or useful in this age of progress. The world moves, and those who do not perceive it are dead to the living issues of the day. I have always advocated the necessity of taking the world as we find it, and following the logic of events. The development of new facts is constantly exploding old theories. The trouble is that some men do not seem to comprehend the new facts."

Asking the pardon of the Senate for the frankness with which he had spoken, Stewart concluded with the plea:

> Let amnesty and suffrage be submitted, and allow each State to act separately, and if the South adopt it, the North must; and if the North does, how can the South refuse? It is safe to say she will not jeopardize her peace and security in any way. Let the plan embody civil rights, impartial suffrage, and repudiation of both rebel debt and claims for emancipated slaves on the one hand, and universal amnesty and restoration of rebels to civil and political rights on the other hand, and the country will finish the work. And when it is done it will be well done.[41]

The basic flaw in Stewart's argument was that, like those he condemned for not keeping abreast of the times, he was unrealistic.
Perhaps, as he said, the people were more advanced than Congress in
their readiness to accept his plan. But in ignoring the problem of
enforcing Negro suffrage in the South and underestimating the opposition to it in the North he exaggerated the power of the ballot.

Stewart was right, however, about the "irreconcilable conflict"
among Republican senators as to the ways and means of implementing a
program. If the debate in the Senate had been allowed to go on un-
checked another failure would almost certainly have been the result.
Instead, Senate Republicans met during a period of five days in a series
of caucuses, where party discipline was applied and amendments to the
resolution were agreed to. It is not yet known exactly what happened in
these secret meetings. According to certain correspondents who got
wind of the proceedings, Sherman's conciliatory plan was discussed at
length and its adoption urged. It seems also that the senators were
assured that House Republicans would accept whatever version of the
amendment the Senate might adopt. Finally, a committee consisting of
the Senate members of the joint committee was commissioned to pull
together the views of the caucus in a proposed amendment. On May 29
Fessenden, the spokesman for this committee, presented its work to
the caucus, which adopted it with only minor changes.[42]

Changes made by the caucus were in the first, third, and fourth
sections. To Section 1 was added a definition of citizenship. Section 3
was removed entirely and replaced by a provision excluding former
Confederate leaders from federal and state offices, a provision almost
identical with the second of the two enabling acts. To Section 4 was
added a provision validating the public debt of the United States. The
question of Tennessee also came up in the caucus meeting. After a
lengthy debate it was decided that, since that state had already acted on
the requirements of the amendment, its congressional delegation
should be admitted immediately.[43]

On May 30 Howard presented the caucus amendment to the Senate.
A debate on Section 1, the civil rights section, followed. Howard and
Fessenden disagreed about the connection of this section with the Civil
Rights Bill. Howard said that the two were related, that the committee
had "desired to put this question of citizenship and the rights of freedmen under the civil rights bill beyond the legislative power of such men
as the Senator from Wisconsin" (Doolittle). Fessenden contended that
the matter had been discussed in the committee before any discussion of
the Civil Rights Bill and that the amendment had been "placed on
entirely different grounds." Whatever the order of discussion in the

committee may have been, there was clearly a connection between the bill and the amendment. The link was John A. Bingham, author of the original civil rights amendment, who had voted against the Civil Rights Bill because he doubted its constitutionality and had insisted on a civil rights guarantee under the Constitution.[44]

The liveliest and most interesting part of the debate on Section 1 had to do with Indian citizenship. Doolittle, assuming that the framers of the amendment had not intended to extend citizenship to Indians, moved to amend it by adding the words "excluding Indians not taxed." Cowan followed with a racist speech in which he made dire predictions as to what would happen to the country if Indians, Mongols, and Gypsies were allowed to migrate into it. His chief concern was with Mongols, a word he used interchangeably with Chinese. With the recently improved means of transportation, he said, "They may pour in their millions upon our Pacific coast in a very short time. Are the States to lose control over this immigration? Is the United States to determine that they are to be citizens? . . . I consider those people to have rights just the same as we have, but not rights in connection with our Government."

Such playing upon the prejudices of fellow senators might well have been a delaying or diversionary tactic by Doolittle and Cowan, neither of whom was any longer a member of the Republican party in any but the most formal sense. Whatever their intentions, the Republican leadership in the Senate—including Fessenden, Howard, and Trumbull—assured their colleagues that Indians were not to be citizens. Of the three, Trumbull's argument was probably the most learned and convincing. The provision that "all persons now in the United States, and subject to the jurisdiction thereof, are citizens" meant, said Trumbull, "subject to the complete jurisdiction thereof." It clearly would not apply to the Navajo or other tribes with whom we make treaties or to those "wild Indians" with whom we have not treaties and over whom we have no jurisdiction. Therefore, to insert the words suggested by Doolittle would in no way clarify the meaning of the amendment.

Howard, although in essential agreement with Trumbull, went a step further. He feared that Doolittle's amendment was an "unconscious attempt . . . to nationalize all the Indians within the limits of the United States." "I do not agree with that," he said, "I am not quite so liberal in my views. I am not yet prepared to pass a sweeping act of naturalization by which all the Indian savages, wild or tame, belonging to a tribal relation, are to become my fellow-citizens and go to the polls and vote with me and hold lands and deal in every other way that a citizen of the United States has a right to do."[45] While they might argue the fine points of the meaning of words and phrases, these Republican Senators, whatever their factions or their loyalties, constituted a solid phalanx against civil rights for Indians. An obvious and easy conclusion from the inconsistency of their arguments is that these men were simply hypocritical, or duplicitous, or that, as was often charged, they were playing politics with reconstruction and the Fourteenth Amendment. Even admitting some validity in such an estimate of them, a fair assessment demands that the matter not be left there.

The plight of the Indian and the treatment of him by Caucasian Americans is, as everybody knows, a persistently tragic theme in American History. Probably no era of Indian relations was more dismal than the one upon which the country entered during the Civil War years, the era of the Chivington massacre and the wars with the Apache, the Navajo, the Sioux, and the Nez Percé which continued for two decades. What senators said about Indians and other alien peoples reflected the prevalence of their racist attitudes and thus makes manifest some similarities between the problems of blacks and Indians. Even so, the presence of the black within the bounds of American society, his importance to the economy, his impact on the American culture, and, above all perhaps, his participation in the war for his own liberation, placed him in an entirely different category from the Indian and led, perforce, to a totally different approach in dealing with him. He shared with the American of European stock, despite racial differences, the experience of being an immigrant to the New World. Thus the symbolic and mythological reaction to him was different from that to the Indian. Given the extent of racial prejudice, what is surprising is not so much the tragic inadequacy of Indian policy—if it can be called a policy—but the effort that was made in Congress to provide the black with a legal and constitutional basis for equality.

Although the Indian question did have some relevancy to reconstruction and to the proposed amendment by challenging the moral stance of its advocates, it was nonetheless ancillary and had very little to do with the congressional decision. It is necessary, therefore, to return to the essentials of the debate. During its final hours Reverdy Johnson argued that only those who were actually in office and thus under oath at the time of their rebellion should be proscribed in Section 3, but his motion to change the amendment was voted down. Doolittle and Sherman again spoke of the unfairness of Section 2 to the western states and urged that representation be based on the number of voters. Garrett Davis of Kentucky spoke for four hours to vacant seats against the amendment, stressing its compromise and partisan nature and the pernicious hand of New England in defeating voter representation. He tried without success to amend Section 4 so as to make the government responsible for "obligations to pay for private property taken for public use" and for bounties promised to slaveholders for military service by their slaves.[46]

Hendricks of Indiana was the leading spokesman of the Democratic opposition, as he had been in the debate on Trumbull's Freedmen's Bureau Bill. His speech of June 4 probed the Republican position at its most vulnerable points and played upon racial prejudices and regional jealousies. Deemphasizing civil rights, Hendricks called on the West and South to protect their agrarian interests against the power of eastern manufacturers. The speech was a combination of anachronism and prescience, appealing to the agrarian tradition of the past as well as to the disturbances of the future that would lead one day to the candidacy of William Jennings Bryan.

He struck first at the secrecy with which Republicans had conducted themselves in bringing forth the amendment: At the beginning of the session, before receiving the president's message, a Republican caucus had decided on the establishment of the Committee of Fifteen which, because of its origin, the nature of its work, and "the secret character of its proceedings," had come to be known as the " 'revolutionary tribunal,' the 'directory,' and the 'star chamber.' " Its first report having been defeated, it had now come forward with a second. And to forestall a second defeat, whose "effect upon the fall elections would be disastrous," another caucus had been called and "We [have] witnessed the astounding spectacle of the withdrawal, for the time, of a great legislative measure, touching the Constitution itself, from the Senate, that it might be decided in the secret councils of a party. For three days the Senate Chamber was silent, but the discussions were transferred to another room of the Capitol, with closed doors and darkened windows, where party leaders might safely contend for a political and party policy." The proposed amendment had been "decided upon in a conclave more secret than has ever been known in this country." "It is hard work," Hendricks said, "to speak when one knows in advance that no argument, however just and forcible, and no appeal, however patriotic, can influence a single vote; that the authority and law of a political party is over every Senator of the majority; and that it remains now only to register the decree of the secret caucus."

Addressing himself to Section 1, Hendricks said that there were unanswered questions on the subject of citizenship, "its rights and duties, its obligations and liabilities," that had taxed the "learning of the departments of the Government." "We have been justly proud of the rank and title of our citizenship," he said, "for we understood it to belong to the inhabitants of the United States who were descended from the great races of people who inhabit the countries of Europe, and such emigrants from those countries as have been admitted under our laws. The rank and title conferred honor at home and secured kindness, respect, and safety everywhere abroad; but if this amendment be adopted we will then carry the title and enjoy its advantages in common with the negroes, the coolies, and the Indians." American citizenship would be no more esteemed than that of Mexico, which defined a "mixed population, made up of races that ought not to mingle—whites, negroes, and Indians—of whom twenty thousand could not cope with four thousand soldiers of the United States of pure white blood on the field of Buena Vista."

Hendricks carried the racial theme on into his discussion of Section 2, whose purpose, he said, was "to constrain every State to confer the right of voting upon the negroes." He did not believe it was good for either race "to be brought into close social and political relations. God has marked the peculiarities of each. He has put them asunder, and it is not the right, much less the duty, of man to join them together." If Republicans believed in Negro suffrage and intended to have it, why did they not in plain words confer it rather than to "seek it by indirection." He spoke of the restrictive policy of Indiana with respect to Negroes, of which he had been an early advocate. Since the beginning of the war, he said, the number of Negroes in the state had greatly increased owing to the lax enforcement of its constitution and laws. But the policy had been to discourage their immigration, "dictated by the desire to protect . . . white labor. The pressure of negroes in large numbers tends to degrade and cheapen labor, and the people have been unwilling that the white laborer shall be compelled to compete for employment with the negro." Negro suffrage, said Hendricks, would encourage Negro migration into the state and would "defeat what experience has shown to be a wise policy."

Should Indiana and other states of the South and West be denied representation while New York or New England, where the Negro population was negligible but where many whites were not allowed to vote, remained fully represented? he asked. To test the good faith of the Republicans on the representation provision, Hendricks proposed an amendment applying the three-fifths clause to the former slave population. If their real objection was the increase of southern representation they would accept such an amendment, but they would not accept it if their purpose was "to reduce the representation of the agricultural sections and then relatively increase the power of the manufacturing interests, and perpetuate a policy that enriches the capital of one section and bears heavily upon the capital and labor of another." Through tariffs, taxes, and the distribution of banking capital, he said, the interests of the eastern states had been built up at the expense of the West. While he rejoiced in the prosperity of any section resulting from "legitimate trade, under equal laws," he called upon "western Senators to hesitate before they surrender a representation that is a reliable support to our great interest, agriculture."

Hendricks branded Section 3 a "harsh and sweeping measure" denying political rights to "many excellent men whose services now in the work of reconciliation would be of the greatest value . . . —men who [had] displayed heroic courage in standing out against the secession movement, but who afterward yielded obedience to and served the established government, *de facto*." "As a penalty for a crime," he said, "this measure is *ex post facto;* and if it were a measure of ordinary legislation would therefore be unconstitutional." Turning to Section 4, to keep the public debt inviolate, he inquired, "Who has asked us to change the Constitution for the benefit of the bond holders? Are they so much more meritorious than all other classes that they must be specially provided for in the Constitution? . . . Are the bond holders not receiving their interest, even in advance, and in gold?" Hendricks concluded with a tribute to the president for his restraint in the use of his great power, in contrast to congressional Republicans who were "straining every brace and timber in the Constitution to secure . . . absolute control." For the Indiana senator, then, the great issue of the forthcoming election was the choice between presidential restoration or congressional reconstruction. He was confident that, despite shouts of "copperhead and sympathizer," the people would choose "reconciliation and Union."[47]

Four days later the Senate passed the amendment by a vote of thirty-three to eleven. Every senator who had attended the caucus voted for it, indicating the political nature of the whole amendment question. The narrowness of the victory and the necessity of resorting to extraordinary measures to achieve it was further evidence of how vital it was for Republicans not to permit the rebel states to return to the Union under Johnson's restoration plan.

On June 13, Stevens presented the Senate's amendment in the House. He was very feeble, and his voice was so low that members had to gather closely around him in order to hear him. He was pleased that the passage of the amendment was imminent, but, he said, "I do not . . . intend so much to express joy at the superior excellence of the scheme, as that there is to be a scheme . . . containing much positive good, as well as, I am bound to admit, the omission of many better things." The next passage shows two sides of Stevens's character that defined his role as leader and that combined to make him one of the remarkable men of his era—the visionary and revolutionary and the political practitioer, the party man par excellence.

> In my youth, in my manhood, in my old age, I had fondly dreamed that when any fortunate chance should have broken up for awhile the foundation of our institutions, and released us from obligations the most tyrannical that ever man imposed in the name of freedom, that the intelligent, pure and just men of this Republic, true to their professions and their consciences, would have so remodeled all our institutions as to have freed them from every vestige of human oppression, of inequality of rights, of the recognized degradation of the poor, and the superior caste of the rich. In short, that no distinction would be tolerated in this purified Republic but what arose from merit and conduct. This bright dream has vanished "like the baseless fabric of a vision." I find that we shall be obliged to be content with patching up the worst portions of the ancient edifice, and leaving it, in many of its parts, to be swept through by the tempests, the frosts, and the storms of despotism.
>
> Do you inquire why, holding these views and possessing some will of my own, I accept so imperfect a proposition? I answer, because I live among men and not among angels; among men as intelligent, as determined, and as independent as myself, who, not agreeing with me, do not choose to yield their opinions to mine. Mutual concession, therefore, is our only resort, or mutual hostilities.

If Congress had had the cooperation of the executive, he continued, "we might have been justified in making renewed and more strenuous efforts for a better plan." "With his cordial assistance the rebel States might have been made model republics, and the nation an empire of universal freedom. But he preferred 'restoration' to 'reconstruction.'" Finally, Stevens appealed to the House to act without delay. "The danger is that before any constitutional guards shall have been adopted Congress will be flooded by rebels and rebel sympathizers." The House of Representatives then adopted the amendment by a vote of 120 to 32.[48]

After six months of deliberation and debate Congress had come up with an amendment to be submitted to the states. But what did this mean with respect to the restoration of the rebel states or the recon- struction of the nation? The immediate answer lay in the enabling legislation that had accompanied the amendment from the committee to Congress. We have seen, in the sharp disagreement between Stevens and Bingham, how uncertain was the fate of the restoration bill. Debate on it continued through the first three weeks of June. A minority from such doubtful Republican states as New York, Connecticut, Indiana, and Ohio supported Bingham in his effort to have the bill adopted. A caucus of the Ohio delegation voted seven to two for the readmission of ex-Confederate states upon ratification of the amendment. But there was firm radical resistance. William D. Kelley of Pennsylvania introduced a reconstruction bill similar to Stevens's. George W. Julian of Indiana reminded the House that it had already passed a bill for Negro suffrage in the District of Columbia and urged that it do the same for the rebel states as a basis for readmission. Then on June 20 the enabling act was tabled, bringing to an end the persistent efforts of its advocates.

Even if the bill had passed in the House it was doomed in the Senate, where on May 29 Sumner moved an amendment to it that would have compelled rebel states to ratify the amendment and institute Negro suffrage to qualify for readmission. It appears that the Senate caucus had assured Sumner that in return for his vote for the amendment the enabling act would be tabled. It was, and that was the end of it.[49]

Although there was little jubilation in the North following the enactment of the amendment, there was a sense of satisfaction that Congress had acted, and Republicans generally agreed that now the party had a platform to stand on for the approaching election. Even some of the Johnson people felt that Congress had moved toward the president. "Few question the abstract justice and wisdom," said Raymond's *New York Times*, "of changing the basis of representation. . . . The exclusion from office of men who added perjury to treason is certainly not severe, . . . and no one can object to declaring the national debt inviolate." The *Chicago Tribune* predicted correctly that the action of Congress had postponed, and not settled, the question of equal political rights for blacks. *Harper's Weekly*, which had clung tenaciously to the hope, if not the conviction, that a break between the president and Congress could be avoided, said, "The ship of state must be trimmed to the breeze of today, not of yesterday nor of tomorrow. Policy is the art of expediency. . . . Mr. Bright, in England, believes in 'manhood suffrage,' but he supports with all his power the new Reform bill which only enfranchises some 40,000 more of the population. Can Bright be fairly accused of betraying the rest of the people?" The president, said *Harper's*, "has often plainly declared his sympathy with the enfranchisement of colored citizens by the States. Unless he misstates his own opinions there is really no substantial difference upon this point" between him and Congress.[50]

The middle ground position occupied by *Harper's* was anathema to the extreme radicals. Even before the Senate voted on the amendment the *National Anti-Slavery Standard* had concluded that Congress had surrendered. Negro suffrage, it editorialized, is the "only vital point in the matter of reconstruction. . . . All other questions are unimportant or will easily settle themselves. A few Senators may resist the Reconstruction plan, but Congress, as a body, has surrendered," in order to save the Republican party. "Our 'political statesmanship' consists of hypocrisy, fear, and compromise. Its pathway, like that of a caravan, is marked by the skeletons of mountebank pretenders who died of chagrin."[51] A few days later Phillips, addressing the Anti-Slavery Society, called for the defeat of the Republican party in the election: "Let that party be broken that sacrifices principle to preserve its own existence."

Frederick Douglass thought the amendment insulting to blacks: "For to tell me that I am an equal American citizen, and, in the same breath, tell me that my right to vote may be constitutionally taken from me by some other citizen or citizens, is to tell me that my citizenship is but an empty name. . . . To say that I am a citizen to pay taxes, . . . obey the laws, support the government, and fight the battles of the country, but, in all that respects voting and representation, I am but so much inert matter, is to insult my manhood."[52]

Congress had faltered, said the *National Anti-Slavery Standard* a few days later, because of a want of confidence in the people, who were "perfectly ready for extreme measures." "They have looked to Congress for leadership in this struggle, and they would gladly have followed Stevens and Sumner and Kelly up to the platform of universal justice. But when Congress faltered, the people doubted, and for the twentieth time in its short history the want of courage and political sagacity in the leader[s] of the Republican party had made shipwreck of its opportunities."[53]

The opposition from the right was almost as vehement as that from the left, and those who hoped the amendment would bring a compromise settlement between the executive and Congress were again destined to disappointment. For the president was as adamant in his opposition to the final amendment as he had been to the proposal of the joint committee of April 30. In a message to Congress on June 22, he explicitly stated his objections.

> Even in ordinary times any question of amending the Constitution must be justly regarded as of paramount importance. The importance is at the present time enhanced by the fact that the joint resolution was not submitted by the two Houses for the approval of the President, and that of the thirty-six States which

constitute the Union eleven are excluded from representation in either House of Congress, although, with the single exception of Texas, they have been entirely restored to all their functions as States, in conformity with the organic law of the land, and have appeared at the national capital by Senators and Representatives, who have applied for and have been refused admission to the vacant seats.

Nor have the sovereign people of the nation been afforded an opportunity of expressing their views upon the important questions which the amendment involves. Grave doubts therefore may naturally and justly arise as to whether the action of Congress is in harmony with the sentiments of the people, and whether State legislatures, elected without reference to such an issue, should be called upon by Congress to decide respecting the ratification of the proposed amendment.

Johnson also informed Congress that Seward, acting in his official capacity as secretary of state, had on June 16 submitted the amendment to the states. To assure that this action would create no erroneous impressions about the administration's position, Johnson said that the actions of the secretary of state were to be "considered as purely ministerial and in no sense whatever committing the Executive to an approval or recommendation of the amendment." "On the contrary," he said,

a proper appreciation of the letter and spirit of the Constitution, as well as the interests of national order, harmony, and union, and a due deference for an enlightened public judgment, may at this time well suggest a doubt whether any amendment to the Constitution ought to be proposed by Congress and pressed upon the legislatures of the several States for final decision until after the admission of such loyal Senators and Representatives of the now unrepresented States as have been, or may hereafter be, chosen in conformity with the Constitution and laws of the United States.[54]

The views of Andrew Johnson about restoration and the Constitution are familiar enough by now that it would be difficult to doubt his sincerity. Despite his errors in judgment and his propensity to reject opportunities for compromise, he did have the quality of consistency. Yet, by late June there was a more tangible explanation of his behavior. At the time of his address there was a movement under way for the formation of a new party to bring together Union-Republicans and Democrats who favored his policies. Johnson was privy to the existence of this movement and had given it his approval. He was ready to take a stand formally against the Republican party. Three days after the president's message to Congress a call was sent out for a "National Union" convention to meet in Philadelphia in August. If the Fourteenth Amendment was, indeed, the platform that Republicans would take to the people Andrew Johnson no longer had any choice but to oppose it.

On July 19 Tennessee ratified the Fourteenth Amendment and thus opened the way for readmission to the Union. Bingham took charge of the readmission resolution in the House and with Democratic support overcame the efforts of Stevens, Boutwell, and other radicals to make Negro suffrage a condition for admission and guided it through to approval. In the Senate the resolution was referred to the Judiciary Committee, which wrote a preamble reasserting the power of Congress over reconstruction. Sumner again tried to insert Negro suffrage as a condition for restoration, but he received almost no support. Fessenden was willing to admit Tennessee before the amendment had become a part of the Constitution but made it clear that hers was a special case and was not to become a precedent for the admission of other states. On July 23, the House having concurred in the Senate changes, the resolution was sent to the president. He signed it, but protested against the conditions for readmission stated in the preamble.

> Among other reasons recited in the preamble for the declarations contained in the resolution, is the ratification, by the state government of Tennessee, of "the amendment to the Constitution of the United States abolishing slavery, and also the amendment (the 14th) proposed by the 39th Congress." If, as is also declared in the preamble, "said state government can only be restored to its former political relations in the Union by the consent of the law-making power of the United States," it would really seem to follow that the joint resolution which at this late day has received the sanction of Congress, should have been passed, approved and placed on the statute books before any amendment to the Constitution was submitted to the legislature of Tennessee for ratification. Otherwise the inference is plainly deducible that while, in the opinion of Congress, the people of a state may be too strongly disloyal to be entitled to representation, they may nevertheless, during the suspension of their "former, proper, practical relations to the Union," have an equally potent voice with other and loyal states in propositions to amend the Constitution, upon which so essentially depend the stability, prosperity, and very existence of the nation.[55]

Meanwhile, in mid-July, a second Freedmen's Bureau Bill was passed. Again, Johnson sent down a veto, but this time it was overridden with votes to spare.[56] On July 28, Congress adjourned sine die.

From October 1866 to February 1867, the ten remaining ex-Confederate states overwhelmingly rejected the Fourteenth Amendment. In Florida, Mississippi, and Louisiana there was not a single vote for the amendment; in Virginia there was one vote for it in the lower house. In Arkansas, whose readmission some members of Congress had expected along with Tennessee, there was a total of three votes for it. North Carolina registered the largest vote for ratification with ten yeas to ninety-five nays in the lower house.[57]

It has been suggested that Andrew Johnson might have changed this, that the South would have followed him if he had advocated ratification of the amendment as a condition of restoration. But were these states simply following the president's advice in rejecting it? Could he have been so persuasive as to turn these huge majorities against the amendment into even narrow majorities for it? It might be more accurate to conclude that Johnson was following the southern states' lead rather than that they were following his. Under the conditions existing in 1866 the Fourteenth Amendment would not be added to the Constitution. Its ratification would come only after Congress had wrested control of the government from the president and instituted its own reconstruction program.

Chapter 7

The Meaning of the Amendment—
For Contemporaries and Historians

THE HISTORY of the Fourteenth Amendment during the century since its adoption has given it an importance far exceeding what its framers could have imagined. And despite the emphasis in congressional debates on Sections 2 and 3, Section 1 has been the basis for important changes in constitutional interpretation. The definition of citizenship laid to rest the constitutional dictum of Roger B. Taney that blacks were not a part of the civil and political population. The greatest impact came, however, from the "privileges and immunities," the "due process," and the "equal protection" clauses. For a decade Congress enacted legislation, under the power granted it in Section 5, protecting the political and civil rights of blacks, but three years before the end of reconstruction the judiciary, in the *Slaughterhouse Case* of 1873, began the process of erosion of civil rights under the amendment that culminated in the *Civil Rights Cases* in 1883 and *Plessy* v. *Ferguson* in 1896. Not until the mid-twentieth century has the amendment fulfilled the hopes of its authors, notably in the *Brown* v. *Board of Education* decision in 1954. The last civil rights act of the Reconstruction era was adopted in 1875; not until 1957 was another one enacted.

A major cause of the failure of the amendment in respect to civil rights was the centralization of business and industrial enterprise under ever larger and more sophisticated corporations, whose legal counselors persuaded the courts to accept a substantive interpretation of "due process" in place of the procedural concept which the framers of the amendment intended. The most notable application of substantive "due process" came in the decisions where courts protected railroads from state regulatory laws and commissions. Thus, while virtually nullifying the amendment as an instrument for civil rights the judiciary protected the property interests of corporations. The relevance of this post-Reconstruction history to the framing of the amendment lies in the interpretation of the amendment by Charles A. Beard and other progressive historians who came on the scene around the turn of the century.[1]

Beard, applying to Reconstruction the economic interpretation he had already developed in earlier works on the Constitution and Jeffersonian democracy, placed great emphasis on the rise of corporate power and substantive "due process" in his account of post–Civil War America. But he did not let the matter rest there; rather, he went on to say that the framers of the amendment had planned it that way; he thus arrived at a "conspiracy theory" of the Fourteenth Amendment. "There is plenty of evidence," Beard wrote in his *Contemporary American History* (1914), "to show that those who framed the Fourteenth Amendment and pushed it through Congress had in mind a far wider purpose—that of producing a general restraining clause for state legislatures." It had been the intention of the Constitutional Convention in 1787, Beard continued, "to check the assaults of state legislatures on vested rights." The Supreme Court under John Marshall had then taken up the cause, using the contract clause of the Constitution, until the succession of states' rights justices to the court had ended the effectiveness of this approach. But, said Beard, the framers of the Fourteenth Amendment had brought forth a new "restriction laid upon state legislatures which might be substantially limitless in its application, in the hands of a judiciary wishing to place the broadest possible interpretation upon it." The evidence Beard needed to prove his assertion that the framers intended the word *person* to be interpreted as an artificial as well as a natural person he found in the argument of Roscoe Conkling before the Supreme Court in December 1882, in the case of *San Mateo County* v. *Southern Pacific Railroad Company*. Conkling, wrote Beard, "unfolded for the first time the deep purpose of the committee, and showed from the journal of that committee that it was not their intention to confine the amendment merely to the protection of the colored race." Conkling's statement that "at the time the Fourteenth Amendment was ratified, . . . individuals and joint-stock companies were appealing for congressional and administrative protection against invidious and discriminating state and local taxes," seemed to substantiate his argument as to the committee's intentions.[2]

In 1882 Conkling had the advantage of being in possession of a copy of the committee journal, which had not yet been published. Nor was it published at the time Beard wrote his *Contemporary American History*. But in 1914, the year of the publication of that book, Benjamin B. Kendrick published *The Journal of the Joint Committee of Fifteen*, making it possible to examine more critically Conkling's argument, which was after all the brief of a defense attorney, not the account of an historian. Even so, when Charles and Mary Beard came out with their majestic *Rise of American Civillization* in 1927 the interpretation had not been changed. Rather, they enlarged upon it and embellished it making John A. Bingham, the author of section 1 and the great spokesman for civil rights, the villain. There were two factions in the committee, said the Beards,

> one bent on establishing the rights of Negroes; the other determined to take in the whole range of national economy. Among the latter was a shrewd member of the House of Representatives, John A. Bingham, a prominent Republican and a successful railroad lawyer from Ohio familiar with the possibilities of jurisprudence; it was he who wrote the mysterious sentence containing the "due process" clause in the form in which it now stands; it was he who finally forced it upon the committee by

ROSCOE CONKLING
Reproduced from the collection of the Library of Congress

persistent efforts. . . . Republican lawmakers restored to the
Constitution the protection for property which Jacksonian judges
had whittled away and made it more sweeping in its scope by
forbidding states, in blanket terms, to deprive any person of life,
liberty, or property without due process of law. By a few words
skillfully chosen every act of every state and local government
which touched adversely the rights of persons and property was
made subject to review and liable to annulment by the Supreme
Court at Washington, appointed by the President and Senate for
life and far removed from local feelings and prejudices.

By 1940 the "conspiracy theory" was under serious attack. Indeed,
Howard Jay Graham, showing that Conkling had been guilty of
bowdlerization and misrepresentation, had all but demolished it. The
Beards, however, ignored the Graham article; in the editions of *The
Rise of American Civilization* after its publication the "conspiracy
theory" remained intact; even the language remained identical with
that of the earlier editions.[3]

It is not the intention of the writer to become deeply involved in the
dispute over the work of Charles A. Beard that has engaged the historical profession during the past quarter-century. The very volume, and
occasionally the acrimony, of the dispute attests to Beard's eminence.
For some thirty years he was the Solon of the community of American
historians. It is his preeminence, and the impact of his work, that
compels us to examine what he has said. His interpretation is important
also because it is a part of the legend of Reconstruction, an era whose
history seems to inspire *l'idée fixe*, embracing simple resolutions to
complex or unanswerable questions, resolutions that do not disturb
existing attitudes or beliefs.[4] Anybody who has taught the history of the
post–Civil War era will know how indelible are certain conventional
notions in the minds of many students about Reconstruction and how
difficult it is to persuade them even to admit to the possibility of
different interpretations and conclusions. This frame of mind may also
be a legacy of America's only civil war.

It may be going too far to say, as two historians do, that Beard was "so
skeptical . . . about the force of the idealistic and humane goals of the
war, . . . and so critical of the capitalist interests that battened on the
war and its legislative results" that he was "unwittingly lending himself
to a pro-Confederate interpretation."[5] The flaw lies not so much in his
being pro-Southern or pro-Northern as in his envisioning the war as
simply another chapter in the ageless conflict between the embattled
farmer and the capitalist. It is the problem of the "activist historian

who," Richard Hofstadter suggests, "thinks he is deriving his policy from his history [but] may in fact be deriving his history from his policy, and may be driven to commit the cardinal sin of the historical writer: he may lose his respect for the integrity, the independence, the pastness, of the past."[6]

Howard K. Beale, in *The Critical Year* (1930), also rested his interpretation of the framing of the amendment on the "conspiracy theory." He also uncritically used Conkling's brief of 1882 to prove the insidious intentions of the radicals. Beale's emphasis is on the centralization of government and the "minimization of state functions" under radical control. Having provided for the "central authority in fields where the state's prerogative had never been questioned . . . [such as] ownership of land, procedure in state courts, qualifications for suffrage, poor laws, state elections, education, and all manner of police regulations," Beale wrote, the radicals now moved to protect the "special privilege and enormous profits" of the industrialists, "in disregard of the interests and welfare of a public that could not always be ignored while it controlled state legislatures."[7]

Both Beard and Beale are made believable by the reasonable accuracy of their account of social and economic changes taking place during the Gilded Age. There were indeed centralizing tendencies; the power of industry was growing apace; the Fourteenth Amendment was used to curb the states in their efforts to control railroads. But their search for a villain—and who could play that role better than the benighted radicals—led them astray in three important respects: first, they ignored the fact that the Fourteenth Amendment was a party measure supported ultimately by members of all factions, by men as far apart as Henry J. Raymond and Charles Sumner; second, they left the term *radical* undefined, failing to distinguish between moderates such as Trumbull and Fessenden and extremists such as Stevens and Sumner; and, third, they attributed to the radicals, however the term may have been defined, more unanimity than actually existed on economic issues.[8] It should be noted that Beale, ten years after the publication of *The Critical Year*, had changed his mind about the radicals. Although he still placed much of the history of the era in the context of the agrarian movement and found connections between Reconstruction and Populism, he could say of the radicals: "They have usually been lumped together in praise or condemnation. Actually they represented strikingly different points of view, tied together only by certain common interests and a common desire to retain power for their party. . . . The Negro wanted forty acres and a mule, but his Republican backers had no serious thought of turning political into social and economic revolution."[9]

If the historians have focused on Section 1 of the amendment, with its civil rights provisions and its implications of conspiracy, contemporaries gave more attention to Section 2, probably because of its relevance to Negro suffrage. Section 2 was a watered-down version of the amendment on representation proposed by the joint committee in January. It was a sop to the Negro suffrage men, some of whom might have believed that it would be an inducement to the states to act, but most of the abolitionist-radical faction made it a focal point of their attack on the amendment. Carl Schurz, writing early in 1867, said that "only the second section of the amendment . . . touches the great question of the source of political power in our system of government." But, he added, "It touches it only to leave it unsolved. And just there is the pivot upon which the whole problem . . . turns."[10] George W. Julian, who had not participated in the debate on the amendment, branded Section 2 "a proposition to the Rebels that if they would agree that the negroes should not be counted in the basis of representation, we would hand them over unconditionally, to the tender mercies of their old masters. It sanctioned the barbarism of the Rebel State Governments in denying the right of representation to their freedmen, simply because of their race and color, and thus struck at the very principle of Democracy [sic] . . . , [and] was a wanton betrayal of justice and humanity."[11]

The radical-abolitionists of the Phillips, Julian, Sumner, and Schurz school were not only appalled by the immorality of Congress's failure; they were also convinced that Congress had thwarted the will of the people. Even the *Nation* shared Phillips's view that the people were ahead of Congress and were ready for Negro suffrage.[12] Whether or not this was so in 1866 is a matter of conjecture. Perhaps a bolder congressional policy would have elicited in the North a larger support than cautious men believed existed there. Perhaps a firmer stand against the president, once it became evident that he would not lead a campaign for black civil and political rights, might have swelled the ranks of the Negro suffrage forces. We have seen Stevens's ebullient estimate of what might have been if the president had been more cooperative. Executive opposition was, indeed, no mean obstacle. The Republican majority in Congress, wrote Carl Schurz, "had they not found in their way a President who, with the maturest incapacity to understand the great tendencies of the times, unites an almost idiotic ambition to control them by autocratic action, and with the temper of a despot [and] the profligate unscrupulousness of a demagogue, . . . would probably have acted upon their true instincts with boldness and consistency."[13]

But despite these possibilities there is not much evidence to show that the northern people were as yet prepared to accept Negro suffrage, or even full civil rights for blacks, especially if doing so would have involved any substantial change in their own race relations, in their own customs and laws relating to the black population. Before the end of 1865 the voters of Connecticut, Wisconsin, Minnesota, the District of Columbia, and Colorado had rejected Negro suffrage by substantial majorities. They were followed by Nebraska territory in 1866, and the trend continued so that by the end of 1868, according to William Gillette, "no northern state with a relatively large Negro population had voluntarily accepted Negro suffrage."[14] In January 1866, the House passed a bill for Negro suffrage in the District of Columbia, but the Senate did not act on it until after the elections in November, when Congress was firmly in Republican hands.

The prevailing attitude among Northerners, especially in the Midwest, was that both blacks and whites would be better off if the two races remained separated. This had been the basis of Lincoln's continuing effort to colonize blacks somewhere outside of the United States which, even if it failed, would have been an adroit political ploy.[15] It appeared to be not only a means of keeping whites and blacks separated but of preventing the dreaded influx of free blacks into the northern states. The decline of colonization as an alternative for managing racial problems came, in part at least, from the dedication of reformers for equal rights, especially after blacks were brought into the armed forces and contributed to the northern victory. But it should also be noted that this change in attitude came toward the end of the war and only after the Lincoln administration had adopted a policy of keeping blacks in the South. The views of the vast majority of northern whites about blacks remained substantially unchanged. "Northerners approached Reconstruction with their racial prejudices largely intact," says George M. Fredrickson. "The Negro was appreciated as an amiable being with some good qualities, whose innate submissiveness had served—and might continue to serve—Northern purposes. But he was expected to remain in his 'place,' defined in a double sense as being, first of all, in the South, and secondly on his own side of the line allegedly established by God and science to ensure that the white race would not be contaminated by an infusion of Negro blood."[16]

It would be too much to expect, therefore, that many members of Congress would have made a last-ditch fight to have Negro suffrage included in the Fourteenth Amendment, whose political implications everybody recognized. Those reformers who did insist on it, castigated the Republican party for its failure, and even threatened to leave the party were for the most part men who did not hold office and thus had no constituents to worry about.[17]

If Section 2 was designed to put pressure on the states to establish Negro suffrage, the wording of the section showed that no such inducement was intended with respect to woman suffrage. Representation would be reduced, said the amendment, "when the right to vote . . . [was] denied to any of the *male* inhabitants . . . in the proportion which the number of such *male* citizens shall bear to the whole number of *male* citizens twenty-one years of age." Leaders of the women's rights movement, such as Susan B. Anthony and Elizabeth Cady Stanton, were shocked by the callousness and hypocrisy of Negro suffrage men toward women's rights. Even those few members of Congress who favored woman suffrage were reluctant to face the ridicule, or even calumny, that would result from advocating it publicly. Benjamin Wade of Ohio was almost alone in his public avowal of it.[18] Sumner felt that it was "not judicious for [women] at this moment to bring forward their claims so as to compromise . . . the great question of equal rights for an enfranchised race."[19] George W. Julian had been converted to the woman suffrage movement twenty years earlier by Harriett Martineau, but for him slavery was always the "previous question . . . , less abstract and far more immediately absorbing than that of suffrage for women." After Congress passed the Fifteenth Amendment, wrote Julian, "I was prepared to enlist actively in the next grand movement in behalf of the sacredness of equality of human rights."[20] But that was two years hence, after the victory of Congress over Andrew Johnson.

The position of the *National Anti-Slavery Standard,* and therefore of Wendell Phillips, was not substantially different from that of Sumner and Julian. In reply to a letter and a woman suffrage petition from Elizabeth Cady Stanton the *Standard* said that it would be hospitable to a good cause but would not pledge its immediate advocacy of woman suffrage. "We do not conceal our conviction," the editorial added, "that this is 'the negro's hour'—an hour which, as it is improved or wasted, may crown with complete victory thirty years toil in his behalf, or once more commit him to the . . . ferocity of the system from which he seems about to escape. . . . Causes have their crises; that of the negro has come; that of the women's rights movement has not come."[21]

The point of all this is that the reformers too, sometimes so insistent on adherence to abstract principles, could at other times defer certain reform objectives in order to achieve others that were more immediate and more pressing. To be sure, many men in Congress were simply opposed to Negro suffrage under the auspices of the federal govern-

ment. Others, such as Howard and Fessenden, agreed to postpone it to
a more opportune time.

Section 3, the exclusion from federal and state offices of Confederate
leaders in lieu of the suffrage restrictions recommended by the committee, was a concession on the part of Congress to make the amendment
more acceptable to the South. It was therefore an answer to those
critics who argued that the original section was intended to prevent the
ratification of the amendment in the southern states. As we have seen,
the alteration of Section 3 was made over the vigorous protest of
Thaddeus Stevens.

Undoubtedly Section 4 was debated less vigorously and at less length
than any other section. Many persons believed it to be unnecessary, a
belief that has been shared by historians. We can see, from the vantage
point of a century, that this was probably true. Even so, the provisions
of that section may have been treated in too cavalier a fashion. The
inclusion of Section 4 as it appeared in the joint committee's
recommendation—the invalidity of debts or obligations incurred in the
Rebellion and of any claim for emancipated slaves—suggests the compromise nature of the amendment. It was inconceivable that any Republican faction would disapprove of such a provision, one which was even
included in Johnson's restoration plan. It does not follow, however, that
there was no concern in the North in 1866 that efforts would be made to
assume southern debts and compensate owners for their slaves. We
have noted the expression of concern by James G. Blaine and others.
Moreover, the committee had heard from a number of witnesses, federal officials in the South during and after the war, that these would be
the primary objectives of the South if, through the resurgence of the
Democratic party, it should find itself once again in a position of power
and influence. A statement of John C. Underwood of New York, a
Lincoln-appointed judge in Virginia, is indicative of the tenor of these
affirmations. The Rebels, said Underwood,

> would attempt either to accomplish a repudiation of the National
> debt, or an acknowledgment of the Confederate debt, and
> compensation for their negroes. I think these would be their
> leading measures, their leading demands; and I think if either the
> rebel debt could be placed upon an equality with the National debt,
> or both could be alike repudiated, they would be satisfied. But the
> leading spirits would claim compensation for their negroes, and
> would expect to get it by such a combination.[22]

Nor can the provisions of Section 4 be fully understood without
considering the economic condition of the country and the financial

condition of the government at the end of the war, the doubling of the cost of living during the war years, and a federal debt of nearly $3 billion, not taking into account some $400 million of legal tender notes—or greenbacks—whose depreciation was sometimes seen as an enforced addition to the debt. This debt, the largest in the nation's history to that time, was galling to a people not accustomed to national debts, which they considered not only unsound financial policy but downright immoral.[23] How to manage the debt, whether to redeem bonds in gold or legal tender currency, and whether to contract the greenback currency and return to specie redemption or to allow a stipulated amount of greenback currency to circulate were matters of great moment as Congress undertook the restoration of the nation, matters on which legislation was debated and passed simultaneously with the efforts at reconstruction on which we have focused our attention. The northern press, too, devoted as much space to these economic and financial matters as to political reconstruction. The milieu in which Congress worked, then, provides part of the explanation of the presence of Section 4 in the amendment.

Neither the Republicans nor the radicals were of one mind with respect to these financial and monetary questions; nor were the business interests with whom, according to progressive historians, the radicals were supposed to be in league.[24] Even so, economic considerations cannot be eliminated from the causal relationships of Reconstruction history. To understand the effect of economic matters it is neccessary to do more than examine the complex and far from consistent relationship of Republicans to the business community; it is also necessary to observe the Democrats.

Even before the end of the war in 1865, and certainly by 1866, a group of midwestern Democrats, abandoning the specie currency tenets of their Jacksonian forebears, had urged upon fellow Democrats the advantages of challenging the Republican party with a platform of cheap greenback currency, to be used not only as a circulating currency but also to redeem bonds. What would emerge as the "Ohio Idea," which appeared in the Democratic platform of 1868, had been formulated and was being tested in state elections two years earlier. Some Republicans saw this as a program of repudiation. "This war will have as its object," wrote one of Jay Cooke's agents, "the issue of paper money directly by the Government, instead of by the agency of a thousand Banks. It will be supported by the plea of economy, and the plea of safety and the old cant about 'the rich richer and the poor poorer.' "[25]

To be sure, not all Democrats subscribed to this "repudiationist," cheap money doctrine, but if the Democracy had indeed found a new issue with which it could appeal to the electorate, the Republican ascendancy, resting on war issues, might be dangerously challenged. The Republican party was, after all, still a sectional, minority party whose origins lay in the struggle over slavery, a fact of which astute Republican leaders were aware. The prospect of a new issue for the Democrats more promising than states' rights, slavery, and Negrophobia helps to explain the caustic remarks of Senator Hendricks labeling Section 4 as the bondholders' section and appealing to the agrarian interests to resist it. It also suggests that when Ben Wade said that Section 4 would "give great confidence to capitalists," he was using the term in a generic rather than a narrow or limited sense. The radicals may have harbored an exaggerated fear of repudiation, but whether or not it was a "phobia," as the leading historian of the framing of the Fourteenth Amendment states,[26] remains open to question.

It is evident from this reprise of the framing of the Fourteenth Amendment that it was a compromise and thus unacceptable to the Sumner, Julian, Phillips school as well as to the Johnson coterie. It is also evident that the amendment had its political purposes. According to Carl Schurz the Republicans, "in order to save their ascendancy, and with it the power of doing better in the future, . . . made a compromise with traditional prejudices of the people, to which the President and his followers were artfully appealing. . . . The result was the Constitutional Amendment now submitted to the State Legislatures for ratification."[27] Even harsher in his judgment than the contemporary Schurz has been the twentieth-century historian Howard K. Beale. "Lawyers and Congressmen," wrote Beale,

> made lengthy speeches on matters of constitutionality, for this gave them an air of erudition, and satisfied the legalistic conscience of their constituents. Nevertheless constitutional discussions of the rights of the negro, the status of Southern states, the legal position of ex-rebels, and the powers of Congress and president determined nothing. They were pure shams.
>
> But for all of the heat and bombast of their enunciation, these constitutional arguments were mere justifications of practical ends. Except the men who made political capital out of them, few cared about constitutional niceties. What vitally concerned the whole country was the practicability and expediency of conflicting Southern programs.[28]

Does it follow, however, from the political purposes and implications of the amendment that the arguments of those who debated it in Congress or introduced it into the 1866 campaign were devoid of theoretical substance or merit and that they were engaging in a cheap charade? If the criteria for the substantive and theoretical worth of the speeches and writings of public figures are to be determined by the absence of political purposes or connections, how do we evaluate, for example, the *Federalist Papers,* Calhoun's *Exposition and Protest,* or Lincoln's trenchant discussion of the meaning of the compact theory in his first inaugural address? Eric McKitrick is illuminating on the subject, as it applies to 1866:

> It would not be wise to assume hypocrisy, claptrap, and sham as a formula for explaining any problem of this magnitude. There were, to be sure, political needs. But had there been no such needs, we would have no problem; it is this very fact that gives the constitutional dimension such great importance. It would be misconceiving the nature of the Constitution to suppose that it was brought into being in the first place for any other reason than the most pressing of political needs. And needs do change—such is the major stimulant under which the Constitution has grown, in its application and meaning. Moreover, constitutional discussion did form an indispensable part of the framework within which men thought in the nineteenth century. Although our political system had developed by then a whole lore of its own, and special ways of responding to problems, we still cannot ignore the legal idiom in which so much of this thinking found expression. Faced with new political requirements, men were still much concerned over the question of how the Constitution would square with them.[29]

The discussion may be carried a step further. The legislators who debated and adopted civil rights measures in 1866 went beyond the Constitution in making their case. Contrary to the notion that America has rejected theory in favor of an overweening pragmatism, these men repeatedly sought a theoretical basis for their arguments. In doing so they invoked not only the Constitution; they went beyond it to Locke, Blackstone, Mill, Grotius, Vattel, Burlamanqui, and so forth. Indeed, the debates on the amendment were carried on at a reasonably sophisticated theoretical level.

One further question relating to the Fourteenth Amendment remains to be briefly examined: Did the amendment and its ratification constitute a plan of reconstruction or restoration? It is a question to which every historian who has examined the Thirty-ninth Congress in any detail—from James Ford Rhodes to Eric McKitrick and W. R. Brock—has addressed himself. The debates on the amendment, and especially those on the enabling act, show the differences among Republicans on the subject. The more extreme radicals rejected the ratification of the amendment as the condition for readmission. But the majority of the party, in and out of Congress, would probably have readmitted other southern states as it had Tennessee upon ratification. To be sure, the failure of the enabling legislation left the country without a specific plan, but the admission of Tennessee left the implication that there was a plan. Kendrick, who examined the question in the greatest detail, found evidence in this of a Republican plot. Tennessee's ratification, said Kendrick,

> gave the politicians the exact opportunity they desired; for, by admitting Tennessee, they could leave the implication to be drawn, that should the other rebel states do what Tennessee had done, they too would be admitted. The radicals were well aware, however, in their own minds, that this was exactly what the other states would never do; for though they might conceivably ratify the Fourteenth Amendment, no one thought for a moment that they would ever evidence the same loyalty which Tennessee had shown.[30]

The matter of a plan of reconstruction was, indeed, left somewhat vague. But it would be hard to prove that anybody intended it that way. Rather, the vagueness resulted from the impasse between those desiring firm conditions for restoration, including Negro suffrage, and those desiring minimal conditions, as evidenced by the disagreement between Stevens and Bingham over the enabling legislation. The failure to resolve this dilemma left men free to adhere to their own beliefs and to state them as the intended and proper course to be taken. Thus it was that Thaddeus Stevens, speaking in Pennsylvania in early September, could say:

> While it was impossible, obstructed as we were, by the President and the Copperheads, to make this a Republic of "liberty and equality," we might have approached it more nearly than we did. We might have treated the rebel States as what they are, in fact, conquered provinces, and, through enabling acts, we could have fixed the qualifications for voters so that every loyal man could participate in the formation of their organic laws. We should thus, with entire certainty, have secured the government to loyal Union men, have formed, in every one of those States, constitutions giving equal privileges to all, and which would have curbed the rising spirit of rebellion which is now rampant in every one of those States,[31]

while two months later, when Congress reassembled, John Sherman stated it as his understanding that when the southern states had approved the amendment they would be readmitted. "If the southern people would now accept [it]," he added, "the people of the United States would hail their acceptance as the most joyful event since the surrender of Lee's army."[32]

James Ford Rhodes, a contemporary of Kendrick's, came to a different conclusion. Congress, said Rhodes, *had* devised a plan of reconstruction embracing the Fourteenth Amendment, the Freedmen's Bureau Bill, and the Civil Rights Bill. It was a plan that "combined reasonableness with justice [in] a system of constructive legislation which may justly command the admiration of congressional and parliamentary historians." It would have been to the advantage of the South, said Rhodes, to accept the congressional plan under which the apportionment of 1862, with the three-fifths provision intáct, probably would have remained in effect until 1872. "What Johnson and the Southerners claimed as their rightful share in the national legislature was offered them for six years, during which they could deliberate on the question of negro suffrage and at the end of which their sixty-one representatives and twenty-two senators . . . would have a part in establishing the machinery for the enforcement of [the second] section."[33]

The absence of a specific and comprehensive plan in late 1866 meant that the course of Reconstruction history would be determined by the exigencies of the time. The crucial decision, which more than anything else determined the subsequent course of reconstruction, was the southern states' rejection of the amendment. Such a move could only have strengthened the radicals and renewed their hopes for a harsher policy. Therefore, John W. Burgess contended, Andrew Johnson

> ought to have done all in his power to influence the reconstructed communities to adopt the proposed Amendment, no matter whether the submission of it to them by the Secretary of State of the United States logically involved their recognition as "States" of the Union by the Administration at Washington, or not. They were not in a position to exact the precise conclusion of a logical process in their favor, especially as it was based on a fallacious premise, and the President did both himself and them a great wrong in not discouraging them from so doing.[34]

Carl Schurz, estimating events from the radical point of view, saw them clearly. "The rejection of the . . . Amendment . . . by the Southern States," he wrote, "is one of the happiest incidents of this great crisis. Congress is again free to act. Since the formation of the Constitution, there never was so great an opportunity for American statesmanship. If it be thrown away, it may not occur again for generations."[35]

The question of whether Congress ought to have acted differently has engaged historians, and some of the best have concluded that it ought to have. "The tragic failure in statesmanship of the Fourteenth Amendment," writes C. Vann Woodward, "lay in the equivocal and pusillanimous way it was presented. In equivocal deference to states' rights, the South was requested to approve instead of being compelled to accept. In this I think the Moderates were wrong and Thaddeus Stevens was right."[36]

A more pertinent question might be: Could Congress have acted differently? Could it have followed the lead of Stevens and Sumner? Technically at least, that was one of the options open to it. But the northern milieu, the continued adherence to states' rights north and south, and especially the rejection of blacks as fellow citizens in any but the most legalistic sense, all but dictated that the radical road would not be the one taken. This estimate seems to be borne out by the subsequent history of Reconstruction and of a century of race relations.[37]

Chapter 8

The Memphis and New Orleans Riots

THE SOUTHERN STATES' rejection of the Fourteenth Amendment represented a continuation of the resistance in the South to federal control. It had begun with the refusal to comply with the requests of Lincoln and Johnson for a token Negro suffrage, had continued with the enactment of the "Black Codes," the pressure against the Freedmen's Bureau, and the animus against the continuing federal military presence—especially the use of black troops—in the South. Smoldering beneath the surface of southern life was a turbulence which on occasion broke out into violence. Two notable occasions in 1866 were the race riots in Memphis in early May and in New Orleans three months later, evidence enough for anti-Johnson people that presidential restoration was a failure and for the Johnson men that a radical policy would not bring a peaceful solution. These riots exacerbated the conflict between the president and Congress and bore significantly on the forthcoming election and on the establishment of a more stringent congressional policy of reconstruction in 1867.

By 1866 social and economic conditions in Memphis made the city ripe for a race riot. A burgeoning Mississippi River city whose population had increased during the past three years from 35,000 to 60,000, its crime rate rose in proportion to its population growth, far outdistancing the capacities of the police force. Despite the warning of Gen. William T. Sherman in 1862 of the need to enlarge the force and make it more efficient, almost nothing had been done. The force itself was hardly more law abiding than the criminal element of the city. "Perhaps nowhere, within the broad area of this country," said one of the city's leading newspapers, "is there another city, in proportion to its population, that supports and harbors a larger number of disreputable women, and their twin companions—gamblers and thieves—than this one of ours."[1] Much of the population growth was due to the influx of foreigners and freedmen, of whom there were more than 16,000 by 1866.

Although there was a great deal of business activity—more, said Whitelaw Reid, than in any other southern city except New Orleans—Memphis had severe economic problems: competition for jobs between blacks and Irish immigrants, a heavy tax burden, unpaid interest on city bonds, a city debt of $200,000, and a recession that began in the spring of 1866.

The presence of black troops in Memphis was galling to white residents. Among the units stationed at Fort Pickering, a base for black troops, was the Third United States Heavy Artillery, a poorly disciplined outfit whose unsavory reputation played into the hands of southern critics of black troops in general. The families and followers of the troops stationed at the fort established themselves in South Memphis, near the fort, where crime and disease became excessive. If the Irish generally resented the blacks, those in this quarter of the city exploited them. In an anonymous letter to Thaddeus Stevens, a citizen of Memphis described this relationship and its effects: "There are along South street, which bounds Memphis on the south, a number of low groceries and grog shops, kept by Irish citizens, who sell liquor to negroes, deal mainly with negroes, buy stolen goods of negroes, and habitually cheat and ill-treat the negroes whenever they have the chance. Between these grocery keepers and many of the blacks there is bitter hate, and when the blacks are in crowds or somewhat under the influence of liquor they often insult the Irish grocery men."[2]

Since the removal of white troops in the fall of 1865, leaving black troops to patrol the city, relations between the races had become even more strained. Sometimes black troops committed crimes against white citizens and insulted them in various ways. There was intimidation, stealing, and an occasional killing. Gen. George Stoneman, commanding the department of the Tennessee with headquarters in Memphis, investigated the actions of black troops and threatened to redress monetary losses of citizens through reduction of soldiers' pay. Some Memphians applauded his efforts, but more would be satisfied only with the removal of all black troops. In April four black regiments were mustered out of the service, but owing to an administrative error they were not paid. Still carrying their sidearms, they were at liberty to roam about South Memphis, where they frequented the grogshops and the houses of prostitution. It was this state of affairs that gave rise to the incidents of April 30 that preceded the outbreak of the riot the following day.

Added to these social and economic conditions was the Memphis press which, if it did not incite the riot, did nothing to hold it in check. Among the conservative, antiradical papers were the *Daily Avalanche* and the *Daily Appeal*, both of which slandered the Freedmen's Bureau, the black troops, and Governor "Parson" Brownlow's radical state government.[3] In opposing a law of May 1866, granting the franchise to blacks but denying it to those who had aided the Confederacy, the *Appeal* proclaimed that "it would be better for the whole black breed to be swept away by a pestilence."

> This may sound harsh but it is true. . . . If one had the power and could not otherwise prevent that curse and inconceivable calamity, in many of the southern states, it would be a solemn duty for him to annihilate the race. The right to vote might just as safely be given to so many South American monkeys as to the plantation negroes of Mississippi and Louisiana.[4]

The *Avalanche* was just as bitter in its denunciation of the bill: "Since [the Radicals] cannot in this part of the State, assassinate, kill and murder rebels, and take possession of their property, they propose to

GEORGE STONEMAN
Reproduced from the collection of the Library of Congress

give a greasy, filthy, stinking negro the right to crowd them from the polls, to exercise those rights of franchise which belong not to indians and negroes, but to white men."[5]

About a week before the riot began the police arrested a black man near the fort, knocked him down, beat him, and carried him away. Blacks witnessing the arrest warned the police that if they carried out an arrest in that manner again they would regret it. The riot broke out on Tuesday, May 1. A crowd of about one hundred blacks had congregated in South Street. According to the congressional committee that later investigated the riot, "their behavior was riotous and disorderly, and fully justified the interposition of the civil authorities." The police came and arrested two black men. As they took the men away some blacks fired their revolvers into the air. The police turned and fired into the crowd; a flurry of fire from both sides followed.[6]

Later that night the police returned to the scene, reinforced by a *posse comitatus* under T. M. Winters, sheriff of Shelby County. The total law enforcement contingent now numbered about two hundred. When they returned they found that the soldiers and former soldiers had returned to Fort Pickering, so that those who remained were women, children, and a few old men. Determined to have their revenge on the blacks, the police and the posse now became a mob that killed people, looted homes, and destroyed property. Among the leaders of the mob were John C. Creighton, judge of the recorder court of Memphis, and Attorney General William Wallace. According to a reliable witness, Wallace, in the role of "captain" of part of the mob, stood by and watched as the men under his command fired on defenseless blacks and burned their houses. Asked by Congressman George S. Shanklin if he believed Wallace had seen what was going on, the witness answered, "I do not think he could help seeing it. They stood for five or ten minutes drawn up in double file, as though for inspection."[7]

Although the number of troops in the city at the time of the riot was small, a detachment of the Sixteenth United States Infantry of 150 men, General Stoneman was strangely cautious in employing them. On the afternoon of the first day of the riot, Sheriff Winters requested that Stoneman send in troops to quell it. The general refused on the ground that "the people of Memphis had been extremely anxious to get rid of United States troops, stating that they were perfectly competent and capable of taking care of themselves." Preferring to test whether they were indeed competent to do so, he decided that federal troops would be used only when it was demonstrable that the riot had got beyond the control of the civil authorities. On the following day Thomas Leonard, a Shelby County judge and a radical, went to Stoneman to request arms for a posse he had assembled. The posse looked disreputable to the general, and he refused to turn over any arms to it. Finally, on the third day, after appeals for protection from northern preachers and teachers whose churches and schools had been burned down and whose lives had been threatened, Stoneman interposed federal authority by issuing an order "forbidding any person without his authority to assemble together any posse, armed or unarmed, white or colored."[8]

Undoubtedly this belated action had an effect on bringing an end to the riot. But Gen. Benjamin P. Runkle, head of the Freedmen's Bureau in Memphis may have been close to the truth in testifying, "I cannot say I think the military authorities stopped the riot." "I think they were rather tired out; it has been aptly expressed by a gentleman who said, 'They had filled their graveyards.' "[9] During the riot 46 blacks and 2 whites were killed and a total of 75 wounded; 91 houses, 4 churches, and 12 school houses were burned; and 100 robberies took place.[10]

After the riot General Stoneman requested of the mayor of Memphis information as to what steps had been taken by civil authorities to apprehend and bring its perpetrators to trial and to provide remuneration to individuals and to the United States government for losses sustained. In answer to the first part of the question Mayor John Park replied, somewhat evasively, that a commission appointed by Stoneman himself, together with the county officials, would assure "that the murderers and incendiaries will be arrested and punished." But because he was restricted by statute, Park claimed, he was unable to make assurances "which could only be made good by the exercise of an usurped power upheld by military force, with which my constituents, the people of Memphis, have had a long time experience even unto nausea." As to remuneration for losses, the mayor knew of "no statute or law authorizing any such appropriation of money," and thus he took it for granted that no action would be taken. William Hunter, judge of the criminal court of Memphis thought the chances of convicting white persons for outrages committed upon blacks would be very remote "with the material we have for jurors."[11] Two months after the riot the *New York Times* reported that no public meeting had been held by the citizens of Memphis "to express approbation or condemnation of the mob." By their silence, the *Times* concluded, they had approved the conduct of the mob.[12]

The northern reaction to the riot was immediate and frequently angry. The *Chicago Tribune*, calling it "The Memphis Massacre," said, "In downright brutality, and wanton, unprovoked diabolism, it makes the atrocities of the great New York anti-negro riot seem honorable and the massacre of Fort Pillow an innocent affair."[13] *Harper's Weekly* also compared the riot with the New York riots of 1863: both had involved "the foreign rabble," and both "sprang from the inhuman prejudice against the colored population which is carefully fostered and influenced by the Democratic party."[14]

The Democratic *New York Evening Post* scoffed at the committee sent by Congress to investigate the riot. What could Congress do except to "discuss the report?" it asked. The *New York Tribune* replied that the committee could, among other things, determine "whether there is a public sentiment in the South that will demand and enforce the protection of Blacks from similar outrages in the future" and whether "further legislation by Congress is necessary to protect Blacks from butchery and rapine."[15]

The New Orleans riot of July 30 was more directly related to reconstruction politics than the Memphis affair. There was more warning in New Orleans of an impending eruption, with men in Washington watching developments in Louisiana and men in New Orleans alert to signs of support from Johnson or the radicals. Deputations went forth, telegrams were exchanged, instructions and advice were requested by civilian and military officials, all of which had a bearing on the tragic events of a hot summer afternoon in New Orleans. Events and actions leading to the riot grew out of the decision of a portion of the constitutional convention of 1864 to reconvene and to modify the constitution. It is necessary, therefore, to review the work of that convention and reconstruction politics in Louisiana during the intervening two years.

The constitution of 1864 in Louisiana resulted from Lincoln's desire to have a government established soon in that commonwealth under the terms of his 10 percent plan. To this end, Lincoln enlarged the authority of Gen. Nathanial P. Banks, commanding general of the Department of the Gulf, and charged him with implementing the program. "Take the matter of State organization into your own hands," Lincoln instructed Banks. "I wish you to take the case as you find it, and give us a free-state reorganization in Louisiana, in the shortest possible time."[16] For a time Banks used the prewar constitution (of 1852) as the instrument of government, modifying it to meet existing circumstances. Soon, however, he acceded to radical demands for a new constitution and called for the election of a new constitutional convention. This convention met from April 6 to July 25, 1864.

To prevent the convention from falling into the hands of slaveholders, Banks ordered that the election of delegates be based upon the white population alone, and thus gave New Orleans a larger representation than the country parishes. He declared also that only whites should vote. These provisions alienated both conservatives and radicals and thus deprived the convention of some leaders from both factions. Untimely military defeats in Banks's ill-fated Red River campaign and Confederate reoccupation of territory deprived some parishes of their representation at the convention—representation that was expected to be there. On several occasions the convention was forced to adjourn for want of a quorum. At other times unsavory tactics were used to achieve a quorum, and the legality of the convention was questioned. Although there were few prominent men in the convention, many of its members were able men. Banks defended it as a convention "composed entirely of men of the people. There were few of the old leaders of opinion in public affairs. They represented, therefore, the heart of the people."[17]

Among the first questions taken up by the convention was that of emancipation. The movement for the "immediate and permanent abolition of slavery" had its opponents, foremost among them Judge Edmund Abell, who probably remained in the convention to protect the interests of slaveholders. He held out against any abolition until provision had been made for compensation of loyal owners and for removal of emancipated slaves from the state. He spoke of the vested rights of slaveholders under the United States Constitution and of the inability of blacks to live without masters.

Judge Edmund H. Durell replied, calling for unconditional emancipation to crush out the "odious rebellion" and leaving the matter of compensation to the "fair sense and justice of the Washington government." Eventually the convention did write into the constitution a clause for the emancipation of slaves, but it memorialized Congress to compensate loyal owners and appointed a committee to correspond with congressional leaders on the subject.[18]

Even before the convention met, General Banks had attempted to make provisions for Negro education, but without much success. After considerable debate on who should bear the tax burden for Negro schools and on the meaning of the word *Negro*, the convention wrote a clause into the constitution for free, segregated public schools. The success of those favoring Negro rights in emancipation and education did not carry through to Negro suffrage. The overwhelming opposition of the convention to anything more than token citizenship for blacks was shown in a resolution adopted by a vote of sixty-eight to fifteen that "the Legislature shall never pass any act authorizing negroes to vote or to immigrate into this State." Even those members who were willing to allow blacks to become citizens, to enter trades and acquire property, were determined that they should never vote.

By the time the convention met Abraham Lincoln had made an appeal, through Governor Michael Hahn, for Negro suffrage in

Louisiana. Following an interview in Washington with a delegation of
free blacks from New Orleans he had written to the Governor:

> My dear Sir: I congratulate you on having fixed your name
> in history as the first free-State governor of Louisiana. Now that
> you are about to have a convention, which among other things, will
> probably define the elective franchise, I hereby suggest for your
> private consideration whether some of the colored people may not
> be let in—as, for instance, the very intelligent, and especially in our
> ranks. They would probably help, in some trying time to come, to
> keep the jewels of liberty within the family of freedom. But this is
> only a suggestion, not to be public, but to you alone.[19]

With this appeal from the president and the continued urging of General
Banks the convention did finally compromise on the suffrage question to
the extent of authorizing the legislature to provide for Negro suffrage.
However, the omission of Negro suffrage, per se, from the constitution
would contribute directly to the riot of July 30.

One reason for the convention's rejection of Negro suffrage was the
presence of representatives of New Orleans working men. Many of
these had been Douglas Democrats in 1860 who had opposed secession
but who had very little sympathy with or concern for blacks. Some
months before the convention they had organized the Working Men's
Union League, whose platform called for the admission of all white men
to suffrage and the abolition of slavery, together with the removal of all
blacks from Louisiana by colonization. These labor delegates won some
important concessions for their white constituents, among them constitutional provisions for the franchise for all white men who had lived in
the state for one year, a revamping of the representation in the legislature more favorable to New Orleans, a nine hour day, and a minimum
wage provision for persons engaged in public works.[20]

Although the new constitution was not all that the president had
hoped for, he was nonetheless eager to have it adopted. In a letter to
Banks of August 9 he wrote: "I have just seen the new Constitution
adopted by the Convention of Louisiana, and I am anxious that it shall
be ratified by the people. I will thank you to let the civil officers in
Louisiana, holding under me, know that this is my wish, and to let me
know at once who of them openly declares for the Constitution, and who
of them, if any, declines to so declare."[21] Mustering all the power and
prestige at their command and with help from the Union League, Banks
and Hahn brought in a large vote for the constitution.[22] If this vote can
be called a victory for Lincoln and his plan of reconstruction, it was a
Pyrrhic one, for without Negro suffrage the constitution was unaccept-

able to congressional radicals. As late as four days before his death in April 1865, Lincoln was still pleading for the restoration of Louisiana under his plan and with the 1864 constitution. "Consider that the new government of Louisiana," said the president in his last speech, "is only to what it should be as the egg is to the fowl, we shall sooner have the fowl by hatching the egg than by smashing it." But, as Roger Shugg has so aptly stated, "there was no agreement at Washington or New Orleans as to what species of egg was desirable."[23]

Just before it adjourned the convention adopted a reconvoking resolution that would be as important for the future as the provisions (or omissions) of the constitution itself. It read: "Resolved that when this Convention adjourns, it shall be at the call of the President, whose duty it shall be to reconvoke the Convention for any cause, for the purpose of taking such measures as may be necessary for the formation of a civil government. It shall also in that case, call upon the proper officers of the State to cause elections to be held to fill any vacancies that may exist in parishes where the same may be practicable." The legislature was also authorized to reconvene the convention in case of emergency. The resolution, it appears, was to provide protection against a rejection of the constitution in the referendum; in which case the convention might again return to its labors. There was, of course, strong opposition to the resolution; opponents argued that with the framing of the constitution the convention had finished the work for which it had been created. If the people rejected the constitution, said the opposition, they could elect another convention which would "represent their views more faithfully." But the resolution was adopted by a vote of sixty-two to twenty-four.[24]

The rejection of the Louisiana government by Congress and the skepticism about its legality at home left it for a time in a state of limbo in which the legislature was unable to accomplish anything of importance. But with the end of the war in 1865 a number of Confederate veterans returned home, took Lincoln's amnesty oath or received pardons from Andrew Johnson, and became active in politics. Indeed, the emergence of Johnson's restoration program was very encouraging to the emerging anti-Free State party. Governor J. Madison Wells, a former Free State leader and Negro suffrage advocate, now deserted his party and went over to the Democrats. Banks, who had been superseded by Gen. Stephen Hurlbut, returned briefly in the spring of 1865 in an unofficial capacity and reported to friends in Washington that since his departure organized "copperhead forces" had found their way to power in the state. Hurlbut and Wells, he said, had removed Union men and replaced them "from among Rebels, secessionists, returned

officers and soldiers, and the worst sort of copperheads." The conservative "momentum became so irresistible," wrote Willie M. Caskey, "that
opposition seems to have found it greatly to its interest to go under-
ground, and to wait for a more opportune season."[25]

While these changes were in progress Governor Wells issued a proclamation calling for elections to state offices and to Congress. Although
a minority continued to press for Negro suffrage, Wells's order included
only male whites at least twenty-one years of age who had lived in the
state for one year prior to the election and who had taken the presidential oaths or received special pardons. The election that followed in
November (1865) was a great victory for Wells and the Democrats,
many of whose candidates were ex-Confederates. The opposition radicals, rejecting the legality of the election, organized themselves into the
"National Republican Association," led by Henry Clay Warmouth,
adopted a platform embracing "universal suffrage" and "universal education" and passed a resolution "that the Civil Government of
Louisiana, as administered by his Excellency, Acting Governor J. M.
Wells, is subversive and destructive of the rights, and liberties of the
loyal people of this State, and that we protest against the Government,
and call upon the President of the United States to appoint a provisional
Governor and organize the State upon the basis of universal freedom
and suffrage."[26]

Asserting that with secession the state had returned to a territorial
status, the National Republicans demanded the election of a delegate to
Congress and nominated Warmouth for that office. In an election ad-
ministered by the Freedmen's Bureau in which blacks were allowed to
vote Warmouth was declared elected. He went to Washington with the
Thirty-ninth Congress and was given a seat on the floor of the House of
Representatives, while the would-be congressmen and senators from
Louisiana looked on from the galleries.[27]

In Louisiana, however, the legislature was in the hands of the Democrats. It convened in special session on November 23, 1865, on order of
Governor Wells and came to be known as the "Black Code Legislature,"
for the laws it passed during the next month. The best known and most
controversial of these was the vagrant law, which read in part:

> All the idle persons who, not having visible means to maintain
> themselves, live without employment; all persons wandering
> abroad and lodging in groceries, taverns, beer-houses,
> market-places, sheds, barns, uninhabited buildings, or in the open
> air, and not giving a good account of themselves; all persons
> wandering abroad and begging, or who go about from door to door,

or place themselves in the streets, highways, passages, or other public places, to beg or receive alms; habitual drunkards who shall abandon, neglect or refuse to aid in the support of their families, and who may be complained of by their families, shall be deemed vagrants.[28]

In the enactment of such laws Southerners were undoubtedly motivated in part by the need to reestablish some social order in the midst of postwar chaos and to have their labor force working again as soon as possible. But their determination to make certain that the South would remain a white man's country was probably more important. A New Orleans Democratic meeting on October 2, 1865, had adopted a resolution "emphatically approv[ing] the views of President Johnson with regard to the reorganization of the State Governments of the South, [and that] we hold this to be a Government of white people, made and to be perpetuated for the exclusive benefit of the white race," and recommending a constitutional convention "at the earliest practicable period, for the purpose of adopting a Constitution expressing the will of the entire people of the State," to replace the constitution of 1864, "the creation of fraud, violence, and corruption."[29]

Early in 1866 the legislature did consider calling for the election of a new constitutional convention; a bill was drawn up to that end but was tabled when a delegation returning from a visit with Andrew Johnson warned that agitation of the constitutional question at that time might embarrass the president and be harmful to his restoration program. The legislature did ratify the Thirteenth Amendment, in accordance with Johnson's plan, but adopted a qualifying clause "that any attempt on the part of Congress to legislate otherwise [than is necessary for the prevention of slavery] upon the political status or civil relations of former slaves within any State, would be a violation of the Constitution of the United States."[30]

Under such a regime, says Donald E. Reynolds, "Louisiana Radicals faced political extinction."[31] In the Spring of 1866 they met to discuss ways in which they might curb Democratic power and assure their own political future. For a time they considered a convention to draw up a constitution for "the territory of Louisiana." Such a scheme, however, would require presidential approval, which they knew would not be forthcoming; nor could they be sure of the necessary two-thirds majority in Congress to override a veto. Knowing that any state constitutional convention would be dominated by Democrats, about the only alternative left them was to use the reconvoking resolution of 1864, despite its questionable legality, and to reconvene the convention.

Expecting that the more conservative members would not participate, the radical rump might then proceed to enact Negro suffrage and to deny the vote to ex-rebels. The rub of the matter was whether Congress would support them.

An informal meeting of members of the convention took place on June 26, in anticipation of the reconvening. Some thirty or forty members attended, far short of a quorum. Judge Edmund H. Durell, president of the convention, refused to attend or to reconvoke it. But Governor Wells, now moving back to the radical side, was there, and proclaimed Judge Rufus K. Howell, the president pro tem, to be president. Howell then announced that the convention would reconvene in New Orleans on July 30, to revise the constitution and to consider the ratification of the Fourteenth Amendment.

Some weeks before the convention convened its organizers dispatched Judge Howell to Washington to determine congressional attitudes toward the movement. Before this visit, Howell "had the impression that there were Congressmen who had suggested the reassembling of the convention, and the submission of their work to Congress for its acceptance." Although he was disappointed to discover that this was not the sentiment of Congress, the men with whom he talked did not raise any legal obstacles and assured him that, while no promises could be made, "if you people adopt a constitution with the principles you mention embodied in it, we will certainly entertain it as favorably as we can as individual members of Congress."[32]

Even before Howell's Washington mission, a Johnson informant had reported to the president his version of conditions in New Orleans.

> I deem it important to inform you [wrote General Gordon Granger] that efforts are being made here to re-convene the State Convention of 1864. This movement is headed by Governor Wells, Gov. Hahn and other malcontents, and has for its object—first to reinstate themselves in office and power. Second—To disfranchise all persons Civil & Military who took part in the Rebellion against the U. S. [,] all registered enemies & persons who left the State during the Butler & Banks regime—third, To declare & render null and void all Elections since the adjournment of the Convention in 1864. Wherein the radical element has not been successful—thereby violently vacating & refilling nine tenths of the offices throughout the state. 4th To enfranchise all negroes who have served in the Army & Navy and Civil departments of the Government without further qualification than proof to that effect.

It is further proposed to give the right of Suffrage to the Negro, based upon property or educational qualifications or both, as may suit the temper of the Convention—The motive of Govr. Wells and other officials is to forestall the next Legislature which they fear will call a Convention & either impeach or legislate them out of office—with the balance (office seekers) their object is a lust of power and thirsting for the spoils. The great mass of the people & I may state, the industrious, peace-loving and law-abiding—those who are anxious and laboring diligently to reunite and restore the Country—are sternly opposed to upsetting and disturbing the present peaceful state of affairs which is daily improving & hourly becoming more generally satisfactory. It is unnecessary for me to point out to the President what this scheme, if they attempt to put it in execution, must inevitably lead to. In my opinion it will inaugurate revolution and terminate in anarchy. So fearful are the leaders of not being sustained or not being able to accomplish their ends, that they have already endeavored to ascertain if the military power would protect them in their deliberations, & enforce their mandates. I can further inform the President that the opposition Press of the North, with the same class of radical agents which did so much to fasten that atrocious "Franchise Law" upon Tennessee, are here, coats off, hard at work trying to hurry forward the Convention."[33]

Clearly, then, the riot that was brewing in New Orleans would be no isolated affair, but would become enmeshed in the struggle between the president and Congress, so central to the history of 1866.

Among the state and city officials with enough authority to influence the convention movement only Governor Wells favored it. In the opposition camp were Mayor John T. Monroe, Lieutenant Governor Albert Voorhies, and Edmund Abell, presiding judge of the first district court of New Orleans. When it became apparent that the convention did indeed intend to reconvene these men set about trying to stop it. Their leader was Mayor Monroe who, on July 25, wrote to Gen. Absalom Baird, in command in New Orleans during the temporary absence of Gen. Philip Sheridan: "It is my intention [said Monroe] to disperse this unlawful assembly, if found within the corporate limits, holding them accountable to existing municipal law, provided they meet without the sanction of the military authorities." Would the General inform him [Monroe] at his "earliest convenience, . . . whether the projected meeting has your approbation, so that I may act accordingly."

Baird's reply of the following day may have been the most sensible statement of the whole controversy. Had his suggestions been listened to and acted upon there would have been no riot. His error was, perhaps, in expecting too much reason and light from men whose passions were aroused by the tensions of the Reconstruction era and who were in no mood to listen to common sense. The assemblage had not so far as he was aware, said Baird, "the sanction or approbation of any military authority for its meeting." The military commanders in Louisiana had "held themselves completely aloof from political" matters. Nor did he intend to provide a military guard for the convention, because "the mayor . . . and [the] police will amply protect its sittings."

If these persons assemble, as you say is intended, it will be, I presume, in virtue of the universally conceded right of all loyal citizens of the United States to meet peaceably and discuss freely

PHILIP H. SHERIDAN
Reproduced from the collection of the Library of Congress

questions concerning their civil governments, a right which is not restricted by the fact that the movement proposed might terminate in a change of existing institutions.

If the assemblage in question has the legal right to remodel the State government, it should be protected in so doing; if it has not, then its labors must be looked upon simply as a harmless pleasantry to which no one ought to object. As to your conception of the duty imposed by your oath of office, I regret to differ with you entirely. I cannot understand how the mayor of a city can undertake to decide so important and delicate a question as the legal authority upon which a convention, claiming to represent the people of an entire State, bases its action.

This doubtless will, in due time, be properly decided upon by the legal branch of the United States government. At all events, the governor of the State would seem to be more directly called upon to take the initiative in a step of this kind, if it was proper and necessary. What we most want at the present time is the maintenance of perfect good order and the suppression of violence. If, when you speak of the projected meeting as one calculated to disturb the public peace and tranquility, I am to understand that you regard the number of persons who differ in opinion from those who will constitute it as so large and the lawlessness of their character so well established that you doubt the ability of your small force of police to control them, you have in such case only to call upon me, and I will bring to your assistance not only the troops now present in the city, but, if necessary, the entire force which it may be in my power to assemble, either upon the land or on the water. Lawless violence must be suppressed, and in this connection the recent order of the lieutenant general, designed for the protection of citizens of the United States, deserves careful consideration. It imposes high obligations for military interference to protect those who, having violated no ordinance of the State, are engaged in peaceful avocations.[34]

Two days later Monroe and Voorhies called upon Baird. Voorhies related the absence of Governor Wells and the fruitless efforts to locate him. Thus the governor's duties had fallen to the lieutenant governor, and Voorhies had a different plan for dealing with the convention. Now, instead of having the mayor and the police arrest the convention, its members were to be indicted by the grand jury of the parish under a writ issued to the sheriff, who would make the arrests. Baird warned them not to proceed in this way. To arrest the conventionists would be in violation of their rights; they would then appeal to him for protection, he said, and "I would feel bound to release them and possibly to arrest the sheriff himself."

Next, both sides turned to Washington for instructions and support. Voorhies telegraphed President Johnson requesting advice as to what the military actions should be if the local authorities attempted to disperse the convention through court action. Johnson replied immediately: "The military will be expected to sustain, not obstruct or interfere with, the proceedings of the courts." On the day Johnson's telegram was received, Baird wired Secretary of War Edwin M. Stanton:

> A convention has been called, with the sanction of Governor Wells,
> to meet here on Monday. The lieutenant governor and city authorities think it unlawful, and propose to break it up by arresting the delegates. I have given no orders on the subject, but have warned the parties that I should not countenance or permit such action without instructions to that effect from the President.
> Please instruct me by telegraph.[35]

Stanton never answered this message. Baird's critics have questioned his wisdom and his motives in his decision to telegraph Stanton instead of the president. Had he communicated directly with the president, they say, he would have received a reply and would have known what to do. Did Baird intentionally wire the secretary expecting no answer or one favorable to the convention? The question was put to him directly by Congressman Boyer, Democratic member of the committee. Why had Baird not telegraphed for instructions directly to the president instead of the secretary of war? Baird replied: "The proper military mode of communication with either the President or Secretary of War would have been through the Adjutant General. I violated that propriety in telegraphing to the Secretary of War directly. I did this thinking I would get a more speedy reply than by sending it through the Adjutant General. Sometimes we took the responsibility of telegraphing in that way. I did not feel justified in passing over the Secretary of War to communicate directly with the President."[36]

A more pertinent and more complex question is why Secretary Stanton failed to reply, and why he did not inform Johnson of Baird's message. Historians differ widely on this point. Howard K. Beale saw Stanton's decision not to reply as a cause of the riot. "No response came [Beale wrote]. Consequently, when the Convention assembled . . . and the riot ensued, the military, undetermined how to act, was useless in 'maintaining order.' It could only restore order after the damage was done."[37] James E. Sefton says that Stanton's failure to reply to Baird's telegram or to inform the president of it "were perhaps the most crucial decisions made by anyone during the entire affair." Although he does not charge the secretary "with deliberate deceit and conniving," he does say that "to ignore an officer's plain request for instructions from the Commander-in-Chief is at least sheer incompetence. . . . It seems clear that had Baird received definite instructions on the specific point of his relations to the civil authorities, the chances of any serious disturbance would have been slim."[38]

Benjamin Thomas and Harold Hyman, Stanton's biographers, while they do not fully exonerate him, are more favorable toward him and give some credence to his version of the case. Six months after the riot Stanton wrote to a friend explaining his role. "There was no intimation in [Baird's] telegram," he said,

EDWIN M. STANTON

Reproduced from the collection of the Library of Congress

that force or violence was threatened by those opposed to the convention or that it was apprehended by General Baird.

Upon consideration, it appeared to me that his warning to the city authorities was all that the case then required, for I saw no reason to instruct him to withdraw protection from the convention sanctioned by the Governor, and in the event of any attempt at arrest, General Baird's interference would bring up the case with all the facts for such instructions as might be proper, and in the meantime under his general authority, he would take measures to maintain peace within his command.

Although Thomas and Hyman do not find this to be a sufficient explanation, they say nevertheless that Stanton was "not so unscrupulously heartless as deliberately to provoke a riot for political advantage." They find it highly probable, however, that he "had a political objective in mind."

He was by no means unaware of the explosive situation at New Orleans. Baird's expressed intention to prevent interference with a Unionist convention, no matter how questionable its auspices, accorded with his own wishes. Stanton knew also that Johnson had no sympathy with the sponsors or the purposes of the convention and that if he was informed of a threatened clash of authority in New Orleans, he would order Baird to support the local authorities. Consequently, he withheld Baird's telegram from the President, but at the same time, not venturing to cross Johnson openly by endorsing Baird's resolution to protect the delegates, he simply neglected to answer the general's telegram.

They remind us that an estimate of Stanton's role in the affair is not divisible from Andrew Johnson's role, that the riot and the events surrounding it must be seen in their relation to the radical-Johnson feud and more particularly the Johnson-Stanton feud. While admitting that Stanton "had no scruples about discrediting Johnson" and that his sympathies were with the Louisiana Unionists, they charge Johnson with irresponsibility in encouraging Louisiana officials in carrying out their intention to arrest convention delegates in contradiction of his own stated policy "that the duty of the United States forces 'is not to interfere in any controversy between the political authorities of the State.' " "The President's worst fault [they say] had consisted . . . in ignoring the regular military channels and using a private telegram to local city and state officials as a means of communicating his wishes to a general of the national army."[39]

Joe G. Taylor, in a recent history of Louisiana reconstruction, also rejects the thesis that Stanton was part of a radical cabal that had "deliberately decided to incite a riot in New Orleans, knowing that this would improve their chances in the election of 1866." "This is a most improbable theory [Taylor writes]. There was no way Stanton could be sure a riot would break out, and the Radicals probably had more to gain if the convention should meet and Louisiana should 'voluntarily' adopt Negro suffrage. But even if Stanton was more Machiavellian and far-sighted than Machiavelli, nothing forced the whites of New Orleans to cooperate with the Radicals by staging a riot to demonstrate rebel intransigence."[40]

Although the riot did not occur until July 30, the events of Friday the twenty-seventh loom large in its history. On the evening of that day a radical rally took place, with a large number of blacks present. Former Governor Hahn was the principal speaker, but it was the speech of Dr. A. P. Dostie that attracted the greatest attention. Dostie, a northern dentist who had settled in Louisiana and had become state auditor under the Banks regime, was well known for his radical convictions, which he stated in forceful language. His remarks at the July 27 rally may have been intemperate; his enemies said they were incendiary and helped bring on the riot. According to the *New Orleans Times*, which quoted from the speech a week after the rally, Dostie said:

> We [Radicals] are 400,000 strong to 300,000, and cannot only whip, but exterminate, the other party. Judge Abell with his Grand Jury may indict us. [Sheriff] Harry Hayes with his *posse comitatus* may be expected there; and the police with more than 1000 men sworn in may interfere with the convention. Therefore let all brave men and not cowards come here Monday (July 30). There will be no such puerile affair as at Memphis, but if interfered with, the streets will run with blood. . . . We are bound to have universal suffrage, though you have the traitor Andrew Johnson against you.

Another report had it that Dostie admonished blacks to come to the convention armed.[41] It is not difficult to imagine that Dostie gave a forceful speech, but it is far from certain that the newspaper account given here is accurate. As Joe G. Taylor points out, this account was published three days after the riot, in which Dostie was killed, by which time "the conservative press of New Orleans had begun picturing the riot as the result of a deliberate Radical conspiracy, and it is possible that the account of Dostie's speech is an invention."[42]

During the three days between the meeting of the twenty-seventh and the convening of the convention tension mounted in New Orleans.

The correspondent of the *New York Tribune* reported "loud threats" of the Rebels to break up the convention. "The Rebel Sheriff, Gen. Harry Hayes, has sworn in a posse of deputies to promote this disruption. Members of the Convention are openly threatened with the lamp-post, but the Union men are resolute and sanguine." The *New Orleans Times* published rumors of secret societies, "irrespective of color," whose purpose was to overthrow "our legitimate and constitutional State authorities, and to maintain by violence the revolutionary attempt of the vampire faction."[43]

On the day of the convention a crowd of whites, some drinking and sullen, gathered in the streets near Mechanics Institute, the hall where the convention would meet. Despite their presence, the convention met at twelve noon, the appointed hour. Discovering that only twenty-five members were present, Judge Howell recessed the convention and sent the sergeant-at-arms in search of other members, so as to have a quorum. Meanwhile, a procession of blacks, in a festive mood with a flag flying and a drum beating, was approaching the hall to demonstrate its support for the convention. As the procession crossed Canal Street a white man knocked a black man down. The black man struck back, and the white man pulled a revolver and fired at him. But the procession moved on to the hall where it halted and cheered the convention. Here a white newsboy—one of a number of boys milling around in the crowd—taunted one of the blacks. A policeman arrested the boy and was taking him away when a black man fired a shot in his direction. The police retaliated by firing a volley into the black ranks. The riot had begun. Now police, firemen, ex-Rebel soldiers, boys, and others joined the attacking mob. Many blacks made their way into the hall where members of the convention still sat without a quorum. The white mob, including policemen, continued the attack, firing into the windows of the building at the virtually helpless persons trapped there. Some were shot down as they tried to escape through the windows. Most braced themselves inside the building against attack. They tried to barricade the two sets of double doors through which the attackers came and defended themselves as best they could with clubs and sticks from broken-up chairs. Three times, with these improvised and inadequate weapons, they drove the attackers back. Some blacks who sought protection by asking to be arrested were shot down in cold blood. Others who managed to have themselves arrested were beaten up and shot on their way to the police stations. Some policemen did try, without conspicuous success, to protect their charges. The Reverend Dr. Horton, chaplain of the convention, tried vainly to stop the slaughter by waving his white handkerchief and pleading for the lives of the convention members and their friends. Both Horton and Dr. Dostie were killed.[44]

Troops from Jackson Barracks, under General Baird's personal command, arrived on the scene about 2:40 P.M., by which time the riot was over. By placing the city under martial law and having his men patrol the streets he may have prevented further violence, but he had arrived too late to prevent the riot or to stop it in its early stages. Undoubtedly the major cause of this failure on the part of the military was Baird's misunderstanding about the time the convention was to meet, which he understood to be 6:00 P.M. instead of twelve noon. Had Baird not been confused about the time the bloodshed and loss of life would have been less than it was, or prevented altogether. Even so, in explaining the absence of troops it is necessary also to consider the reluctance of the military to become involved in local political affairs and its tendency to place too much trust in the local law-enforcement establishment. Although Baird was more alert to conditions in New Orleans than General Stoneman had been to those in Memphis, the reaction of the two generals was not altogether dissimilar. Indeed, General Sheridan had instructed Baird not to "allow the military to become involved in any political discussions or matters of that kind . . . [and that] the military was not to be used, except in case of a breach of the peace . . . such that life and property of citizens depended upon the military, and not upon civil authority."[45]

On the morning of the thirtieth Lieutenant Governor Voorhies had visited with Baird to discuss the employment of the military during the meeting of the convention. Baird told him that he had received no instructions from Washington but that no arrests were to be made "without the sheriff first bringing the writ to me for my endorsement, and that the convention should be permitted to proceed." He feared that if he sent troops to the convention site his motives might be questioned and that he would be accused of "organizing a military guard for the convention." But he would consent to "bring a few companies into the city and post them in the streets, somewhere not adjoining the convention building, but a short distance from it." He proposed the posting of four companies in the streets one hour before the convention. Voorhies, Baird testified, seemed pleased with this arrangement and assured him that his friends would not "misinterpret my motives."[46] But because of Baird's confusion about the time the troops were not there; the riot occurred and 34 blacks and 4 whites were killed and 119 blacks and 27 whites were wounded.[47]

Baird's confusion about the time of the convention reminds us of the importance of chance or accident in determining the turn of historical events and of how inadequate scientific analysis of causality can sometimes be. Without probing deeply into why a responsible general—whose very profession dictated an acute sense of time—should err in this particular way, we may at least raise questions about it. Did Baird harbor a subconscious wish not to have his troops ready to intervene? Did he perhaps prefer, without being fully aware of it, that events should take their own course without him?

General Sheridan returned to New Orleans during the night of July 31. He found the city still in a state of great excitement, necessitating the continuation of martial law. The following day he reported to General Grant by telegram:

> You are doubtless aware of the serious riot which occurred in this city on the 30th. A political body, styling itself the convention of 1864, met on the 30th, for, as it is alleged, the purpose of remodelling the present constitution of the State. The leaders were political agitators and revolutionary men, and the action of the convention was liable to produce breaches of the public peace.
>
> I had made up my mind to arrest the head men, if the proceedings of the convention were calculated to disturb the tranquility of the department; but I had no case for action until they committed the overt act. *In the mean time, official duty called me to Texas, and the mayor of the city, during my absence, suppressed the convention by the use of their police force, and in so doing attacked the members of the convention and a party of two hundred negroes, and with firearms, clubs, and knives, in a manner so unnecessary and atrocious as to compel me to say that it was murder.* About forty whites and blacks were thus killed, and about a hundred and sixty wounded. Everything is now quiet; but I deem it best to maintain a military supremacy in the city for a few days until the affair is fully investigated. I believe the sentiment of the general community is great regret at this unnecessary cruelty, and that the police could have made any arrests they saw fit without sacrificing lives.

On August 3 the *New York Times* published this message, but with a key passage—shown in italics—deleted. Sheridan, indignant, requested of Grant's headquarters who was guilty of this "violation of military honor." Grant assured him that "your dispatches did not get into print from these headquarters." Later W. W. Warden, a *Times* correspondent, testified that the dispatch had been given to him by Johnson's secretary, with the permission of the president. The incident was brought into the campaign, which was beginning at the time.[48]

Within twenty-four hours Sheridan was viewing the riot as more

infamous than he had at first reported. "The more information I obtain
. . . , the more revolting it becomes," he wired Grant on August 2. "It
was no riot. It was an absolute massacre by the police, which was not
excelled in murderous cruelty by that of Fort Pillow. It was a murder
which the mayor and police of the city perpetrated without the shadow
of a necessity. Furthermore, I believe it was premeditated, and every
indication points to this."

Although, in his testimony before the committee, Sheridan indicated
that he would have acted more forcefully than did Baird, he nonetheless
exonerated his subordinate commander. When asked to explain why the
military had been brought in so late he replied: "I am unable to answer
the question. I can say this, that I can see no object why the military
should have been present, unless it was to have prevented the police
from perpetrating a massacre, and in order to have guarded against
that it was necessary for General Baird to pre-suppose that the police
were going to be the assailants and rioters. It was not reasonable for
him to suppose this, because it was their business to be there for the
preservation of the peace." The police force, said Sheridan, "was amply
sufficient to preserve the peace," and "twenty policemen were sufficient
to have arrested the convention without violence."[49]

During the days immediately following the riot, some men explained
it as the result of a conspiracy by radicals to further their own political
purposes. Not unexpectedly, this was the way Gideon Welles saw it.

> There is little doubt [Welles wrote] that the New Orleans riots had
> their origin with the Radical Members of Congress in Washington.
> It is a part of a deliberate conspiracy and was to be the
> commencement of a series of bloody affrays through the States
> lately in rebellion. . . . There is a determination to involve the
> country in civil war, if necessary, to secure negro suffrage in the
> States and Radical ascendency in the General Government. . . .
> Stanton is evidently in deep sympathy and concern with the
> Radicals in this matter, though he studied to conceal it.[50]

With only slight variations Congressman Benjamin M. Boyer, Democratic member of the investigating committee, suggested such a conspiracy in his minority report: "To provoke an attack on the colored
population, which was expected to be suppressed by the military before
it had seriously endangered the white leaders, appears to have been
part of the scheme of the conventionists. This would afford an excuse for
congressional investigation, resulting in congressional legislation favoring the ultimate design of the conspirators, viz., the destruction of the
existing civil government of Louisiana." Although he made no direct

charge of conspiracy against his radical colleagues in Congress, he clearly implied it. "If there be any members of the federal government who are indirectly responsible for the bloody result," he wrote, "they are those members of the present Congress, whoever they may be, who encouraged these men by their counsels and promised to them their individual and official support."[51]

Historians of Louisiana Reconstruction have generally accepted the conspiracy theory, or some corollary of it, during the first half of the twentieth century. Willie M. Caskey, writing in the 1930s, in summing up the results of the riot, said that the "conspirators" had succeeded in overthrowing the restoration government of Lincoln and Johnson. Although the public officials were "not officially suspended for some months . . . to all intents and purposes [they] had been rendered impotent" by the imposition of martial law after the riot. In attempting to prove his point, Caskey quoted extensively from Welles's diary.[52] John R. Ficklen, whose history was published in 1910, was not so blatant as Caskey in labeling the conventionists and their friends as conspirators. But, relying heavily on Boyer's minority report, he concluded that without "encouragement from certain radical congressmen . . . and the presence of Federal troops in New Orleans the convention would not have ventured to meet."[53]

Undoubtedly the riot contributed directly and indirectly to the overthrow of the Conservative-Democratic goovernment in Louisiana— directly by the imposition of martial law and a diminution of the power of elected officials, indirectly by becoming an issue in the national election. Nor could the radicals have been anything but pleased with the political turn of events. It would be hard to prove, however, that they conspired to overthrow the government or the constitution of Louisiana. Indeed, the evidence seems to point in another direction. The adherents of the conspiracy theory have made much of the effort of radical Congressman George Boutwell to postpone the adjournment of Congress until the convention had completed its work of revamping the constitution so as "to accept it, and thus give it validity as the Constitution of the State." For "if Congress should not be in session, [the argument continued] a long time must elapse before action could be taken; the new government of the State might fail to get a foothold, and the country would experience a very serious calamity."[54] Even if congressional radicals had followed Boutwell's lead and postponed adjournment, the case against them as conspirators would have been dubious, for there is no evidence of collusion to bring on a riot. But Congress did adjourn, just two days before the convention met, and was thus not in session to exploit whatever advantage the riot might have given it.

The actions of Judge Durell, president of the 1864 convention, leading to his decision not to reconvene it, further discredit the conspiracy theory. If Durell had some doubts about the legality of the reconvoking resolution, he also had them about the prospects of cooperation from radicals in Congress. Thus on June 18 he telegraphed Boutwell, Stevens, and Fessenden asking their advice: "Shall I call this convention," he asked, "and when, now or in the fall? Please telegraph reply, and write full advices. I am strongly pressed to issue the call, and desire your earliest answer immediately." He received no reply. As the revisionist historian Donald E. Reynolds says, "This wire proves fallacious the assertions by several historians that Durell refused to act because he felt he lacked the legal power to do so." It also strongly suggests that there was no radical conspiracy. "Certainly," Reynolds continues, "had the Radicals been conspiring to achieve a coup in Louisiana, they would have pledged their aid to Durell. The necessity of appointing a president pro tem of the rump convention made the legality of the reconvocation more questionable than ever. This step might not have been necessary had the Radicals pledged their support when Durell asked for it."[55]

Joe G. Taylor, another revisionist, accepts Reynolds's rejection of the conspiracy theory, but goes on to explain its origin and its peristence for more than seventy years. The tendency of the press in Louisiana was at first to play down the riot, says Taylor, but "the national reprecussions could not be ignored," so that a new line of argument was developed, "that the whole affair had been planned in Washington for the benefit of the Radical Republican party."[56]

The riots at Memphis and New Orleans demonstrated that the debate over reconstruction in 1866 was not confined to Washington. Further evidence of this would be forthcoming in the election campaign of the summer and fall, when the New Orleans riot, especially, would be used by each side to show the righteousness of its cause.

Chapter 9

The Voice of the Electorate

NEVER IN AMERICAN HISTORY has there been a mid-term election—and seldom a presidential one—so important as the election of 1866. It was the culmination of the great debate between Andrew Johnson and the congressional Republicans, which had been going on since the previous December. Historians have treated the election in scrupulous detail,[1] and contemporaries recognized its magnitude. "It was a deadly struggle between the Executive and Legislative Departments, . . . both of which had been chosen by the same party," said James G. Blaine in his memoirs. "This peculiar fact imparted to the contest a degree of personal acrimony and political rancor never before exhibited in the biennial election of representatives to Congress."[2] Greeley's *New York Tribune* editorialized that the "canvas had elements unknown, which make it more complex and important than any preceding. . . . All the old questions that led to the Rebellion are summed up in this new dilemma."[3] The *New York Herald* believed it to be more important than the election of the first Congress of the United States.[4]

The question of readmission of the southern states to representation in the national Congress was, of necessity, the major issue of this first political campaign since the end of the war. The election might also have been a referendum on pressing postwar economic and social problems such as tariffs, the national debt, currency and banking, public land policy, federal aid to railroads, and the demands of the labor movement, but neither Andrew Johnson nor his radical enemies wanted it that way. Often the debate descended to the level of demagoguery and buffoonery, especially on the part of Johnson and some radicals, behavior that has played into the hands of historians determined to blame one side or the other. Although the antics of Andrew Johnson, whose inability to engage in dignified public discussion we have already seen, cannot be ignored, his traducers responded with an invective that was equally irresponsible. Unfortunately, the acrimony and bombast of these men has overshadowed a more enlightened discussion by other men of the Fourteenth Amendment and its bearing on restoration.

Between mid-August and the end of September there were four conventions that provided a structure or outline for the campaign and indicated the direction in which it was going. The first and most important was the National Union convention in Philadelphia, followed by the Southern Loyalists convention of September 3, also in Philadelphia, and later by two Soldiers and Sailors conventions, the pro-Johnson assembly at Cleveland and the anti-Johnson one at Pittsburgh in late September. Earlier in the year the Grand Army of the Republic, the great northern veterans organization committed to Republican ascendancy, had been organized in Illinois and Indiana. Its representatives were present "in force" at the Pittsburgh convention, where they formally took their stand with the Republicans and seized the occasion to extend their organization, and their influence, from the Midwest into the East. Late in the year the G.A.R. held its first national encampment in Indianapolis.[5]

The origins of the National Union party are to be found early in the year. As the conflict between president and Congress intensified, the possibility of forming a new party around Andrew Johnson and his program was in the minds of many men. It was James Gordon Bennett, however, the erratic and idiosyncratic publisher of the *New York Herald*, who first gave the idea wide publicity. Just why Bennett should have become a champion of Andrew Johnson's cause is not easy to determine; he was not known for his loyalty to anybody for very long, and he disagreed with the administration on some important economic issues. The explanation is probably to be found in Bennett's hatred of the radicals, whom he branded as "niggerlovers," and whom he held responsible for the war. In any case, an affinity developed between Bennett and the president, which was sometimes advantageous to both. The *Herald* could expect to benefit from being close to the White House and the president could enjoy the favorable publicity of New York's most widely circulating paper. As early as January the *Herald* had cast Johnson in the mold of a national hero: "Standing above political parties, and recognizing no party but that of the great mass of the American people, he has it in his power to so shape events that all opposition will only bring defeat and grief to those who attempt it. But he must bear in mind that the cunning and artful party leaders, both in and out of Congress, will not be deterred . . . from their efforts to force him into their party meshes." A fortnight later the *Herald* reported rumors from Washington of new party alignments and proceeded to call for the organization of "A Great Conservative National Party."[6]

The next move came in mid-April, following the passage of the Civil Rights Bill over Johnson's veto, when a "National Union Executive Committee" was established; the committee arranged for a soldiers and sailors serenade to the president for April 18. On this occasion Johnson spoke, in a fashion somewhat redolent of February 22 and foreshadowing his speeches of the campaign. Passing up the opportunity to discuss calmly his policy of states' rights and restoration Johnson again passionately defended himself and attacked his enemies:

> I think I have given some evidence that I am sincere and earnest; and now I want to know why it is that the whole train of slanderers, and calumniators and traducers have been barking and snapping at my heels? Why is it that they array themselves against me? . . . Where were they during the rebellion? In the Senate I raised my voice against it; and . . . did I not leave my place in the Senate—a place of emolument, ease, and distinction, and take my position where the enemy could be reached, and where men's lives were in danger? While I was thus exposed personally and publicly, and in every way, some of my present traducers and calumniators were far from the foe, and were enjoying ease and comfort. But I care not for them; I care not that slander, that foul whelp of sin, has been turned loose against me. I care not for all that. . . . They have turned the whole pack loose to lower me in your estimation. Tray, Blanche and Sweetheart, little dogs and all, come along snapping and snarling at my heels. But I heed them not.[7]

After the serenade several pro-Johnson clubs were formed, which merged in May to become the National Union Club, led by Alexander W. Randall and Montgomery Blair. This club arranged for another serenade where, it was hoped, cabinet members would be present and would make public their attitudes about the movement. The serenade did not work out as planned. Speed, Seward, and Harlan did not appear. Welles, who opposed "these methods of calling out public men," was ill-at-ease when the crowd assembled and stated only that he "approved the policy of the administration and was for the union of the States and the rights of the States." Only McCulloch among the Cabinet members, it seems, spoke in an unambiguous way.[8]

On June 11 several organizers of the movement—Cowan, Doolittle, Randall, and Orville H. Browning among them—met with Johnson to discuss their plans. Browning's account of the meeting shows that no persuasion was needed to get the president's approval and encouragement:

The President said his only ambition was to bring all the states back to their proper relations to the general government, and give unity, tranquility and prosperity to the Country, and he was then ready to retire. He did not believe this could be done whilst the Congress was in the hands of the radicals. He thought their measures revolutionary, and if persisted in would subvert the government and ruin the Country. To rescue the power from their hands, and avert such a calamity he was willing to put in all the capital he had. He would give $20,000 in cash, and all the influence he had as Chief Executive. The patronage of the government and the Presidency for the next term could be used by the true friends of the Country to accomplish the desired results [etc.]. We all thought a convention of the friends of the country should be called at an early day.[9]

By this time Doolittle had emerged as the leader of the movement. On June 15 he had breakfast with Welles for the purpose of continuing the discussions. Together they called on the president, who concurred with their view that "a prompt call for a national convention of friends of the Union should be issued." Doolittle agreed to prepare the call, which he felt ought to be signed by those members of the cabinet who agreed with it.[10] Two days later Doolittle brought Welles a first draft of his call for the convention. Welles was displeased because it did not contain an outright repudiation of the Fourteenth Amendment, which Welles thought was one of the purposes of the movement. "An alarm should be sounded," he said, "warning the people of the movements that are being made to alter the organic law, and insidiously change the government." Although Doolittle saw some merit in Welles's argument, he was reluctant to oppose the amendment because he wanted Henry J. Raymond, chairman of the National Repulican Committee, and others, to sign the call. Welles was also fearful that Seward had had a hand in it and that "the call, if not the convention itself is . . . perverted to an intrigue in behalf of the old Whig party, on which Weed and Seward rely." He also feared that there may have been an "understanding" between Seward and Stanton "in concert with the Radicals" and that Seward was "prompting Doolittle."[11]

These differences among men in the inner circle calling for a convention are significant in that they were never resolved. Those who felt that the amendment should be rejected were, for the most part, Democrats; those who would accept it were Republicans. Thus, nearly two months before the convention met there were signs that to effect a coalition of Democrats and moderate Republicans in a new party would be difficult if not impossible. These structural weaknesses in the movement will become clearer when we examine more carefully the role of Henry J. Raymond in the National Union party.

On June 23, Johnson met at the White House with Doolittle, Seward, McCulloch, Cowan, Browning, Randall, and Welles to prepare the final draft of the call. On the twenty-sixth it was made public.[12]

The National Union movement became the occasion for the reorganization of Johnson's cabinet, which friends had been urging upon him for some time. Doolittle sent letters to all cabinet members, eliciting their attitudes toward the movement. Favorable replies came from those who had been involved in preparing the call, but three others—Dennison, Speed, and Harlan—resigned. Stanton, however, neither replied nor resigned. When asked point-blank what he thought of the convention he admitted that he opposed it. He had not answered Doolittle's letter, he said, because "I did not choose to have Doolittle or any other little fellow draw an answer from me."[13]

The call for the convention, which said nothing about the Fourteenth Amendment, was in essence an endorsement of Johnson's restoration policy and his states' rights position: "The rights, the dignity, and the equality of the States in the Union, including the right of representation in Congress, are solemnly guaranteed by [the] Constitution." It asserted the right of each state "to prescribe the qualifications of its own electors" and to "order and control its own domestic concerns." It was an invitation to people throughout the country who loved the Union and could "rise above personal and sectional considerations" to assemble "as friends and brothers under the national flag."[14]

The invitation included Democrats, without whom the whole movement would have been doomed. But the presence of Democrats might be embarrassing, and with only the conservative minority of the Republicans supporting the movement the Democrats might take it over. We are reminded at this point of that earlier conversation between Johnson and Governor Morton at the time of the Civil Rights veto, when the question of a new party arose and Morton had warned Johnson that "all roads out of the Republican party led into the Democratic party." Is it possible that in rejecting this sage advice the president intended that the National Union movement would be the instrument for the resurgence of the Democracy? It appears that he did not have any such plan in mind or that he had not given much thought to the question of which party, per se, would control the government. His thinking on the meaning and prospects of the forthcoming Philadelphia convention were ambiguous. Shortly after the call for the convention he told Henry J. Raymond that he "did not want any new party, nor did he want the

Democratic party restored to power. He wanted Congress to restore the Union, and if those who favored this would take hold of it, . . . he felt sure the people would sustain them and that the next Congress would be overwhelmingly on our side. He declared his wish that this matter be settled within the Union party." He believed, said Raymond, that the Philadelphia convention "would have a very salutary effect on public sentiment, and would cause the leaders of the Radical movement to pause."[15] Yet a few weeks later, when the Democrats were becoming a liability to the president, he could say, "Let parties sink into insignificance. If a party must be maintained let it be based on the great principles of the Constitution."[16]

The Democratic conundrum, which bedeviled the National Union party throughout its brief history, became evident even before the convening of the Philadelphia convention. Three weeks before the convention Montgomery Blair, from an old and influential Democratic

HENRY J. RAYMOND
Reproduced from the collection of the Library of Congress

family, had invited a Democratic committee from Ohio to a meeting of the National Union Executive Committee. One of the visitors was Clement L. Vallandigham, the famous Ohio Copperhead whom Lincoln had banished to the Confederacy. Orville H. Browning described the incident in his diary: Blair had invited the guests without the knowledge of other members of the committee. "I protested against admitting them. . . . [said Browning]. I was not willing that Mr. Vallandigham should become identified with us[.] The committee sustained me, and they were not admitted. . . . I thought the whole thing was intended by Blair and Vallandingham [*sic*] to get recognition for him and to identify him with the friends of the Philadelphia Convention[.] The scheme failed[.]"[17] The committee's rejection of Vallandigham is not the last we shall see of him. He showed up at the convention, where his presence became a *cause célèbre*.

On August 14 the convention assembled in Philadelphia in the "Wigwam," a building constructed for the occasion to accommodate some 10,000 people. In addition to the delegates was a throng of visitors and correspondents who crowded into the hotels.

The convention opened in a dramatic way, when Postmaster General Randall, on viewing the approach of the delegates announced to the crowd, "Gentlemen of the Convention, I have to announce to you the approach of the delegates from Massachusetts and South Carolina, arm-in-arm." At that moment the huge Governor James Orr of South Carolina and the diminutive Gen. Darius N. Couch of Massachusetts did indeed appear, arm-in-arm. Following them came the remaining delegates from those two states, also arm-in-arm. It was all prearranged, and in keeping with the plans of the leaders not to allow anything to destroy the illusion of unity. Also, to preserve the illusion, no open debate on the convention's resolutions was permitted until the managers decided that the time had come to vote on them. Southerners flocked to this convention, the first since before the war with delegates from all the states, although Alexander Stephens, who fully endorsed the movement, thought it discrete to stay away. But the Copperheads Fernando Wood of New York and Clement Vallandigham were there. Wood, seeing that he was persona non grata, withdrew gracefully from the New York delegation; but Vallandigham withdrew only under pressure. He prepared a letter of withdrawal, which the Ohio delegation insisted on reading to the convention. That delegation also passed a resolution unanimously recognizing the right of Vallandigham "to hold a seat in this convention; that we should regard his exclusion . . . as an unjust and unreasonable infringement of the rights of the democracy [in his district], and are ready to stand by him in the assertion of his rights and the rights of his constitutents." However, they consented to his withdrawal "for the sake of harmony and good feeling, . . . and in order to secure the great ends for which [the convention] was called."[18] After a speech by Doolittle, the permanent chairman, the convention got down to the business of preparing its "Declaration of Principles" and its "Address to the People," in which Henry J. Raymond was the leading figure.

From the outset, Raymond's role in the National Union movement was a difficult one and one wonders why he allowed himself to be a participant and to deliver the main address to the convention. From our vantage point it appears that he had everything to lose and nothing to gain. It was never his intention to participate in the formation of a new party and thus "to forfeit my standing as a member of the Union party" or to jeopardize his position as its national chairman. When Doolittle called upon Raymond and read him the first draft of the "call," Raymond "suggested that its terms were too broad—that it would admit all who had been in rebellion against the Government, and whose political sympathies had been with them, while it would exclude many who had stood by the Government, but who now desired national action questions resulting from the war." A few days later Raymond published in the *New York Times* an article stating simply that he favored a national convention "for the purposes of adopting, if possible, a platform of principles upon which the Northern and Southern States could take common political action."

Even though Raymond did not sign the call for the convention, a Republican congressional caucus assailed him "for having engaged in a conspiracy . . . to destroy the Union party." Raymond answered that he believed the convention would strengthen the party and that if he found this not to be so he would oppose it. Actually, he was skeptical of the movement as it was being shaped by Doolittle and its other leaders and was a reluctant participant in it. Why, then, did he go along? It appears that he was a victim of his loyalty to Andrew Johnson and that he allowed himself to be persuaded by Seward, not only to attend the convention but to write its "Address to the People." Seward, it seems, successfully assuaged Raymond's fears that the convention might fall into "the hands of former rebels and their Copperhead associates." In Seward's view, the convention was "simply for consultation. It was not a party convention, nor need it affect in any way the party standing of those who should take part in it." As a Union man Seward "did not admit the right of anybody to turn him out of [his] party; but he claimed the right to meet and consult with any portion of his fellow citizens." He appealed to Raymond to join the movement to *prevent* it from falling into the hands of the Copperheads. Seward then enticed Raymond into a conversation with Johnson at the White House, where the president and the secretary of state prevailed upon him to play the role expected of him.[19]

In preparing the "Address" at Philadelphia, Raymond finally learned that his fears about the convention were now without foundation. He read the "Address" first to the convention's committee on resolutions which, not altogether pleased with it, passed it on to a subcommittee of thirteen to prepare the final document. This committee was dominated by Southerners who objected to several of Raymond's key passages. One of these was a statement on the harmful effects of slavery on the South and the nation; Raymond finally acquiesced in the removal of this whole passage. Another, on the Fourteenth Amendment, asserted "the right of Congress and the States to make Amendments and [suggested] that some enlargement of the powers of the National Government, in

WILLIAM H. SEWARD

Reproduced from the collection of the Library of Congress

the respects covered by the [amendment] . . . , might be desirable."
The subcommittee rejected this passage on the grounds that it might be
construed as favoring the amendment. Southerners were also sensitive
to the use of the words *rebellion* and *insurrection* and requested that
they be deleted. Although Raymond felt that such words were necessary "to describe in accurate language the legal character of the acts
referred to," he did rewrite the "Address" so as to make it less objectionable to the South.

Southerners and Northern Democrats made similar objections to
some clauses of the "Declaration of Principles." The fifth clause, asserting the supremacy of the national constitution was changed so as to
leave no doubt that among powers reserved to the states was that "to
prescribe the qualifications for the elective franchise therein, with
which right Congress cannot interfere." There was also disagreement
on the seventh clause, which originally read: "That it is with proud and
unfeigned satisfaction that we recur to the conduct of the American
soldier all through the recent conflict—his courage, his endurance merit
our highest encomiums." Senator Hendricks felt that this clause was
ambiguous. "What soldier does it mean?" he asked. Senator Cowan said
the intention was "to include the soldiers of *both armies.*" Southerners
concurred in this, but some Northerners vehemently opposed it. A
Michigan delegate said that he "had sacrificed his political position at
home by consulting the sensitiveness of the South. He would do so no
longer. It was that which had prepared the way for the rebellion, and he
did not mean to repeat the mistakes of former years . . . he could never
consent to extend equal applause to the men who had been in arms
against the Government." To preserve harmony, the committee omitted the resolution altogether, but inserted another one simply stating it
to be the "duty of the National Government to recognize the services of
Federal soldiers and sailors . . . by meeting promptly and fully their
just and rightful claims."[20]

The "Declaration" concluded with an avowal of confidence in Andrew
Johnson, "a Chief Magistrate worthy of the nation, and equal to the
great crisis upon which his lot is cast [to whom] we tender . . . in the
discharge of his high and responsible duties our profound respect, and
assurances of our cordial and sincere support."

The longer, and more important, "Address" was a lucid restatement
of Johnson's states' rights and restoration policy. The former Confederate States, it said,

> are, one and all, in an attitude of loyalty toward the government,
> and of sworn allegiance to the Constitution of the United States. In

no one of them is there the slightest indication of resistance to this authority, or the slightest protest against its just and binding obligation. . . . There is no section of the country where the Constitution and the laws of the United States find a more prompt and entire obedience than in those States and among those people who were lately in arms against them; or where there is less purpose or less danger of any further attempt to overthrow their authority. [Yet Congress had proclaimed that] the Federal Government may now claim over the States, the territory, and the people involved in the insurrection, the rights of war,—the right of conquest and of confiscation, the right to abrogate all existing governments, institutions, and laws, and to subject the territory conquered and its inhabitants to such laws, regulations, and deprivations, as the legislative department of the government may see fit to impose. . . . Such action finds no warrant in the Constitution, but is at war with every principle of our government, and with the very existence of free institutions.

The "Address" rejected the "laws of war" as the basis for congressional policies and actions, for they "relate solely, so far as the rights they confer are concerned, to wars waged between alien and independent nations, and can have no place or force . . . in a war waged by a government to suppress an insurrection of its own people, upon its own soil, against its authority."[21] In this important passage, the convention sought to undermine the theoretical foundation upon which Congress rested its case for reconstruction against the president's restoration.

Merely to read these declarations issuing from the Philadelphia convention is to understand why the National Union movement could never serve Republican unity. The radicals would, of course, reject it, and with no reference to the Fourteenth Amendment it would be unacceptable to the most conciliatory moderates. The National Union convention had taken its stand as the adversary, not merely of the radical minority in Congress, but of the Republican majority. For Henry J. Raymond the result was tragic; permitting himself to be used by the convention, he paid the price of banishment by his party and the end of his political career.

Whatever the difficulties inherent in the movement, they did not dampen the enthusiasm of the delegates or their followers. John A. Dix wrote to Johnson that the convention was "the most able, harmonious and enthusiastic body of men of such magnitude I have ever met in my long acquaintance with political affairs. I cannot be mistaken when I say it ensured the success of your patriotic and unwavering efforts to heal the breach between the two great sections of the Union."[22] Dix, and many others, yearned for an end of postwar turmoil, which now appeared to be at hand. This first truly national convention in six years had given Southerners an opportunity to show their loyalty to the Union and their moderation; Andrew Johnson, with such a movement back of him, might lead the nation to peace. As Howard K. Beale has said, "The National Union Convention was a huge Johnson rally."[23] But despite the euphoria, the movement never became a party. If its program precluded Republicans from joining it, the Democrats might use it to their advantage without disrupting their ancient party ties. Less than a month after the convention some of the early advocates of the movement saw its basic weaknesses and were drifting away from it.

Before adjournment the convention appointed a committee, consisting of two delegates from each state and Reverdy Johnson as chairman, to call on the president at the White House and to present him with a copy of the proceedings. "In you, Mr. President," said the chairman at the White House meeting, "the convention recognize a chief magistrate devoted to the Constitution and laws and the interests of the whole country. The course of Congress in holding ten States as subjected provinces is at war with the very genius of our Government and prejudicial to the peace and safety of the country."[24] In a passionate reply, Johnson gave his listeners a foretaste of what would follow when he entered personally into the campaign. Professing to be overwhelmed by the occasion and by the faith the convention had shown in him, he said, "I think we may justly conclude that we are acting under a proper inspiration, and that we need not be mistaken that the finger of an overruling and unerring Providence is in this great movement." The executive department had tried "to restore the Union, to heal the breach, to pour oil into the wounds which were consequent upon the struggle. . . . [But] we find a disturbing and marring element opposing us."

> We have witnessed in one department of the Government every endeavor to prevent the restoration of peace, harmony, and Union. We have seen hanging upon the verge of the Government, as it were, a body called, or which assumes to be, the Congress of the United States, while in fact it is a Congress of only a part of the States. We have seen this Congress pretend to be for the Union, when its every step and act tended to perpetuate disunion and make a disruption of the States inevitable. Instead of promoting reconciliation and harmony, its legislation has partaken of the character of penalties, retaliation, and revenge. This has been the course and the policy of one portion of your Government.

In contrast, "the humble individual who is now addressing you . . . takes his stand upon that charter of our liberties the [Constitution] as the great rampart of civil and religious liberty." Having been taught in his youth to hold it sacred, "and having done so during my whole public career, I shall ever continue to reverence the Constitution of my fathers and to make it my guide."

The executive department, he said, had been accused of being "despotic and tyrannical. Let me ask this audience of distinguished gentlemen to point to a vote I ever gave, to a speech I ever made, to a single act of my whole public life, that has not been against tyranny and despotism." It was Congress that had "encroach[ed] step by step upon constitutional rights, and violate[d]. day after day and month after month, fundamental principles of Government." Having "passed through every position, from alderman of a village to the Presidency of the United States," he had had "enough to gratify a reasonable ambition." If he had wanted authority or desired to perpetuate his own power, "how easily could I have held and wielded that which was placed in my hands by the measure called the Freedmen's Bureau Bill. . . . I could have proclaimed myself dictator."

As to the Philadelphia convention, for which the committee spoke, Johnson considered its proceedings "equal to, if not more important than, those of any convention ever assembled in the United States." When compared with Congress "whose policy, if persisted in, will destroy the country," he regarded it as more important than any convention since 1787 and its declarations "equal to those contained in the Declaration of Independence." They were, indeed, "a second Declaration of Independence."[25]

A fortnight after the adjournment of the National Union Convention, just as Andrew Johnson began his Swing Around the Circle, the Southern Loyalists met, also in Philadelphia. Among the southern delegates at this assembly were H. C. Warmouth and Thomas Durant of Louisiana, Albion W. Tourgée of North Carolina, John Minor Botts of Virginia, and Governor "Parson" Brownlow of Tennessee. Durant was selected as temporary chairman and James Speed of Kentucky, the former attorney general of the United States, as permanent chairman. To swell their ranks and to demonstrate that theirs too was a national movement a number of men were invited from the northern states. A large delegation from Pennsylvania, headed by Governor Curtin, came, along with such Republican luminaries as Oliver P. Morton, Lyman Trumbull, Zachariah Chandler of Michigan, and Carl Schurz, who at the time was editor of a Detroit newspaper. After assembling together in Independence Square, the Northerners and Southerners proceeded to form separate conventions, with most of the attention focused on the southern group.

In his address, Speed spoke of the recent National Union Convention "which came here to simply record its abject submission to the commands of one man. . . . [But] the loyal Congress of the United States had refused to do his commands; and whenever you have a Congress that does not resolutely and firmly refuse, as the present Congress has done, to merely act as the recording secretary of the tyrant at the White House, American Liberty is gone forever."[26]

In its "address" the convention made an "appeal for protection and justice to the friends and brothers in the States that have been spared the cruelties of the Rebellion and the direct horrors of Civil War. . . . Our last hope, under God, is in the unity and firmness of the States that elected Abraham Lincoln and defeated Jefferson Davis." What followed was a bill of particulars against Andrew Johnson, who had "resorted to the weapon of traitors to bruise and beat down patriots," had "practiced upon the maxim that none but traitors shall rule," had removed from office "brave men, who had fought the great battle for the Union" and replaced them with "avowed rebels," had "corrupted the local courts by offering premiums for the defiance of the laws of Congress, and by openly discouraging the observance of the oath against treason," had "pardoned some of the worst rebel criminals . . . , including some who have taken human life under circumstances of unparalleled atrocity." "In every State south of Mason and Dixon's line," it read, "his policy has wrought the most deplorable consequences—social, moral, and political."[27]

The northern pro-Johnson press, led by the *New York Herald*, lashed out at the Southern Loyalists' Convention. Labeling it the "Nigger-Worshippers' Convention," the *Herald* said, "Such an aggregation of the freaks of nature, physically and mentally, in the shape of humanity, was never seen before." Why was the original "Southern Loyalists' Convention" now being called the "Loyalists' Convention"? Probably because "the managers found that it would be a very beggarly affair if confined to the 'white trash' of the South," for "in the sense in which the radicals use the word 'loyalist' there are but few white men in the South who come under the designation."[28]

Just as the presence of Copperheads had embarrassed the National Union Convention, so the presence of blacks and the question of Negro suffrage embarrassed the Southern Loyalists' Convention. Despite the protests of some white delegates that they would not attend the convention along with blacks, the blacks were admitted; but they were all but ignored. Frederick Douglass, their leader, was made a member of a committee to tour the North during the Campaign, but only over the noisy protests of some delegates. Morton of Indiana, while he had abandoned Johnson and his program, still rejected Negro suffrage and pleaded with Theodore Tilton "to prevail on Frederick Douglass to take the first train . . . home, in order to save the Republican party from detriment."[29]

While the convention was in progress Thaddeus Stevens addressed a crowd in Bedford, Pennsylvania, where he vehemently defended the rights of black people: "I care not what you may say about negro equality—I care not what you may say of radicalism, these are my principles, and with the help of God I shall die with them." But two days later Stevens expressed his private concern about too much display of Negro rights at the Southern Loyalists' Convention: "A good many people here are disturbed by the practical exhibition of social equality in the arm-in-arm performance of Douglass and Tilton. It does not become radicals like us to particularly object. But it was certainly unfortunate at this time. The old prejudice, now revealed, will lose us some votes. Why it was done I cannot see except as a foolish bravado. The Massachusetts and S. Carolina [performance] was disgusting enough. This I fear will neutralize it."[30]

The convention's difficulties with its black delegates gave the *Herald* an opening for another caustic attack. Since it was the "niggers" who "form the great majority of the Southern loyalists, why," queried the *Herald*,

> is not the Convention composed chiefly of these blacks? Why were not some of the distinguished and numerous Pompeys, Caesars, Scipios, George Washingtons, and Tom Jeffersons chosen as delegates? If they are intelligent enough to have the elective franchise and are entitled to all the privileges of white men, it is flat usurpation on the part of . . . the Convention to keep them out. Why does not Fred Douglass denounce this hypocrisy? He ought to see to it that the political tricksters do not use him and his race for their own benefit. Not only ought the Southern negroes to be most largely represented, but one of them ought to be President of the Convention.[31]

The conflicts within both Philadelphia conventions and their vulnerability to the attacks of their enemies show the continuing bitterness and prejudices of the war years and how difficult it would have been to make the election a national referendum on the really important matters awaiting solution. There was nothing to indicate that 1866 would be a year in which either restoration or reconstruction would be achieved.

The decision of Andrew Johnson to enter personally into the campaign of 1866 was a most unusual one. Rarely in mid-nineteenth century America did presidents or presidential candidates enter these contests. There was an unwritten but well understood rule that such activity was beneath the dignity of the presidential office. "It [had] been the decorous habit of the Chief Magistrate of the Country," said James G. Blaine, "when upon a tour of his fellow citizens, to refrain from all display of partisanship, and to receive popular congratulations with brief and cordial thanks."[32] But an invitation from the citizens of Chicago to a ceremony for the laying of the cornerstone of a monument to Stephen A. Douglas was irresistible to the president and was the occasion for his famous Swing Around the Circle. Some of Johnson's friends, knowing his penchant for careless and provocative statements in his public appearances, were apprehensive about the tour. Welles reluctantly agreed to go but would have been "glad to be relieved and [had] never at any time advised the excursion."[33] Thomas Ewing, while sympathizing with Johnson for the abuse he had taken from the radicals and fearing for his life, urged him not to go.[34]

Also, the appropriateness of the president's participation in a celebration for Stephen A. Douglas was questioned. The *New York Herald* applauded the decision of the president to attend what would be "one of the most striking ceremonial events of the kind ever witnessed in the country."[35] But James Russell Lowell, writing in the *North American Review*, was of a diametrically opposite view.

> Who was Stephen A. Douglas [Lowell asked] that the President, with his Cabinet and the two highest officials of the army and navy, should add their official dignity to the raising of his monument, and make the whole country an accomplice in consecrating his memory? His name is not associated with a single measure of national importance, unless upon the wrong side. So far was he from being a statesman, that, even on the lower ground of politics, both his principles and his expression of them were tainted with the reek of vulgar associations.[36]

Actually, there is something explicable and reasonable in Johnson's visit to Douglas's tomb; for he was appealing to the non-Copperhead Democrats, of whom Douglas was an exemplar. In theory and practice, Johnson's scheme of restoration rested on convictions about the Constitution and the nation that were remarkably similar to Douglas's principles of localism and states' rights. And, if we may be permitted a conjecture, it is difficult to see how Douglas, if he had lived through the war and into the Reconstruction era, could have been elsewhere than solidly in the Johnson camp.

Confident that he could win over the people if he could meet them face-to-face, the President and his party set out from Washington on August 28 on the famous Swing Around the Circle, which took them north along the eastern seaboard to Philadelphia and New York, up the Hudson to Albany, thence west to Chicago via Cleveland and Detroit, through Springfield, Illinois, to St. Louis, then east again to Louisville, Indianapolis, and Pittsburgh, and back to Washington on September 15. In the party were the president's daughter, Mrs. Patterson, General Grant and Admiral Farragut, Secretaries Seward, Randall, Welles, and Mrs. Welles, along with some fifty others including secretaries. By their very presence the two military heroes, without public utterances, lent their prestige to the president's cause; but they were reluctant fellow travelers. On the other hand, Seward, a strong advocate of the journey, became, next to the president himself, its greatest liability. He had long since lost all credibility with the radicals and many moderates. Sumner, writing to John Bright during the tour, said of him: "Seward seems to have lost his wits as well as principles."[37] The *Nation* accused him of having forgotten civilized usages and of "vie[ing] with the President in rant and indecency" and of speaking "nothing but churlish nonsense, mingled with doctrines utterly subversive of free government."[38]

The Democrats were equally contemptuous of Seward. Campaigning in Missouri, Francis P. Blair, Jr., classed Seward with Stanton "and the rest of the scoundrels . . . the President has about him." One of Blair's hopes for the National Union movement was that it would drive both Stanton and Seward from the cabinet while organizing the Democratic party.[39] At various points during the journey there were slights and thinly veiled insults to the secretary of state. In introducing the president and his party to an assembly at the New York state capitol, Governor Fenton deliberately ignored Seward, who stood next to the president. Even in Auburn, New York, his home town, Seward received a cold reception. Toward the end of the tour he fell gravely ill with cholera and was forced to leave the party. It appeared for a time that he might not survive.[40]

If the secretary of state did not enhance the campaign, it was still Johnson himself who did the most harm. While repeatedly disclaiming any intention of making a speech, Johnson did make speeches, actually the same speech over and over again. Only the degree of intemperance distinghished one from another. As was his wont, he repeated endlessly the story of his humble background, his trade as a tailor, his climb up the political ladder from village alderman to the presidency. Early on, in New York, he took up the theme that, with the rebellion "crushed in the South," he now intended "to fight out the battle with Northern traitors." His speeches were studded with first-person pronouns—"I", "Me", "My", and "Myself"—so that soon his critics were labeling his restoration policy as "My Policy."

The first serious encounter with an audience occurred at Cleveland where, despite the hostile feeling toward the president in an enclave of radicalism, the city officials prepared a reception due the president of the United States. With complete insensitivity to what the occasion called for, Johnson entered into a harangue against his enemies. Soon the audience was giving it back to him, and the whole thing because senseless and ludicrous. "Notwithstanding the subsidized gang of hirelings and traducers," said Johnson, "I have discharged all my duties and fulfilled all my pledges, and I say . . . that if my predecessor had lived the vials of wrath would have poured out upon him." Somebody in the crowd answered, "Never." "Three cheers for the Congress of the United States."

Johnson: "I called upon your Congress that is trying to break up the Government."

"Cries from the audience: 'You be d——d.' Cheers mingled with hisses . . . 'Don't get mad, Andy.' "

Johnson: "Who can come and place his finger on one pledge I have ever violated, or one principle I have ever proved false to." A voice: "How about New Orleans? Hang Jeff Davis."[41]

Gauche as was the Cleveland encounter, it was not the worst. Five days later Johnson spoke from the portico of the Southern Hotel in St. Louis. He had barely begun to speak when somebody in the crowd called out, "New Orleans." Johnson responded with his explanation of the riot in that city, concluding with an accusation against Congress for having caused it: "every drop of blood that was shed is upon their skirts, and they are responsible for it." For this and for other things, Johnson claimed, he had been traduced and maligned: "I have been called Judas Iscariot and all that. . . . There was a Judas, and he was one of the twelve apostles. Oh! Yes, the twelve apostles had a Christ [A voice, 'And a Moses, too'; laughter]. The twelve apostles had a Christ, and he never could have had a Judas unless he had twelve apostles. If I have played the Judas, who has been my Christ that I have played the Judas with? Was it Thad. Stevens? Was it Wendell Phillips? Was it Charles Sumner? [Hisses and cheers.] These are the men that . . . compare themselves with the Savior; and everybody that differs with them in opinion, and to try to stay and arrest their diabolical and nefarious policy, is to be denounced as Judas. ['Hurrah for Andy!' and cheers]."[42]

In Indianapolis Morton and other political leaders did not put in an appearance at Johnson's meeting. Violence broke out, and the president found it impossible to speak. But there were cries for Grant, whose presence Johnson had counted on to help his cause. By this time, however, the taciturn general had become thoroughly disenchanted with the journey. The correspondent of the *New York Herald* reported him as saying, "I am disgusted with this trip. I am disgusted at hearing a man make speeches on the way to his own funeral." He was also disgusted to be traveling in the company of and being introduced by John Hogan, a St. Louis Copperhead who accompanied the party from St. Louis to Washington and assumed the role of introducing the dignitaries.

Toward the end of the journey city and state officials were openly avoiding the president's appearances. The mayor of Pittsburgh explained why: "I should be pleased to assist in doing honor to the Chief Magistrate of the United States, if I had a reasonable expectation he would refrain upon the occasion . . . from stigmatizing those whose views of reconstruction coincide with my own, as traitors on the Northern side of the line. The speeches made by Andrew Johnson in other cities prevent me from believing that he will. I am therefore constrained, from motives of self-respect, to decline your invitation."[43]

The radicals must have been delighted with Johnson's conduct during the Swing Around the Circle, for it gave them just the opportunity they needed to launch a remorseless attack on him. A party of speakers from the Southern Loyalists' Convention in Philadelphia was dispatched to follow on the heels of the president; they were joined by others along the route. Among them were Andrew Jackson ("Jack") Hamilton, a former Texas secessionist turned Unionist and radical; Gen. Benjamin Butler; Governor "Parson" Brownlow of Tennessee, whose avowed purpose was to "wipe out the moccasin tracks of Andrew Johnson and William H. Seward [and of the] untamed and unmitigated Copperheads who are sliming and crawling along" behind them.[44] "By the assassination of Abraham Lincoln," said Charles Sumner,

> the rebellion . . . vaulted into the Presidential chair. Jefferson Davis was then in the casements at Fortress Monroe, but Andrew Johnson was doing his work. . . . Witness Memphis; witness New Orleans. Who can doubt that the President is the author of these tragedies? Charles IX of France was not more completely the author of the massacre of St. Bartholomew than Andrew Johnson is the author of those recent massacres which now cry for

judgment. . . . The blood of Memphis and New Orleans must cry out until it is heard, and a guilty President may suffer the same retribution which followed a guilty King. . . . Next to Jefferson Davis stands Andrew Johnson as [the Republic's] worst enemy.

Carl Schurz added, "If there is any man that ought to hang . . . it is Andrew Johnson."[45] Others charged him with drunkenness and immorality. Radicals in Ohio and Wisconsin accused him of being implicated in Lincoln's assassination.[46] Speaking in Cincinnati in early October, Ben Butler announced that Congress had already won the election and that its next order of business was the impeachment of the president.[47] In Pennsylvania Thaddeus Stevens told his constituents:

I cannot begin to attempt to unfold the policy of that man, in whom the people confided as a true patriot, and whom we have now found to be worse than the man who is incarcerated in Fortress Monroe. . . . You all remember that in Egypt the Lord sent frogs, locusts, murrain and lice, and finally demanded the blood of the first born of all the oppressors. Almost all of these have been sent upon us. More than the first born has been taken from us. We have been oppressed with taxes, and debts, and He has sent us more than lice, and has afflicted us with Andrew Johnson.[48]

Probably more effective in the campaign against Johnson than the radical onslaught was the work of two gifted satirists, Thomas Nast, the famous cartoonist for *Harper's Weekly,* and David R. Locke, better known by his nom de plume, Petroleum V. Nasby. Nast opened his attack with a cartoon on the Philadelphia convention, which he labeled "The Tearful Convention." In the center were the leading delegates of Massachusetts and South Carolina, arm-in-arm, bounded on right and left by a Confederate crocodile shedding copious tears and a Yankee serpent also weeping. At top center were the delegates again, with animal heads, entering two-by-two as in Noah's ark. Flanking this were delegates embracing on the left, and on the right Vallandigham and Wood being ejected from the convention. At botton center was a lachrymose Andrew Johnson overcome with emotion upon receiving the report of the convention's proceedings. To Andy's right and left were more delegates over the captions "Patriotic Sentiment" and "Unbroken Harmony," but with their mouths padlocked shut.[49] Another Nast cartoon published just before the November election showed "King Andy" crowned and seated on his throne, flanked by Welles and Seward, who presided over the execution of the leading radicals; at "King Andy's" feet sat a despondent and shackled "Liberty." An earlier cartoon had death as a ghostly apparition hovering over the slaughter at New Orleans and issuing a "Timely Warning to Union Men."[50]

If the shafts of Petroleum V. Nasby were not so stinging as Nast's, they were probably equally effective, and they were unremitting. Nasby presented himself as the "Late pastor of the Church of the New Dispensation, Chaplain to His Excellency the President, and [Postmaster] at Confederate X Roads, Kentucky"; his comments on the campaign were published in the form of public letters. He opened with an explanation of how he became a delegate to the National Union Convention.

> I wuzn't elected nor nothin, and hedn't any credentials; but . . . the door-keeper wuz a Dimokrat, and my breath helped me; my nose, which . . . blossoms like a lobster, wuz of yoose; but I spect my hevin a gray coat on, with a stand up collar, with a brass star onto it, wuz wat finished the biznis. . . . Doolittle, who wuz the Cheerman, winked at Randall, and nodded his head, when Randall announced that THE DELEGATES FROM SOUTH KARLINY, AND THE DELEGATES FROM MASSACHOOSITS, WOOD ENTER ARM IN ARM! With a slow and measured step they cum in; and, at a signal from Randall, the cheerin commenst—and sich cheerin! Then Doolittle pulled out his white hankercher, and applied it to his eyes. . . . I saw a comin back the good old times when thirty-four States met in convensun, and let eleven rule em; and ez I contemplated the scene, I too wept, but it wuz in dead earnest.
>
> "Wat are you blubberin for?" asked a enthusiastic delegate in front uv me, who wuz a swabbin his eyes with a handkercher.
>
> "I'm a Postmaster," sez I, "and must do my dooty in this crisis. Wat are you sheddin pearls for?" retorted I. "Are you a Postmaster?"
>
> "No," sez he; "but I hope to be;" and he swabbed away with renood vigger.
>
> "Wat's the matter with the eys uv all the delegates?" sez I.
>
> "They've all got Post Offisis in em," sez he; and he worked away faster than ever.

Nasby then followed Johnson on his tour and reported on his progress. At Cleveland, he said, "we begun to get into hot water."

> Here is the post to which the devil uv Ablishnism is chained, and his chain is long enough to let him rage over neerly the whole State. I am pained to state the President wuzn't treated here with the respeck due his station. He commenst deliverin his speech, but wuz

made the subjeck uv ribald laffture. Skasely hed he got to the pint uv swingin around the cirkle, when a foul-mouthed nigger-lover yelled "Veto!" and another vocifferated "Noo Orleens!" and another remarked "Memphis!" and one after another interruption occurred until His Highness wuz completely turned off the track, and got wild. He forgot his speech, and struck out crazy, but the starch wuz out uv him, and he wuz worsted. Grant, wich we hed taken along to draw crowds, played dirt on us here, and stepped onto a boat for Detroit, leavin us only Farragut ez a attraction, who tried to git away ditto, but wuz timely prevented. The President recovered his ekanimity, and swung around the cirkle wunst, and leavin the Constooshn in their hands, retired.

And so the lampooning went, all the way back to Washington. Nasby concluded his lengthy account with a brief postscript: "I forgot to menshun that at Chicago we laid the cornerstone uv a monument to Douglas. The occurrence hed entirely slipped my memory."[51]

The reception Johnson received upon his return to Washington was quite in contrast to the scenes at Cleveland, St. Louis, Indianapolis, and Pittsburgh, and it must have warmed his heart. Whether it was a truly spontaneous greeting may be questioned, but the Washington city council, the mayor, and various patriotic organizations arranged for him to be greeted with the fanfare and ceremony befitting a victorious national leader on his return from the campaigns. Johnson was convinced that he had successfully made his case to the people. Despite radical opposition, wrote Gideon Welles, "the people were, and are, obviously with him. The President himself has sanguine belief that he has so aroused his countrymen that they will sanction his measures for reestablishing the Union on the Constitutional lines and oppose the Radicals' revolutionary measures."[52] But these were the illusions of the leader, too immersed in his cause to see reality, for by the time Johnson returned to Washington the victory was passing to the radicals. The National Union party was not working out as a middle alternative between Democracy and radicalism; in some states the Democrats were taking it over, and it was no longer a viable political force.

Events in New York—where with leaders such as Raymond, Weed, and John A. Dix, there was reason to be hopeful—are illustrative of the malaise afflicting the new party. Weed, the architect of the movement in New York, planned to have the war Democrat John A. Dix nominated for governor with the support of Dean Richmond, the state Democratic leader. It was far from certain that Richmond actually approved of the scheme, but his death a short time before the state convention made the whole question academic. When the convention met in Albany on September 11, the Democrats brazenly took charge and nominated Mayor John T. Hoffman of New York City, a Copperhead-Tammany Democrat. Meanwhile, the Republicans had nominated Reuben E. Fenton, a radical.[53]

We have noted the difficulties of Henry J. Raymond at the Philadelphia convention. The collapse of the National Union party in New York was the coup de grâce ending his political career. Already the National Committee of the Republican party had expelled him, an action approved immediately by the New York Republican State Convention. Invited by a group of conservative Republicans to run again for Congress, Raymond, in a long public letter, declined their invitation and made known his decision to withdraw from active political life. Reflecting upon his participation in the Philadelphia movement, he said, "I believed, and I still believe, that I was endeavoring to do a useful and patriotic work, fully in harmony with the principles of the Union party. . . . I am now as I was when elected two years ago,—as I have always been, and shall always remain,—a member of the Union party. . . . With the Democratic party, as it has been organized and directed since the rebellion broke out, I have nothing in common . . . and shall regard its re-established ascendancy in the government of the country, State or national, as a public calamity." But because he no longer had the approval of a large body of those who had voted for him and "a seat in Congress ceases to have for me any attraction, or to offer an opportunity for useful public service," he had best "consult my self-respect, as well as the sentiments of my constituents and the interest of the Union cause, by withdrawing my name for the canvass altogether."[54]

A few days later Raymond repudiated Andrew Johnson. "We have tried very hard to hold our original faith in his personal honesty, and to attribute his disastrous action to errors of judgment and infirmities of temper," he said. "The struggle has often been difficult, and we can maintain it no longer."[55] Another reason for Raymond's abandonment of Johnson was the serious decline in the circulation of the *New York Times* as the president became more and more unpopular.[56]

Even before the *Times* turned away from Johnson, the *New York Herald* had begun to waver in its support. The tenuous position of Raymond, the Democratic dominance of the National Union party in New York, and the dangerous decline in the *Times*'s circulation made its decision explicable. But for Bennet's *Herald* to abandon Johnson must have been unthinkable to men around the president. After all, the *Herald* had issued the first call for the new party, had been glowing in its praise of the president and acrimonious in its attack on the radicals.

Its correspondent reported the president's campaign in the most meticulous and glowing detail. Yet more than a week before Johnson returned to Washington the editorial tone of the paper had changed. It began with the elections in Vermont and Maine in September. Although the election in Vermont, where the radicals won, was not viewed by the *Herald* as necessarily a bad omen, it was a warning that they were "stripped for action all over the North, and intend that it shall be no child's play; and from all the signs of the times, if these radicals are successful, we may certainly look to a reign of terror."[57] Two days later, however, with the imminence of the Maine election, the *Herald*'s editorials took on a more ominous tone. Now there was real danger of a radical victory and of an " 'irrepressible conflict' between a radical Congress and a Conservative administration." The "tone and spirit" of the radical campaign was comparable to "the revolutionary fermentations of Paris which preceded the bloody Jacobins and their reign of terror." If another radical Congress should be elected "we may look before the expiration of the next session of the present Congress for the removal of Andrew Johnson from the White House, through his indictment by the House of Representatives and his impeachment by the Senate, with Chief Justice Chase in the chair." Such an event would insure "such a reconstruction of the government as will save the people any further trouble in its regulation short of a sanguinary revolution." The next chapter of "civil commotion and bloodshed" would not take place in the southern states, which had "had enough of fire, sword and flame, slaughter and destruction to last them at least for several generations." It would "break out among the clashing political elements of our Northern cities, and woe to those by whom these fires shall be kindled." Such dangers could be avoided with a conservative victory. But, asked the *Herald*, "Are the conservative masses of the North awake and at work, and do their leaders comprehend the urgent necessity for vigorous action? Or are they more intent upon the spoils than the triumph of the President's policy?"[58]

On the day of the elections in Maine, September 10, the tone of the editorial was calmer. The real struggle for control of the Fortieth Congress, it said, would not take place in Maine, which lay in a "distant eddy, in which the great running currents of public opinion [were] comparatively only lightly felt," but in the October elections in Pennsylvania, Ohio, and Indiana.[59] However, the decisiveness of the radical victory in Maine was such as to require a "larger explanation." The *Herald* found it in the riots in New Orleans and Memphis, where "the ugly fact stands forth in gloomy relief that Southern whites and negroes sympathizing with the Northern radical party were deliberately murdered by Southern desperadoes and municipal officials who had been notoriously active as Southern rebels in the late rebellion."[60]

Without waiting for the October elections, the *Herald* now changed its political stance. The election in Maine having demonstrated the futility of Johnson's cause, he was now called upon to adopt a statesman-like policy by making a truce with Congress and actively cooperating with the "fixed and predominant public opinion of the North" for the restoration of the southern states on the basis of the Fourteenth Amendment. Such a policy would be closer to Johnson's policy than to Thaddeus Stevens's. The *Herald* now became aware that Congress did properly have a role in the restoration process. Under the war powers and in the absence of Congress, it said, the president had "an almost unlimited power of discretion. . . . But with the reassembling of Congress this business constitutionally reverted from the Executive to Congress, the law making department. . . . Upon this point there should have been no controversy . . . as to the right of Congress when in session to legislate upon Southern reconstruction." Nor would the President have to make any "sacrifice of principle or consistency . . . in supporting [the] constitutional amendment." The rupture between the president and Congress had been unwise and unfortunate for the administration, and to persist in the quarrel would "result in nothing but mischief." Delay would only play into the radicals' hands; the only course open to Johnson was to cooperate with Congress in the ratification of the amendment, to use his influence with the southern states to that end, to bring about a speedy restoration on the Tennessee model, and possibly to prevent his own impeachment. Now the newspaper most adamant in its promotion of the National Union party, with its rejection of the Fourteenth Amendment, assured its readers that the amendment was not a Jacobin measure after all and admitted that Johnson had made a mistake in not accepting it.

Belatedly calling on the president to establish himself on the middle ground between the two extremes, the "radical Copperhead" and the "radical niggerhead" factions, the *Herald* beseeched him to issue a proclamation calling on the governors of the southern states to convene their legislatures for the purpose of ratification. Belatedly the *Herald* saw that there was, or had been, a moderate middle-of-the-road faction with which Johnson might have cooperated. But what the *Herald* failed to see was that it was too late. Repeatedly, as has been shown, the moderates had appealed to the president to join them. Repeatedly they had been rebuffed. Now, especially since Johnson's Swing Around the Circle, the contest was no longer one between him and the radicals but between him and Congress. Finally, the *Herald* came to grips with one of the essential realities of national politics in 1866; it regretted that Andrew Johnson had not also done so. Learning that he had authorized "an emphatic denial" that he would modify his policy and recommend ratification of the amendment to the southern states, the *Herald* lamented that he was passing up a "golden opportunity" leading "to the conclusion that he comprehends neither the advantages nor the dangers of the present situation."[61]

The fears expressed by the *Herald* were well founded. The Republicans carried all four October states—Pennsylvania, Ohio, Indiana, and Iowa. In Ohio the Republicans overcame some early factionalism and combined to win over strong Democratic opposition. Governor Jacob D. Cox, who had been a leader in the Johnson movement in the state, repudiated the president and became president of the anti-Johnson Soldiers and Sailors Convention in Pittsburgh in late September. In his speech to the convention Cox charged Johnson with being "false to his principles."

> It was not pleasant to find ourselves brought face to face with this fact; but now, seeing that the fact is so, seeing that we are pledged to recognize the truth, that it has entered into the minds of some to exalt the Executive department of the government into a despotic power, and to abase the representative portion of our government into the mere tools of despotism—learning that this is the case, we now, as heretofore, know our duty, and knowing dare maintain it.[62]

In Indiana the vigorous campaign of Oliver P. Morton, who threw all of his great authority and prestige against Johnson, was a decisive factor. In November the Republicans carried the remainder of the northern states as well as West Virginia and Missouri. The Democrats won in Delaware, Maryland, and Kentucky. The Republican majorities in the fortieth Congress would enable it to override presidential vetoes and thus to proceed with its own reconstruction policy.[63]

In the feverish atmosphere of the last six weeks of the campaign rumors were rife that one side or the other would use force to take over the government. In the midst of this turmoil the Grand Army of the Republic came into being. Founded as an organization to assure Union veterans of their bounties, to assist them in finding jobs, and to continue the camaraderie of the war years, the G.A.R. soon turned its attention to politics, with the primary mission of preventing Democrats from coming into the control of the government, to "vindicate the rights of the American people at the polls as nobly as they did in the field." Those who had saved the Union by putting down the rebellion were "resolved to repeat the chastisement of the same spirit of evil, now clothed with the treacherous garb of 'my policy' at the ballot box." They felt themselves entitled to "the dispensation of the fruits of their victory and a controlling voice in shaping the destiny of this great Republic."[64]

Some men who hated and feared the radicals urged Johnson to protect himself and the government with military force. Congress was revolutionary, wrote one of these, and the president was "as much bound to put it down as was Abraham Lincoln to wage the war to suppress the late rebellion." An Ohio correspondent thought Johnson should issue a call for 500,000 volunteers, and assured him that Ohio would send 50,000 in thirty days to do its part in preventing the destruction of the government.[65]

A clamor arose again to get rid of Secretary of War Stanton and to replace him with either Sherman or Grant. A rumor circulated that Sherman would be brought to Washington as secretary of war and that Stanton would become minister to Spain; but there was uncertainty now whether Sherman still supported Johnson, as he had earlier. Although the rumor reached the general, he received no official communication from the president. Even if the offer had been made, it is unlikely that Sherman would have accepted it. His brother, Senator John Sherman, appealed to him not allow his name to be connected with the administration. By doing so, wrote the senator, "You lose in every way. . . . it connects you as a partisan with Johnson—just what he wants, but what you ought to dread."[66]

The rumors circulating about the G.A.R. appeared to have some credence, enough at least that Johnson commissioned one Charles O'Beirne to investigate them. O'Beirne discovered a considerable distribution of arms to members of the organization, who did not always know for what purpose they were intended. But the leaders, said O'Beirne, in cooperation with Morton and other mid-western governors, meant violence and that "nothing will avert it but a positive[,] determined[,] and fearless attitude of the President backed up by preparations and reliable armed force to execute his constant prerogatives." He viewed Indiana as "a fit country for military occupation . . . to keep down the Radicals."[67]

The reports were frightening enough that Johnson did take steps to protect the government. General Grant visited Baltimore, a city of tension where mobs were wont to become violent, where he disposed the troops to defend against an attack. He also reported to the president that of the 2,224 troops in the vicinity of Washington only 1,550 were effectives. This prompted Johnson, on the eve of the November elections, to order Stanton to prepare "at once" to insure the safety of the government "and thus discourage any attempt for its possession by insurgent or other illegal combinations."[68]

Although the possibility of violence, or even a coup d'état, cannot be discounted, the rumors, the threats, and the ominous reports seem to reflect more accurately the unsettled state of the country a year and a half after the end of the war. Even in the best of times hyperbole is a characteristic of American politics, of the biennial national rites; and these were not the best of times. As yet, the nation had achieved neither restoration nor reconstruction, and the prospects for doing so were not auspicious. If either side had seriously contemplated a coup, the decisiveness of the election doomed it. For the congressional party it was no longer necessary, except as a countermeasure in the event the president might act. And for the presidential party it would have been too risky.

Despite the threats, the fears, and the chaos that characterized the campaign, a French traveler in America and commentator on the American scene felt that Americans had reason to congratulate themselves on both the conduct and the results of the election. He said: "This victorious and nevertheless peaceful struggle of a parliamentary assembly against a head of government has for us an instructive and curious side. Accustomed as we are to all the other spectacles, we cannot see without interest mingled with some surprise and even admiration, what good sense, what steadfastness, what spirit of justice the United States have displayed in coming through without a crisis which elsewhere would have set off a civil war."[69]

Chapter 10

How Johnson Lost—The Historical Debate

THE FOREGOING NARRATIVE might appear to be an adequate explanation of the results of the election of 1866. But historians have chosen not to let the question rest there. Instead, they have engaged in a lengthy debate on whether Andrew Johnson might have won and how he might have done it. In a way, the question is irrelevant, because Johnson lost, and the task of the historian is to examine what did happen rather than what did not happen. But because possibilities sometimes illuminate actualities the debate is not altogether academic.

Howard K. Beale, who wrote in the tradition of Charles A. Beard and the progressive historians, developed the thesis that Johnson's great mistake was his failure to form a third party based on economic issues. Although technically there were two parties, Beale argued, "actually there was chaos. . . . When the war ended and peacetime issues again began to interest men, the stage was set for a political upheaval." Had Johnson, then, "launched . . . an attack upon the economic views of the eastern wing of the Radical party, had he used his 'Swing 'round the Circle' to arouse the West upon this subject, he could have marshalled all the latent discontent of the West to his support, and could have split the Radical party at one blow." His "fatal error in political judgment" was his assumption that nothing could be "safely and permanently done in regard to restoring the currency, diminishing taxation and establishing the prosperity of the country on a sound and enduring basis until representation from all the States [was] present in Congress."[1] In acting on this false assumption, said Beale, Johnson played into the radicals' hands; for they knew that "underneath the quarrel over 'reconstruction' lay the great economic differences that had divided men for generations, and new problems that were to become great political issues before the century closed—the regulation of big corporations, government subsidies to business, taxation and government expenditures, currency and banking problems, and the tariff. On many of these questions Johnson could have secured more support than Stevens or Sumner."[2]

It would not have been enough, Beale continued, for Johnson merely to campaign on the great economic issues. To bring into being and to sustain a third party he would have had to use the patronage effectively. Many of the leading men in the Johnson camp appealed to him to do so, among them Governor Morton, before he went over to the radical side.

> Were I in your place, [Morton wrote] I would not fail to employ every power and instrumentality in my hands to sustain my policy, and the friends who sustain it. While it is understood that members of Congress can oppose you, and in breaking down your policy break down your administration and yet control your patronage, you may expect to have opposition and to fail. The resolute wielding of your patronage in favor of your friends, inside the Union party, cannot fail to build you up with the people and disarm the Opposition in Congress.[3]

Because Johnson "had not grown up in the northern party system, but had been superimposed upon it by chance," because the key men as well as the petty office holders "looked upon him as an intruder," said Beale, Johnson did nothing until it was too late, allowing the Radicals to use the "full force of his own patronage against him."[4]

At every point the Beale interpretation has been challenged by revisionist historians. W. R. Brock has succinctly summarized the difficulties we have already noted in the Philadelphia movement and examined its prospects as a third party. It illustrated, said Brock, "the classic difficulties of third party movements in America."

> It had to create its own organization, risk capture by one of the existing parties, or content itself with a minor role. Its chances of local success were increased [by] the decentralization of American parties, but its chances of national success were diminished by the need to capture or create organizations in so many different States. Developing only a superficial strength at the national level, and very little elsewhere, the movement failed to capture the Republican organization or to create its own in any State; and it retained influence at the time of the elections only by alliance with the Democratic party, which was proof in Republican eyes that its real purpose was the restoration of the secessionists to power.

Its tragedy was "that it did not bring Southerners into contact with men such as Bingham and Trumbull, who were near enough to the main stream of Republican thought to speak with confidence about its strength without giving the impression that everyone north of the Mason-Dixon Line was an ardent supporter of Sumner and Stevens. The Southerners met only those Northerners who had committed themselves to unqualified support of the State rights position or those like Raymond who had muzzled themselves against their better judgment."[5]

Perhaps because of his faith in economic forces as political prime movers, Beale was too optimistic in his assessment of the chances of a third party movement in 1866. Nor was he altogether accurate in his statement that Johnson waited too long to use the patronage weapon. He began to use it against some of his real or imagined enemies as early as December 1865, and continued the practice throughout the campaign, removing 1,283 postmasters and a large number of customhouse and internal revenue officials. A case in point was his campaign in Illinois against Lyman Trumbull, who was to come up for reelection in 1867. The Illinois senator was so threatened by Johnson's firing of federal officials that he introduced an amendment to an appropriations bill that would have held up the salaries of these appointees, and thus set off a debate that went on for more than three weeks before the amendment was finally voted down. Sherman argued effectively against the amendment on the grounds that by such misuse of the patronage Johnson would lose more votes than he would gain and thus persuaded both moderates and radicals to join him in defeating it.[6]

As Eric McKitrick has shown, patronage did indeed have its limitations as a political weapon: It could be "a set of silken threads useful for binding [an] organization more securely" among men "not already determined to follow other paths." It was "an adjunct of power, but hardly a perfect synonym for it."[7] W. R. Brock also shows how Johnson violated the principles necessary to the successful use of patronage. "It was accepted," wrote Brock,

> that the patronage might be used to succor those factions in the party which the President favored, but it was against the rules, as normally understood, to use patronage against the party itself. An attempt to disrupt the normal channels of recommendation and advice offended individuals and supplied grievances for hundreds of men all down the party ladder. . . . Johnson could have used patronage to build up a moderate faction against the Radicals, but he could not beat both moderates and Radicals because there was no other party group to which he could turn. . . . The acceptance of a Johnson appointment became an act of desertion, and there were

even cases in which a man became suspect because he had not earned dismissal.

Thus, Brock concludes, "Johnson's attempt to use patronage to break up the Republican party and to promote the National Union Movement . . . was . . . hopeless from the start."[8]

Interesting as are the historians' comments on patronage and the nature of third parties, they are really ancillary to the main debate on the economic issues. Before recounting and analyzing this debate in detail, a summary account of financial matters such as the national debt, the condition of the currency, the national banking operation, and the tariff will be useful.

In September 1865, the national debt was nearly $3 billion—the highest in the nation's history to that time, held in a profusion of securities bearing different rates of interest and maturing over different periods of time. The most important, and the most troublesome, of these securities were the 5-20 bonds, which had been successfully marketed by Jay Cooke and Company and paid for in legal tender (greenback) currency. Investors in 5-20s were uneasy because the government was authorized to redeem them as early as 1867, just five years after the original date of issue. Under the law the interest on these bonds was to be paid in gold, but there was no such provision for repaying the principal, an omission that led to a decade-long controversy.

Related to the debt was the matter of legal tender currency, greenbacks not redeemable in coin, issued to meet the mounting expenses of the war. By the end of the war, Congress had authorized some $450 million of these United States notes. Their value relative to gold rapidly declined, bringing a gold premium of 185 as early as 1864, and they were an important cause of wartime inflation. Whether to redeem the greenbacks in gold, whether to curtail their circulation or reduce their volume was perhaps the most difficult financial problem facing the government at the end of the war.[9]

In addition to a huge national debt and legal tender currency, the Civil War had brought forth a national banking system in place of the chaotic and variegated banking operation in existence since the demise of the Second Bank of the United States during Andrew Jackson's administration. Because the purpose of this new system, established under the Banking Acts of 1863 and 1864, was primarily to help finance the war, it was far from a perfect instrument for implementing a rational monetary policy. Even so, its existence represented a kind of victory for the Federalist-Whig tradition that had continued within the

Republican party. The acts of 1863 and 1864 provided that associations with a specified amount of capital might be chartered as national banks through the purchase of federal bonds deposited with the Comptroller of the Currency in the Treasury Department. Upon depositing the bonds the banks received national banknotes to the amount of 90 percent of their value; the notes might then be loaned out at interest and would circulate as currency. The total note issue was restricted, however, to $300 million. In 1866 the total national banknote circulation was around $280 million, an amount about equal to the circulation of state banknotes. But in that year, a 10 percent tax on state banknotes drove them out of circulation.[10]

To Secretary of the Treasury Hugh McCulloch fell the responsibility of coping with postwar problems of finance and currency. Believing that the greenbacks demanded the most urgent and most immediate attention, even before the end of 1865 he had begun his policy of contraction,

HUGH McCULLOCH
Reproduced from the collection of the Library of Congress

or withdrawal of greenbacks from circulation, for the purpose of resuming specie payments. McCulloch's experience in finance had begun thirty years earlier when, a migrant from New England, he settled in the town of Fort Wayne, Indiana. There he became manager of a branch of the State Bank of Indiana, of which he became president in 1857. He had gone to Washington as comptroller of the currency, and in 1865 Lincoln made him his third secretary of the treasury. McCulloch's ideas about currency stemmed from his banking experience; that is, "He favored a well-directed central bank similar to the Bank of England which should control the issue of notes and the discount rates for the entire country." His pronouncements on what to do about greenbacks, says Robert P. Sharkey, "reflected . . . a rigid, conservative, and essentially unimaginative mind. . . . He could see little merit and much positive evil in greenbacks. They were controlled by none of the rules of experience and legal restrictions by which a well-secured bank currency was made to serve the needs of the business community." He even doubted their constitutionality. Failing to perceive that tampering with their volume might set off an economic depression, McCulloch brought to his task not "the delicacy of a scalpel" which it called for but "the bluntness of a meat axe."[11]

During a visit to Fort Wayne in October 1865, at a dinner given in his honor, McCulloch made his views public. "I am not one of those who seem disposed to repudiate coin as a measure of value, and to make secured paper currency the standard," he said.

> On the contrary, I belong to that class of persons who, regarding an exclusive metallic currency as an impracticable thing among an enterprising and commercial people, nevertheless look upon an irredeemable currency as an evil which circumstances may for a time render a necessity, but which is never to be sustained as a policy. By common consent of the nations, gold and silver are the only true measure of value. They are the necessary regulators of trade. I have myself no more doubt that these metals were prepared by the Almighty for this very purpose, than I have that iron and coal were prepared for the purposes for which they are being used. I favor a well-secured convertible paper currency—no other can to any extent be a proper substitute for coin.
>
> The present unconvertible currency of the United States was a necessity of the war; but now that the war has ceased, and the Government ought not to be longer a borrower, this currency should be brought up to the specie standard, and I see no way of doing this but by withdrawing a portion of it from circulation.[12]

McCulloch opposed the greenbacks for reaasons other than their effect on the economy.

> There are other objections to the present inflation, [he said].
> It is, I fear, corrupting the public morals. It is converting the
> business of the country into gambling, and seriously diminishing
> the labor of the country. This is always the effect of excessive
> circulation. The kind of gambling which it produces is not confined
> to the stock and produce boards, where the very terms which are
> used by the operators indicate the nature of the transactions, but it
> is spreading through our towns and into the rural districts. Men are
> apparently getting rich, while morality languishes and the
> productive industry of the country is being diminished. Good
> morals in business, and sober, persevering industry, if not at a
> discount, are considered too old-fogyish for the present times.[13]

Although McCulloch did not go all the way to the advocacy of specie as the only proper currency, he was close enough to that position that he would have trouble as finance minister in post–Civil War America. Other men, with less experience in financial matters, saw more clearly that an expanding economy, even more subject now than before the war to periodic depressions, called for a policy more open, more flexible, and less doctrinaire than McCulloch's. Upon assuming the post of secretary of the treasury in March 1865, he announced that his "chief aim" would be "to institute measures to bring the business of the country gradually back to the specie basis, a departure from which . . . is no less damaging and demoralizing to the people than expensive to the government." Because under existing laws he could not go as far as he wished, with his first annual report in December 1865 he requested of Congress additional power to retire greenbacks for the purpose of resuming specie payments. The lower house responded promptly by passing a resolution, by a vote of 144 to 6, pledging its cooperation with the treasury in contracting the currency "with a view to as early a resumption of specie payments as the business interests of the country will permit."[14]

The vote on the House resolution was not, however, a true indication of sentiment either in or out of Congress on contraction. When Congressman Justin S. Morrill, on February 21, 1866, reported from the Ways and Means Committee a bill granting the secretary his requested authority it met with a stormy protest. Thaddeus Stevens, who favored greenbacks, thought it gave McCulloch too much power. Samuel Hooper of Massachusetts was wary about tampering with the currency, which affected the value of property and the economic interest of the whole country. He foresaw that a larger amount of money would be required to carry on the country's business and feared that "some other paper money, not so good [as the greenbacks] may be allowed to take its place, by which the country would be further than ever from a currency convertible into coin." William D. "Pig Iron" Kelley, a Pennsylvanian who, like Stevens, favored high protection and cheap currency, said: "Let a contraction begin and depositors check heavily upon their balances and it will affect every bank, and the next act of the Secretary of the Treasury will be to notify the banks that, owing to depreciation in the market value of Government securities, they must increase their deposits to secure the redemption of their notes. I warn gentlemen to withhold from any man the power, at this time, when we are just coming out of such a war, to contract our currency or even to threaten its contraction."[15]

Further debate on the measure, commonly known as the Loan Bill, was postponed at that time, but when it was taken up three weeks later the debate was just as sharp as ever, with the radicals almost evenly divided on it. When Morrill finally brought it to a vote, on March 16, it was defeated by the narrow margin of seventy to sixty-five, with forty-nine not voting. Garfield's motion to reconsider led to further debate, after which the bill was sent back to the committee. On March 23 Morrill brought it out again, amended to provide "that of United States notes not more than $10,000,000 may be retired and cancelled within six months from the passage of this act and thereafter not more than $4,000,000 in any one month." After another brief exchange, this bill finally passed by a vote of eighty-three to fifty-three, with forty-seven not voting.[16]

In the Senate the Loan Bill had much easier sledding. Reported without amendment from the Finance Committee by its chairman, Fessenden, it passed by a vote of thirty-two to seven, but only after a sharp exchange between Fessenden and Sherman, two of the Senate's leading moderates. "If Senators will read this bill," said Sherman, "they will find that it confers on the Secretary of the Treasury greater powers than have ever been conferred, since the foundation of this government, upon any Secretary of the Treasury." Fessenden charged Sherman with impugning the good intentions of McCulloch by implying that "he had a purpose to accomplish, and that he would not hesitate to take any means in his power to accomplish it, improperly against the manifest will of Congress, against the interests of the country, and against his own interests as Secretary of the Treasury." Sherman replied that his argument was based on his optimism about the country and its economy, whose future will be hopeful, bouyant, joyous. . . . I do not wish to cripple the industry of the country by adopting the policy of the Secretary of the Treasury, . . . by reducing the currency, by crippling the operations of the government, when I think that under any probability of affairs in the future, all this debt will take care of itself. . . . No one who heeds the rapid development of new sources of wealth in this country, the enormous yield of gold now, the renewal of industry in the south, the enormous yield of cotton, the growing wealth of this country, and all the favorable prospects that are before us, doubts the ability of this government before [the] debt matures to reduce it to four or five per cent interest.[17]

Sherman's efforts were unavailing. The Loan Bill passed the Senate and was signed by President Johnson on April 12. But its enactment was hardly a victory for the Secretary of the Treasury; indeed, he was bitterly disappointed with it. "This was not what I wanted," said McCulloch, "for I knew there would be months in which much more than four millions could be withdrawn without affecting the market; and other months when the withdrawal of a much smaller amount would cause considerable stringency. What I did want was authority to retire the legal-tender notes as rapidly as it could be done, without affecting injuriously industry and trade."[18] He continued with his efforts at contraction under the terms of the Loan Act until February 1868, when a law was passed by large majorities in both houses of Congress suspending any further reduction of the currency.[19]

Some businessmen who could not agree to continued expansion of the volume of greenbacks but who feared contraction of the currency sought a solution through an adjustment in the national banking system. The total note issue of $300 million authorized under the National Banking Act was clearly inadequate. Much of the enmity against the banking system and the demand for revision came from businessmen west of the Alleghenies, where banknotes were much more scarce than in New York and New England. The argument therefore had a regional character that was missing from the greenback question. Early in 1866 two bills were introduced in the Senate for redistribution of banknotes, neither of which was reported out of committee. The intensity of feeling on the issue was shown, however, in the next Congress, when Senator Sherman introduced a bill calling for a banknote increase of $20 million to be distributed to states with less than a $5 per capita note circulation, a measure clearly designed to aid the western states. The debate on this bill, says Irwin Unger, "became a bitter and undignified sectional dogfight among Republican Senators." Although Sherman's bill failed, the Senate did pass a bill allocating to the West and the South some of the original $300 million, only to see it fail in the House. The disagreement over the banking system, says Unger, continued "until time homogenized the soft money interest in the late '70's." It was "an important point of distinction between agrarian and business versions of financial dissent."[20]

Just as the financial demands of the Civil War shaped the issues of currency and banking during Reconstruction, so it shaped the tariff question. Tariff schedules during the fifteen years before the war, although not strictly in accordance with the principles of free trade, were moderate. Except for the brief crisis of 1857 these were years of prosperity which, together with the predominance of the Democratic party, account for the low tariffs. In May 1860, the House of Representatives passed a bill introduced by Justin S. Morrill, chairman of the Ways and Means Committee, which the Senate would not accept until March 1861. Although the Morrill tariff did increase duties on iron and wool, its real purpose was to appeal to Pennsylvania and to some western states in the election of 1860. It did not, according to Professor F. W. Taussig, form any "part of the financial legislation of the war, which gave rise in time to a series of measures that entirely superseded [it]."[21]

With the coming of the war and the vastly increased need for revenue additional tariff laws were enacted, the first in August and the second in December 1861, levying duties on sugar, tea, and coffee and raising them on a number of other items. From that time until the end of the war every session of Congress enacted laws raising import duties. Beginning in 1862 the principle of compensation was applied—that is, the passage of tariffs to compensate manufacturers for high internal taxes. Except for these internal taxes, it would have been difficult to carry tariff measures through Congress; with them it was relatively easy. But the men framing these laws were protectionists who went beyond the principle of compensation or of tariffs for revenue only. The tariff of 1864 is a notable example. This "crude and ill-considered" bill, wrote Professor Taussig, "established protective duties more extensive than . . . any previous tariff act in our country's history; it contained flagrant abuses, in the shape of duties whose chief effect was to bring money into the pockets of private individuals." The two houses of Congress devoted only five days of debate to this important bill. Helping to push it through were lobbyists from recently formed organizations such as the National Association of Wool Manufacturers and Woolgrowers, the New England Cotton Manufacturers Association, the American Iron and Steel Association, and the National Manufacturers Association. The tariff of 1864 is of particular significance because it was only slightly changed over a period of twenty years. Men came to accept it as established tariff policy, either forgetting or ignoring that those who passed it defended it as an exceptional measure designed to meet the exigencies of war.[22]

In the summer of 1866 the House, urged on by Justin S. Morrill, passed a highly protective measure, only to see it fail in the Senate. In the following year a bill providing for downward revisions, framed by David A. Wells, Special Commissioner of the Revenue, passed the Senate but was not voted on in the House because of the failure to muster the necessary two-thirds majority to suspend the rules and discharge the Committee of the Whole from further consideration of the bill. Soon thereafter, however, the Woolens Act of March 2, 1867, was passed, raising duties on raw and manufactured wool to the highest level to that time.[23]

It would have been strange indeed, if not irresponsible, if historians had not weighed these economic questions in their interpretations of Reconstruction history. Whatever flaws or unwarranted conclusions revisionist historians may have found in Howard K. Beale's economic interpretation, Beale did address the problem in greater detail and with more thorough scholarship than his predecessors or his revisionist detractors. The very fact that the revisionists have used his work as a point of departure, have found the need to oppose him so compelling, attests to his influence. Writing in the late 1950s and the 1960s, when the progressive school was no longer in vogue, the revisionists have made some incisive criticisms of the Beale thesis. At some points, however, they may have gone too far.

In making his case that a proper use of economic issues might have thrown the election to Johnson, Beale argued that "most of the factors that in subsequent years underlay Greenbackism, the Granger Movement, Populism, Progressivism, and the Farm Bloc were at work in 1866." Oliver H. Kelley, founder of the Grange, said Beale, worked out the details of the organization from his observations during a southern trip early in the year. Although acknowledging that some northeastern radicals opposed contraction of the currency, Beale saw in this issue an East-West regionalism, with the "loudest outcry" against contraction coming from the West. His analysis of the Loan Bill led him to the conclusion that the East favored contraction while the West was divided or opposed to it. (This is hardly a valid conclusion, because it is impossible to know whether men regarded the bill as something less than McCulloch wanted or as granting him the authority to contract the currency.)

An estimate of greenbacks and contraction as campaign issues calls for some understanding of where Andrew Johnson stood in respect to them. Beale's assertion that he "leaned to the inflationist view" and that "his sympathies led him to align himself with the poorer people, and to suspect the financial interests" is not altogether convincing. The evidence Beale offers for this conclusion is simply that in 1868, "when McCulloch prepared a veto message for the bill repealing the contraction law, Johnson refused to use it, and allowed the bill to become a law." But in the earlier part of his administration, said Beale, Johnson "abided by the advice of his Secretary of the Treasury, and refrained from interference in favor of the inflationists." Beale found McCulloch's position "economically sound but politically injudicious." For if the administration had taken a stand more favorable to inflation "the deflationist demands of Morrill and other leading radicals could have been used to organize a powerful political opposition that would have split the Republican party."[24] Also, according to Beale, the administration missed a golden opportunity in not demanding the redemption of government bonds in legal tender currency instead of gold and in not demanding taxation of bonds. "In their Northern campaign for the control of the South," he said, "the Radicals capitalized their position with the bondholders. Thousands supported the Radicals as the party that would secure and enhance the value of their government securities. The Conservatives failed to organize the opposition of thousands of others who looked with suspicion on a party that used the government for the services of bondholders."[25]

In his discussion of national banknotes Beale correctly pointed out divisions between East and West. "The banks' power to issue currency," he said, "was particularly resented." Although greenbacks and banknotes circulated as currency there was a difference between them, for greenbacks "had no other backing than the willingness and ability of the government to redeem after it had met all other obligations," whereas banknotes were guaranteed by government bonds. An Illinois farmers' convention protested against McCulloch's plan of withdrawing greenbacks and substituting banknotes. In December 1866, Beale related, an Illinois Congressman introduced a resolution "to inquire into the expediency of withdrawing national bank currency and winding up the national banks and furnishing the country . . . with greenbacks, or other currency of similar character." When the resolution was tabled another Illinoisan proposed one to prohibit any reduction in the number of greenbacks because it was "to the interest of the whole people of the United States that the Government should issue all bills intended and designed to circulate as money." The vote on the resolution, which was tabled, showed the East opposed fifty-four to twelve while the West approved it forty-one to thirty-six. In his annual message of December 9, 1866, Johnson attacked the unwarranted profits of bondholders under the National Banking system. But he kept silent during the campaign, said Beale, "waiting until the South should be restored before he turned to other matters."[26]

Beale gave his greatest emphasis to the tariff, which he believed to be the most important of the economic questions. "After the new industrial system had depended for years on a war tariff never repealed, [he wrote] that war tariff ceased to be such, and became an integral part of the new economic order." In commenting on the harmfulness of the new tariff system on the general economy, he continued: "Cutting off the extra protection of the war period would have forced manufacturers back to efficient methods and normal production. It would have ruined some; it would have meant temporary depression for all during a period of adjustment. But it would have established the new industrial America upon the non-protective basis operative in the days before the War." In what may have been the most vulnerable part of his tariff argument Beale said, "Northeastern Radicals were the leading protectionists. An underlying cause of their Radicalism was dread of tariff reduction which they felt a combined West and South would force through Congress if the Southern members were seated."[27]

Beale examined in detail the activities of the woolen manufacturers and the woolgrowers that led to the Woolens Tariff Bill of 1867. The woolgrowers, faced with a dangerously declining market for their product after the war were persuaded by the Woolen Manufacturers, under the leadership of John L. Hayes, to join forces in a convention at Syracuse, New York, in December 1865, where they organized to demand a higher tariff on both products. They succeeded in having their schedule included in the tariff of 1866; then with the failure of this general tariff measure, the wool and woolens schedule was presented as a separate bill and called up by Senator Sherman to become the Wool and Woolens Act of 1867. Although both growers and manufacturers were active in the wool lobby, the force and leadership came from the manufacturers who, according to Beale, "played a significant part in the election" of 1866. "In spite of the Conservative failure to capitalize it, the tariff question would have injured the Radical cause, had not this clever maneuver won the support of the Western wool-grower. Sheep owners still opposed protection in the abstract, but they accepted this particular tariff because it promised to aid them personally."[28]

Among the revisionist historians who have challenged the Beale interpretation none has been more effective than Stanley Coben in his now famous article, "Northeastern Business and Radical Reconstruction: "A Re-examination," published in 1959.[29] The Beale thesis—that radicals and northern businessmen acted together through the Republican party to control the national government to enact protective tariffs, national banks, and sound currency against the futile efforts of the West to check them—said Coben, could not stand up under careful scholarly investigation: A close "examination of the important economic legislation and congressional battles of the period, and the attitudes of businessmen and influential business groups, reveals serious divsons on economic issues among Radical legislators and northern businessmen alike; . . . neither business leaders nor Radicals were united in support of any specific set of economic aims." Coben went on to show how the "tariff split northeastern businessmen more than any other issue," with "highly protectionist Pennsylvania interests on one side and influential low-tariff groups in New England and New York on the other."[30] "Leading business interests of New England and New York," he contended, "believed they lost more than they gained from high post-war tariffs. Had reconstruction politics allowed them a choice, it seems likely that these important groups would have preferred a return to the coalition which had produced the low tariff of 1857—a coalition which included the South."[31]

Coben also found similar differences over currency questions. Businessmen feared "that goods bought at high prices with inflated greenbacks might have to be sold at much lower prices" if McCulloch was allowed to proceed with his contraction policy. Their objections were louder and more widespread as the result of a recession that set in in 1866 and continued through 1867. William D. "Pig Iron" Kelley and Thaddeus Stevens, representing the iron and steel interests of Pennsylvania, were leaders in the inflation movement. One reason was to maintain the premium on gold, which had the effect of raising the cost of foreign goods, and therefore served as a kind of protective tariff. But such a policy was harmful to importers, bankers, and to some established manufacturers in New York and New England.[32] Coben concludes that "northeastern businessmen had no unified economic program to promote. Important business groups within the region opposed each other on almost every significant economic question, and this lack of a common interest was likewise reflected in the economic views of Radical congressmen." It seemed clear to Coben "that factors other than the economic interests of the Northeast must be used to explain the motivation and aims of Radical Reconstruction."[33]

Coben's argument, that there were differences among radicals and businessmen on economic issues, is difficult if not impossible to refute.

Even Beale was not dogmatic on this point. However, Coben does not specifically challenge Beale's argument that economic issues could have been used to advantage by Andrew Johnson in the election of 1866. This task was undertaken by the revisionist historian Eric McKitrick, who took an unequivocal stand in opposition to Beale's argument. Admitting that economic problems were the source of some dissatisfaction, McKitrick questioned whether they were available as party issues and how they might have been used in a political campaign. "In the Populist period of a generation later," said McKitrick, "these economic questions did come to acquire enough cohesiveness to warrant the organizing of political activity around them, but there is not much evidence that many people saw the urgency of such activity in 1866. . . . The likelihood is that Andrew Johnson or anybody else at this time would have brought greater difficulties upon himself by raising these economic issues than by leaving them alone."[34]

Although admitting that by 1866 there was some support for inflation and considerable opposition to McCulloch's contraction policy, McKitrick doubts "that such sentiment was strong enough to be organized in any way by either party" or that it could have replaced reconstruction as the key issue or split the Republican party. "Such sentiment as existed was [he said] . . . of a nature quite different from the popular 'greenbacker' impulse of a few years later, and it would be a great mistake to suppose that the 'money of the people' angle on legal tenders had much meaning in 1866. . . . The natural reaction of most people . . . was a more or less undifferentiated desire . . . to retrench," to pay the public debt, "and get back to normal."

As evidence to support this statement McKitrick cites the approval by the House of Representatives on December 18, 1865, of McCulloch's report, which demonstrated that "at the level of theory . . . a virtually perfect harmony prevailed." But in his account of the Loan Act of April 1866 McKitrick glosses over the sharp debate that occurred as well as McCulloch's bitter disappointment with the measure. He concludes that Johnson, "had he decided . . . to turn inflationist, would have gained nothing but confusion. He would have reversed the policy of his own administration and probably made himself even less popular than he already was."[35] Granting that in the Midwest there was a good deal of antiprotectionist feeling, he said that Republican Congressional leaders "did what politicians had always done in such crises: . . . they adjusted and compromised." In Illinois, for example, the most powerful antitariff state, McKitrick found that the strongest opposition pressures were exerted within the Republican party and that "the adjustments were intra-party adjustments rather than occasions for political warfare."

In summing up his argument on economic questions as political issues McKitrick wrote:

> The whole question, indeed, could be turned squarely around. Since the Republican party was so solidly united on the problem of reconstruction, why should we not speculate on how the President, had he been so minded, might best have used that unity in the interest of such ends as a rational tariff program, an intelligent policy on money, and a judicious federal regulation of corporate enterprise? To have co-operated with Congress and the party on reconstruction might really have made President Johnson a figure of towering moral authority on a sweeping range of other matters. Thus fortified, upon what great objects might he not have shed his enormous prestige? What vistas might not have been open to him then, in the work of making this disorderly Republic a model of economic enlightenment?[36]

Despite the general excellence of McKitrick's book—there is probably none better on the Johnson years—his assertion that the tariff, currency, and banking were without merit as campaign issues in 1866 cannot be accepted uncritically. One might wonder just what his criteria are for determining what was and what was not an effective political issue. Even in our own time, with the profusion of public opinion polls and projections of all kinds there remain subtleties and uncertainties about the electorate's response to the issues. Would not these subtleties and uncertainties have been even more prevalent in the early Reconstruction years? And if the economic questions did not appear to be issues before the campaign opened, who can say whether, with some prodding from the president, they might not have become so.

If the space devoted to these economic questions in northern newspapers is indicative of how successfully they might have been used as campaign issues one must conclude that they ought to have been exploited, for they were given as much, possibly more, space than Reconstruction per se. No paper was more strident in its attack on the National Banking system than the pro-Johnson *New York Herald.* As early as June 23, the *Herald* was blasting the banks as the creations of Salmon P. Chase and Jay Cooke and Company, whose friends and supporters had enriched themselves at the expense of the government through "this vast and dangerous monopoly." National Bank notes, said the *Herald,* should be replaced with greenbacks and interest-bearing bonds bought up and cancelled, at a saving of $25 million a year. In August and September the *Herald* attacked McCulloch and his contraction policy—his "Specie-Mania." The secretary's experience as an Indiana banker, it said, had been too limited for him to understand high finance, and had led him to underestimate the country's prosperity. He might learn some valuable lessons if he would remove himself from the confines of his office to visit and to observe what went on in the centers of trade.

Amidst the *Herald*'s paean to the Philadelphia convention, its declaration of principles, and its address there was one discordant note:

> The financial shortcomings of Congress, its schemes and jobs,
> taxation and tariff, are unfortunately entirely omitted. . . .
> But the omission can easily be made up in the State and
> Congressional meetings which it is now necessary to hold at once to
> carry out the campaign so successfully inaugurated. . . . Let the
> mass meetings which are to be held in support of [the Philadelphia
> Convention] incorporate a condemnation of the financial feature of
> the radical Congress, and the issue is made complete. No power can
> then arrest its progress or prevent its complete and overwhelming
> triumph at the polls.[37]

It is evident, then, that the *Herald*, the most ardent champion of Johnson and the Philadelphia movement, fully expected that economic matters would have an important place in the campaign.

While the *Herald* insisted that the economic questions would become important, *Harper's Weekly*, supporting Congress, feared that the tariff, especially, might be, and warned its readers not to be led astray by it; it was "essential to remember [said *Harper's*] that the paramount question [was] still the restoration of the Union."

> To vote for a candidate who is opposed to protection, or who is
> an absolute free-trader, but who thinks that Congress has no right
> to prescribe conditions for the restoration of the late rebel States to
> their full relations to the Union is to prefer the lesser to the greater.
> It is always possible to reverse or repeal a tariff. But the conditions
> upon which reorganization is to be founded can neither be amended
> nor abolished. The vital bond of the Union party is not financial but
> political. . . . The heartiest Union men differ radically upon the
> tariff question. Whatever, therefore, . . . tends to excite the
> feeling and acrimonious debate upon this subject tends to a division
> or paralysis of the party. . . . Every individual Union man should
> reflect that such an issue is not a party question, and while he would
> naturally prefer a Representative who sympathized with his views
> upon the subject, he must not forget that it is still better to take a

candidate who is wrong upon the tariff than one who is wrong upon reconstruction.[38]

McKitrick, himself, has told us that Joseph Medill, editor of the *Chicago Tribune,* "was as strong against the tariff [of 1866] as any man in" Illinois. Yet, McKitrick added, "no newspaper ever flogged Andrew Johnson with less mercy over reconstruction than did the Chicago *Tribune.*"[39] Is it not logical to ask here whether Medill might not have been more merciful if Johnson had taken a stand against the tariff bill? Undoubtedly Howard K. Beale exaggerated the differences between East and West on both tariff and greenbacks. But the sectional differences over national banknotes, which McKitrick ignores, were very real. This is a point on which Beale and Irwin Unger agree.[40]

To be sure, as McKitrick suggests, the organization of economic issues for use in the political campaign would have posed some problems for Andrew Johnson. But would they have been so formidable as to rule out such an approach? Although an advocacy of greenbacks might have split some Republicans off from the congressional party, Johnson would have been forced to repudiate a cabinet member whose loyalty to him and to his restoration program had been unwavering since the beginning of his administration. However, some stance in opposition to the maldistribution of national banknotes and to the tariff of 1866 would have been easier to take. Nor would it have been necessary for him to develop elaborate or expert arguments on these issues. How many elections in our history have shown that finely drawn and concise arguments on the issues are not necessary for victory, that they may indeed have harmful rather than beneficial effects? The Jacksonians' campaign of 1828 and Franklin Roosevelt's in 1932 are obvious examples. And of course there was Lincoln, whose use of obfuscation could be brilliant. A mere expression by Andrew Johnson of his awareness of the importance of the economic issues, as the nation moved into the complexities of the postwar era, would have fallen on some receptive ears. And if such an appeal had been combined with presidential advice to the southern states to ratify the Fourteenth Amendment, as a congressional act representing adherence to and not rejection of Johnson's plan, who can say what the result might have been? Since this was not the course taken, we cannot know. But surely it could not have been more disastrous than the tragic Swing Around the Circle.

Knowing what we do about Andrew Johnson and the impact of his battle with Congress over Reconstruction, it would have been asking too much of him to conduct such a campaign. Had he done so, he would not have been Andrew Johnson, and the history of Reconstruction and

of the United States during the past century would have been different
from what it is.

THE ELECTION OF 1866 ended the first and most decisive phase of the
contest between Johnson and Congress over Reconstruction. Soon
Congress would go ahead with its own reconstruction program, embraced in a series of reconstruction acts that would all pass over presidential vetoes. Before that, however, the debate was briefly renewed
during the last month of 1866 and the early weeks of 1867. The occasion
was the assembling of the Thirty-ninth Congress for its second session.

On December 3, Johnson sent his annual message to Congress. It
showed beyond any question that his bitter experiences of the past year
had not caused him to budge an inch from his established position on the
issues of reconstruction. He restated the argument from a year earlier
that under his plan the rebel states had been restored to the Union.
Upon this question, he said, "my convictions, heretofore expressed,
have undergone no change, but, on the contrary, their correctness has
been confirmed by reflection and time." In challenging the "conquered
territories" theory Johnson invoked the Crittenden Resolution of 1861
and Lincoln's proclamation of September 22, 1862, both of which had
stated that the only valid objective of the war was the preservation of
the Union. Not only did the members from the excluded states have the
constitutional right to take their seats in Congress, Johnson asserted,
their return "would alleviate the present condition of those States, and
by inducing emigration [would] aid in the settlement of fertile regions
now uncultivated and lead to an increased production of those staples
which have added so greatly to the wealth of the nation and the commerce of the world."

There was, of course, a radical response to Johnson's message, but
this time the radicals were in a position to do more than debate. They
could begin to act. Within a few days they were busy pushing a bill
through Congress for Negro suffrage in the District of Columbia. Such a
bill had passed the House in the previous session, and now Charles
Sumner took the lead in getting Senate approval.

Expressing views almost identical with those of the president, Gideon Welles showed in his diary that the administration's war with
Congress had not ceased. "There is not a Senator who votes for that bill
who does not know that it is an abuse and wrong," he wrote.

> Most of the negroes of this District are wholly unfit to be electors.
> With some exceptions they are ignorant, vicious, and degraded,
> without patriotic or intelligent ideas or moral instincts. There are

among them worthy, intelligent, industrious men, capable of
voting understandingly and who would not discredit the trust, but
they are exceptional cases. As a community they are too debased
and ignorant. Yet fanatics and demagogues will crowd a bill
through Congress to give them suffrage, and probably by a vote
which the veto could not overcome. Nevertheless, I am confident
the President will do his duty in that regard. It is pitiable to see how
little sense of right, real independence, and what limited
comprehension are possessed by our legislators. They are the tame
victims and participators of villainous conspirators.

Early in January the bill passed and was promptly vetoed, on January 7,
1867. The following day Congress passed it over the veto. Emboldened
by the victory Congress proceeded, before the end of the month, to
legislate for Negro suffrage in the territories.

As congressional Republicans looked forward to the year ahead they
were aware that the Fortieth Congress, elected in 1866, would not
normally meet until the following December. What mischief might the
president do during the hiatus of nine months? The fruits of the political
victory of 1866 might be thrown away as had been those of the military
victory during the absence of Congress in 1865. To prevent it, Congress
passed an act on January 22 which provided that the Fortieth Congress
would begin on March 4, immediately upon the termination of the
Thirty-ninth. Then on March 2, on the eve of its termination, the
Thirty-ninth passed the first Reconstruction Act establishing five military districts over the ten unrestored southern states, each to be under
the command of a general officer. Congress had wrested control of
reconstruction from the executive, and the experiment in congressional
reconstruction had begun.

Appendix
Notes
Selected Bibliography
Index

Appendix

Thirteenth, Fourteenth, and Fifteenth Amendments to the Constitution of the United States

Thirteenth Amendment

SECTION 1. Neither slavery nor involuntary servitude, except as a punishment for crime whereof the party shall have been duly convicted, shall exist within the United States, or any place subject to their jurisdiction.

SECTION 2. Congress shall have power to enforce this article by appropriate legislation. [December 18, 1865]

Fourteenth Amendment

SECTION 1. All persons born or naturalized in the United States, and subject to the jurisdiction thereof, are citizens of the United States and of the State wherein they reside. No State shall make or enforce any law which shall abridge the privileges or immunities of citizens of the United States; nor shall any State deprive any person of life, liberty, or property, without due process of law; nor deny to any person within its jurisdiction the equal protection of the laws.

SECTION 2. Representatives shall be apportioned among the several States according to their respective numbers, counting the whole number of persons in each State, excluding Indians not taxed. But when the right to vote at any election for the choice of electors for President and Vice President of the United States, Representatives in Congress, the Executive and Judicial officers of a State, or the members of the Legislature thereof, is denied to any of the male inhabitants of such State, being twenty-one years of age, and citizens of the United States, or in any way abridged, except for participation in rebellion, or other crime, the basis of representation therein shall be reduced in the proportion which the number of such male citizens shall bear to the whole number of male citizens twenty-one years of age in such State.

SECTION 3. No person shall be a Senator or Representative in Congress, or elector of President and Vice President, or hold any office, civil or military, under the United States, or under any State, who, having previously taken an oath, as a member of Congress, or as an officer of the United States, or as a member of any State legislature, or as an executive or judicial officer of any State, to support the Constitution of the United States, shall have engaged in insurrection or rebellion against the same, or given aid or comfort to the enemies thereof. But Congress may by a vote of two-thirds of each House, remove such disability.

SECTION 4. The validity of the public debt of the United States, authorized by law, including debts incurred for payment of pensions and bounties for services in suppressing insurrection or rebellion, shall not be questioned. But neither the United States, nor any State shall assume or pay any debt or obligation incurred in aid of insurrection or rebellion against the United States, or any claim for the loss or emancipation of any slave; but all such debts, obligations and claims shall be held illegal and void.

SECTION 5. The Congress shall have the power to enforce, by appropriate legislation, the provisions of this article. [July 28, 1868]

Fifteenth Amendment

SECTION 1. The right of citizens of the United States to vote shall not be denied or abridged by the United States or by any State on account of race, color, or previous condition of servitude.

SECTION 2. The Congress shall have power to enforce this article by appropriate legislation. [March 30, 1870]

Notes

**Chapter 1:
Andrew Johnson Tries
Restoration**

1. Walter L. Fleming, ed.,
   *Dcoumentary History of
   Reconstruction*, 2 vols. (1906–7;
   reprint ed., New York:
   McGraw-Hill Book Co., 1966),
   1:51–53.
2. Ibid., pp. 57–59.
3. Carl Schurz, *Speeches,
   Correspondence and Political
   Papers of Carl Schurz*, ed.
   Frederic Bancroft, 6 vols. (New
   York: G. P. Putnam's Sons, 1913),
   1:279–374.
4. Rembert W. Patrick, *The
   Reconstruction of the Nation*
   (New York: Oxford University
   Press, 1967), p. 55.
5. Kenneth M. Stampp, *The Era of
   Reconstruction* (New York:
   Alfred A. Knopf, 1965), pp. 70–72.

**Chapter 2:
The Assembling**

1. "Clemency and Common Sense,"
   Atlantic Monthly 16 (December
   1865): 757–59.
2. David Donald, *Charles Sumner
   and the Rights of Man* (New
   York: Alfred A. Knopf, 1970),
   pp. 226–28.
3. Ibid., pp. 237–38.
4. It may be significant that Stevens
   did not ask for a guarantee against
   infringement of the Constitution.
   Also, the law of nations was soon
   to become one of the pillars on
   which Stevens's reconstruction
   policy would rest.
5. Fawn M. Brodie, *Thaddeus
   Stevens, Scourge of the South*
   (New York, W. W. Norton, 1959),
   231–33; Richard N. Current, *Old
   Thad Stevens: A Story of
   Ambition* (Madison: University of
   Wisconsin Press, 1942), pp.
   214–17.
6. Eric L. McKitrick, *Andrew
   Johnson and Reconstruction*
   (Chicago: University of Chicago
   Press, 1960), p. 82*n*.
7. Lawanda Cox and John H. Cox,
   *Politics, Principle, and
   Prejudice, 1865–1866* (London
   and New York: Macmillan, Free
   Press, 1963), pp. 140–42.
8. Benjamin J. Kendrick, *The
   Journal of the Joint Committee of
   Fifteen on Reconstruction, 39th
   Congress, 1865–1867* (New York:
   Columbia University Press,
   1914), pp. 142–43.
9. Ibid., pp. 144–45.
10. Italics added. James D.
    Richardson, ed., *A Compilation
    of the Messages and Papers of the
    Presidents, 1789–1897*, 10 vols.
    (Washington, D.C.: Bureau of
    National Literature and Art,
    1896–99), 6:356–68.
11. McKitrick, *Johnson*, p. 91.
12. Richardson, ed., *Messages and
    Papers*, 6:356.
13. Ibid., p. 360.
14. Ibid., pp. 360–61.
15. Quoted in Cox, *Politics,
    Principle, and Prejudice*, p. 152.
16. Mary L. Hinsdale, ed.,

Garfield-Hinsdale Letters;
Correspondence Between James
Abram Garfield and Burke
Aaron Hinsdale (Ann Arbor:
University of Michigan Press,
1949), pp. 76–77.

17. Shelby M. Cullom, *Fifty Years of*
    Public Service (Chicago: A. C.
    McClurg and Co., 1911), pp.
    147–49.

18. Cox. *Politics, Principle, and*
    Prejudice, pp. 131–39.

19. McKitrick, *Johnson*, 107–10.

20. U.S., Congress, House,
    Congressional Globe, 39th Cong.,
    1st sess., 1865, 36, pt. 1:73;
    Emmerich de Vattel, *The Law of*
    Nations or the Principles of
    Natural Law Applied to the
    Conduct and Affairs of Nations
    and of Sovereigns, translation of
    the edition of 1758 by Charles G.
    Fenwick (Washington, D.C.:
    Carnegie Institution, 1916), pp.
    336–40.

21. Vattel, *Law of Nations*, pp.
    350–51.

22. There is an interesting anomaly
    here. Calhoun had argued at the
    time of the nullification crisis that
    protective tariffs were
    unconstitutional because they
    were, in effect, taxes on exports,
    forbidden by the Constitution.
    Now Stevens argues that an
    export tax will serve as a
    protective tariff.

23. House, *Congressional Globe*,
    39th Cong., 1st sess., 1865, 36,
    pt. 1:74–75.

24. Senate, *Congressional Globe*,
    39th Cong., 1st sess., 1866, 36,
    pt. 1:707; Kendrick, *Joint*
    Committee, p. 182.

25. The *Independent*, April 12, 1866,
    quoted in Kendrick, *Joint*
    Committee, p. 182.

26. Current, *Old Thad Stevens*,
    p. 216.

27. Brodie, *Stevens*, p. 110.

28. Kendrick, *Joint Committee*,
    p. 168.

29. Brodie, *Stevens*, p. 200.

30. Ibid., p. 26.

31. Alexander K. McClure, *Abraham*
    Lincoln and Men of War-Times
    (Philadelphia: Times Publishing
    Co., 1892), p. 287.

32. William R. Brock, *An American*
    Crisis: Congress and
    Reconstruction, 1865–1867
    (London: Macmillan & Co., 1963),
    p. 81.

33. McClure, *Abraham Lincoln and*
    Men of War-Times, p. 286.

34. Kendrick, *Joint Committee*,
    pp. 162–63.

35. Brodie, *Stevens*, pp. 180–81.

36. Ibid., p. 150.

37. Ibid., p. 86.

38. Brock, *American Crisis*, p. 128.

39. Kendrick, *Joint Committee*,
    pp. 195–96.

40. Brodie, *Stevens*, p. 243.

41. Brock, *American Crisis*, p. 130.

42. The committees were organized
    as follows: 1st,
    Tennessee—Grimes, Bingham,
    and Grider; 2d, Virginia, North
    Carolina, and South
    Carolina—Howard, Conkling,
    and Blow; 3d, Georgia, Alabama,
    Mississippi, and
    Arkansas—Harris, Boutwell, and
    Morrill; 4th, Louisiana, Florida,
    and Texas—Williams,
    Washbourne, and Rogers. See
    Kendrick, *Joint Committee*,
    pp. 47–48.

43. Howard K. Beale, *The Critical*
    Year: A Study of Andrew
    Johnson and Reconstruction
    (New York: Harcourt, Brace &
    Co., 1930), p. 94.

44. Patrick, *Reconstruction of the*
    Nation, pp. 65–66.

45. McKitrick, *Johnson*, p. 331.

46. Hans L. Trefousse, ed.,
    Background for Radical
    Reconstruction: Testimony

Taken from the Hearings of the Joint Committee on Reconstruction (Boston: Little, Brown and Co., 1970), p. 9.

47. Ibid., p. 51.
48. U.S., Congress, House, Joint Committee on Reconstruction, *Report of the Joint Committee on Reconstruction*, 39th Cong., 1st sess., 1866, H. Rept. 30, pt. 2, pp. 114–23.
49. Ibid. pt. 4, pp. 129–32.
50. Ibid., pp. 132–36.
51. Ibid., pt. 2, pp. 129–36.
52. Ibid., pt. 3, pp. 158–66.
53. Ibid., p. xii.
54. Ibid., pp. ix–x.
55. Ibid., pp. xi, xx.
56. Ibid., p. xvi.
57. Ibid., pp. xviii, xix.
58. John W. Burgess, *Reconstruction and the Constitution, 1866–1876* (New York: Charles Scribner's Sons, 1902), p. 86.

Chapter 3:
Howard, Trumbull, and the Freedmen

1. Mark M. Krug, *Lyman Trumbull: Conservative Radical* (New York: A. S. Barnes and Co., 1965), pp. 236–38; Jacobus ten Broek, *Equal Under Law* (New York: Macmillan, Collier Books, 1965), pp. 194–95 (originally published, 1951, as *The Antislavery Origins of the Fourteenth Amendment*); Harold M. Hyman, *A More Perfect Union: The Impact of the Civil War and Reconstruction on the Constitution* (New York: Alfred A. Knopf, 1973), pp. 449–50.
2. W. E. Burghardt DuBois, "The Freedmen's Bureau," *Atlantic Monthly* 87 (1901): 356.
3. *National Anti-Slavery Standard*, November 23, 1861, quoted in

James McPherson, *The Struggle for Equality: Abolitionists and the Negro in the Civil War and Reconstruction* (Princeton: Princeton University Press, 1964), pp. 158–59.
4. McPherson, *Struggle*, pp. 155–66; Willie Lee Rose, *Rehearsal for Reconstruction* (1964; reprint ed., New York: Knopf, Vintage Books, n.d.), pp. 3–62, 152–54; George R. Bentley, *A History of the Freedmen's Bureau* (1955; reprint ed., New York: Farrar, Straus & Giroux, Octagon Books, 1970), pp. 5–12.
5. Rose, *Rehearsal*, pp. 327–28.
6. Bentley, *Freedmen's Bureau*, pp. 21–23, 59–60.
7. Oliver Otis Howard, *Autobiography of Oliver Otis Howard*, 2 vols. (New York: Baker & Taylor Co., 1908), 2:164.
8. Quoted in John G. Sproat, "Blueprint for Radical Reconstruction," *Journal of Southern History* 23 (1957):34.
9. Ibid., pp. 36–37.
10. Howard, *Autobiography*, 2:209–10.
11. Bentley, *Freedmen's Bureau*, p. 56.
12. McPherson, *Struggle*, pp. 167–68, p. 187.
13. John T. Trowbridge, *The Desolate South, 1865–1866: A Picture of the Battlefields and of the Devastated Confederacy* (1866; reprint ed., Boston: Little, Brown and Co., 1956), pp. 181–84.
14. Quoted in Bentley, *Freedmen's Bureau*, pp. 136–37.
15. John Richard Dennett, *The South as It Is, 1865–1866*, ed. Henry M. Christman (New York: Viking Press, Compass Books, 1967), pp. 52–53.
16. See, for example, the report of General Grant, submitted to the president on December 18, 1865.

Grant admitted that he had not given the Freedmen's Bureau much attention, but had heard this complaint in conversations. Edward McPherson, *The Political History of the United States of America during the Period of Reconstruction, from April 15, 1865, to July 15, 1870* (1875; reprint ed., New York: Greenwood Press for the Negro Universities Press, 1969), pp. 67–68; Paul Skeels Pierce, *The Freedmen's Bureau: A Chapter in the History of Reconstruction* (Iowa City: State University of Iowa, 1904), pp. 56–57.

17. Bentley, *Freedmen's Bureau,* pp. 77, 80, 84, 149–51.
18. Sidney Andrews, *The South Since the War* (1866; reprint ed., New York: Arno Press and the *New York Times,* 1969), p. 224.
19. Trowbridge, *Desolate South,* p. 156.
20. Pierce, *Freedmen's Bureau,* pp. 87–91.
21. Ibid., pp. 94–98.
22. Quoted in Bentley, *Freedmen's Bureau,* p. 169; see also Howard, *Autobiography,* 2: 313.
23. Bentley, *Freedmen's Bureau,* pp. 63–64, 169–74.
24. Ibid., pp. 175–76.
25. In the spring and summer of 1866 Johnson, reacting to the recent *Milligan* decision, ordered that where civil courts were open civilians were to be tried in them and not in military courts. He also issued proclamations ending the rebellion in the former Confederate states. See Bentley, *Freedmen's Bureau,* pp. 65, 68, 152–68.
26. Ibid., pp. 90–93.
27. Ibid., p. 95; McPherson, *Struggle,* pp. 408–9; Howard, *Autobiography,* 2:234–35.
28. Howard, *Autobiography,* 2:238–40.

29. Rose, *Rehearsal,* pp. 305–6.
30. Ibid., pp. 37–38; Bentley, *Freedmen's Bureau,* pp. 31–34, 81, 94–95.
31. Howard, *Autobiography,* 2:279–80; Bentley, *Freedmen's Bureau,* pp. 115–16.
32. McPherson, *Reconstruction,* pp. 72–74.
33. Senate, *Congressional Globe,* 39th Cong., 1st sess., 1866, 36, pt. 1:316, 318.
34. Ibid., p. 318.
35. Ibid., p. 317.
36. Before the end of 1866 a Southern Homestead Act was passed, for the purpose of establishing freedmen on public lands. However, it was never implemented and was repealed during the working out of the compromise of 1876–77 that brought Rutherford B. Hayes to the presidency. See Paul W. Gates, "Federal Land Policy in the South, 1866–1888," *Journal of Southern History* 6 (1940):303–30.
37. Senate, *Congressional Globe,* 39th Cong., 1st sess., 1866, 36, pt. 1:322.
38. McKitrick, *Johnson,* p. 281, citing Senate, *Congressional Globe,* 36, pt. 1:364–67.
39. McKitrick, *Johnson,* p. 280.
40. Howard, *Autobiography,* 2:280.
41. Cox, *Politics, Principle, and Prejudice,* pp. 177–78.
42. Gideon Welles, *Diary of Gideon Welles,* 3 vols. (Boston and New York: Houghton Mifflin Co., 1909–10), 2:393–94, 397, 415.
43. Ibid., pp. 398, 433, 435.
44. Ibid., p. 432–33.
45. Brock, *American Crisis,* pp. 108–9.
46. Welles, *Diary,* 2:434–35.
47. Richardson, ed., *Messages and Papers,* 6:400.
48. Ibid., p. 401.
49. Ibid., pp. 402–3.

50. Ibid., pp. 404–5.
51. Ibid., p. 403.
52. Ibid., p. 404. Italics added.
53. *Harper's Weekly*, March 3, 1866, p. 130.
54. Quoted in McKitrick, *Johnson*, pp. 290–91.
55. Gaillard Hunt, *Israel, Elihu, and Cadwallader Washburne* (New York: Macmillan Co., 1925), p. 119.
56. Kendrick, *Joint Committee*, *p. 234.*
57. Senate, *Congressional Globe*, 39th Cong., 1st sess., 1866, 36, pt. 1:937.
58. Ibid., p. 943.
59. Ibid., p. 943.
60. McPherson, *Reconstruction*, pp. 58–63.
61. Welles, *Diary*, 2:439.
62. Hugh McCulloch, *Men and Measures of Half a Century: Sketches and Comments* (New York: Charles Scribner's Sons, 1888), p. 393.
63. Welles, *Diary*, 2:439.
64. Fessenden to Elizabeth F. Warriner, February 25, 1866, William Pitt Fessenden MSS, Bowdoin, College, Brunswick, Me.
65. Quoted in Brodie, *Stevens*, p. 256.
66. McKitrick, *Johnson*, pp. 295–96.

Chapter 4:
Trumbull and Civil Rights

1. McPherson, *Reconstruction*, pp. 78–81.
2. Senate, *Congressional Globe*, 39th Cong., 1st sess., 1866, 36, pt. 1:474–75.
3. Ibid., p. 475.
4. Ray to Trumbull, February 7, 1866, Lyman Trumbull MSS, Library of Congress, Washington, D.C.
5. Senate, *Congressional Globe*, 39th Cong., 1st sess., 1866, 36, pt. 1:476.
6. Saulsbury and Charles Sumner, the great champion of Negro suffrage, were in agreement on this point, but with a difference. Saulsbury feared that there would be Negro suffrage under the Civil Rights Act; Sumner lamented that its authors did not include Negro suffrage.
7. Senate, *Congressional Globe*, 39th Cong., 1st sess., 1866, 36, pt. 1:480.
8. This passage was written in 1974, at a time of violent resistance in Boston to the busing of students for purposes in integration.
9. Quoted in Cox, *Politics, Principle, and Prejudice*, p. 144.
10. Welles, *Diary*, 2:458–59.
11. Ibid., pp. 455–60; Cox, *Politics, Principle, and Prejudice*, pp. 143–50; Brock, *American Crisis*, pp. 116–17.
12. Patrick W. Riddleberger, *George Washington Julian, Radical Republican* (Indianapolis: Indiana Historical Bureau, 1966), pp. 214–15.
13. William Dudley Foulke, *Life of Oliver P. Morton*, 2 vols. (Indianapolis: Bowen-Merrill Co., 1899), 1:466–67; McKitrick, *Johnson*, pp. 308–9.
14. Quoted in Foulke, *Morton*, 1:474–76. In his early political career before the formation of the Republican party, Morton had been a Democrat.
15. McKitrick, *Johnson*, pp. 310–11; Cox, *Politics, Principle and Prejudice*, pp. 196–97.
16. James Ford Rhodes, *History of the United States from the Compromise of 1850 to the McKinley-Bryan Campaign of 1896*, 8 vols. (New York: Macmillan Co., 1920), 6:64–65; McKitrick, *Johnson*, pp. 298–305.

17. John Sherman, *John Sherman's Recollections of Forty Years in the House, Senate and Cabinet*, 2 vols. (New York: Werner Co., 1895), 1:368–69.
18. Welles, *Diary*, 2:460–64.
19. George Fort Milton, *The Age of Hate: Andrew Johnson and the Radicals* (New York: Coward-McCann, 1930), p. 310, quoting Moore's diary.
20. Richardson, ed., *Messages and Papers*, 6:413, 407.
21. Ibid., p. 412.
22. Lawanda Cox and John Cox, "Andrew Johnson and His Ghost Writers: An Analysis of the Freedmen's Bureau and Civil Rights Veto Messages," *Mississippi Valley Historical Review* 48 (1961):460–79. Andrew Johnson MSS, Library of Congress, Washington, D.C., Series 1, [March 27, 1866].
23. Horace White, *The Life of Lyman Trumbull* (Boston and New York: Houghton Mifflin Co., 1913), p. 272.
24. Burgess, *Reconstruction and the Constitution*, p. 68.
25. J. G. Randall and David Donald, *The Civil War and Reconstruction*, 2d ed. (Lexington, Mass.: D. C. Heath, 1969), p. 594.
26. Beale, *Critical Year*, pp. 88–90. What is most surprising about Beale's account is that, in a detailed study of the politics of the year 1866, he says nothing about the proceedings in the New Jersey legislature, which are germane to the matter and were an important part of the Senate debate. Also, Beale fell into the familiar trap of categorizing as radicals all those who opposed the veto.
27. David M. Dewitt, *The Impeachment and Trial of Andrew Johnson, Seventeenth President of the United States. A History* (New York: Macmillan Co., 190), pp. 67, 80.
28. Ibid., pp. 175–76; James G. Blaine, *Twenty Years in Congress: From Lincoln to Garfield, with a Review of the Events which Led to the Political Revolution of 1860*, 2 vols. (Norwich, Conn.: Henry Bill Publishing Co., 1893), 2:156–57.
29. Brock, *American Crisis*, p. 114.
30. McKitrick, *Johnson*, pp. 319–23.
31. Ibid., pp. 320–23; White, *Trumbull,* pp. 261–65; Brock, *American Crisis*, p. 114; Dewitt, *Impeachment*, pp. 66–80; Blaine, *Twenty Years*, 2:156–61.
32. Brodie, *Stevens*, pp. 263–64.
33. Rachel Sherman Thorndike, ed., *The Sherman Letters: Correspondence Between General and Senator Sherman From 1837 to 1891* (New York: Charles Scribner's Sons, 1894), p. 276.
34. Brock, *American Crisis*, p. 115.
35. As much as any other president in our history, with the possible exception of Richard Nixon, Johnson allowed himself to be cut off from those very contacts which might have made his administration effective.
36. In the summer of 1971 I happened to be present in the Strangers' Gallery of the House of Commons when the prime minister, Edward Heath, was taking questions from the opposition. I was struck by the harshness of the language and the accusatory tone of the opposition members. But the prime minister, accustomed to handling such barbs, either ignored them or disposed of them with wit or aplomb, and thus left himself free to discuss important mattrs. In this situation of direct confrontation, it was clear that for

the prime minister to have been led into a personal dispute would have been very damaging to him and his party.

Chapter 5:
Struggle for an Amendment—
First Phase

1. Joseph B. James, *The Framing of the Fourteenth Amendment* (Urbana: University of Illinois Press, 1956), pp. 12–14.
2. Kendrick, *Joint Committee*, pp. 198–99
3. ten Broek, *Equal Under Law*, pp. 145–48.
4. Blaine, *Twenty Years*, 2:190–91.
5. Sumner, "Clemency and Common Sense," p. 759.
6. Blaine, *Twenty Years*, 2:194.
7. Ibid., p. 195, italics added.
8. House, *Congressional Globe*, 39th Cong., 1st sess., 1866, 36, pt. 1:142–46; McKitrick, *Johnson*, pp. 113–15; Burgess, *Reconstruction and the Constitution*, pp. 59–61; Alfred H. Kelly and Winfred A. Harbison, *The American Constitution* (New York: W. W. Norton, 1963), pp. 480–81, 463–64.
9. Kendrick, *Joint Committee*, pp. 39–46; James, *Framing*, pp. 52, 55–56; Francis Fessenden, *Life and Public Services of William Pitt Fessenden*, 2 vols. (Boston: Houghton Mifflin Co., 1907), 2:22; Brock, *American Crisis*, pp. 131–32.
10. The appearance of the words *person* and *citizen* in the various proposals made during the framing of the Fourteenth Amendment take on added significance because of Roscoe Conkling's assertion sixteen years later of the intention of the committee to protect corporations as legal persons and the subsequent acceptance of the "conspiracy theory" by Charles A. Beard and others. In this instance the language of the subcommittee was that representation would be based on "the whole number of citizens . . . in each State." Stevens sought to insert a definition of citizenship so that it would be understood that citizens were "all persons born in the United States, or naturalized, excluding Indians." Conkling then moved to strike out the word *citizen* and to include the word *person*. A few days later Conkling offered an explanation in the House. "Many of the large States," he said, "now hold their representation in part by reason of their aliens, and the legislatures and the people of these States are to pass upon the amendment. It must be made acceptable to them." See James, *Framing*, p. 359, and Kendrick, *Joint Committee*, pp. 52–53. Even though this discussion took place over the matter of representation—covered in Section 2 of the final amendment—and the "conspiracy theory" arose from the use of the word *person* in the first, or civil rights, section, it appears to be relevant. If Conkling had any idea at this time that the committee had a "corporate person" in mind, there is no evidence of it. For a more detailed discussion of the "conspiracy theory," see chapter 7.
11. House, *Congressional Globe*, 39th Cong., 1st sess., 1866, 36, pt. 1:351–57; James, *Framing*, pp. 59–61.
12. James, *Framing*, pp. 62–63.
13. Ibid.

14. Fessenden, *Fessenden*, 2:25–26, 36.
15. Blaine, *Twenty Years*, 2:199–200.
16. Ibid., pp. 201–2.
17. Donald, *Sumner and Rights of Man*, pp. 240–47.
18. Blaine, *Twenty Years*, 2:203; James, *Framing*, pp. 70–71.
19. James, *Framing*, p. 74.
20. Fessenden, *Fessenden*, 2:56.
21. *National Anti-Slavery Standard*, February 10, 1866.
22. *Nation*, February 1, 1866; *Harper's Weekly*, February 10, 1866; see Kendrick, *Joint Committee* for a summary of northern press opinion.
23. Donald, *Sumner and Rights of Man*, pp. 247–54; McKitrick, *Johnson*, pp. 340–41.
24. *Dictionary of American Biography* (1935–36), vol. 9, pt. 2, pp. 13–15; William M. Stewart, *Reminiscences of Senator William M. Stewart of Nevada*, ed. George Rothwell Brown (New York: Neale Publishing Co., 1908), passim.
25. Kendrick, *Joint Committee*, pp. 252–55; McKitrick, *Johnson*, pp. 341–43; James, *Framing*, pp. 94–95; Stewart, *Reminiscences*, pp. 214–18.
26. ten Broek, *Equal Under Law*, pp. 213–14.
27. House, *Congressional Globe*, 39th Cong., 1 st sess., 1866, 36, pt. 2:1063–64.
28. Kendrick, *Joint Committee*, pp. 63–81, 226–62.
29. Brock, *American Crisis*, pp. 136–39.
30. Fessenden, *Fessenden*, 2:22–24.
31. Ibid., p. 26. Italics added.

Chapter 6:
Congress Adopts the Amendment

1. *Cincinnati Commercial*, March 28, 1866.
2. James, *Framing*, p. 94.
3. Phillips to Sumner, March 24, 1866, quoted in James, *Framing*, p. 111.
4. *Chicago Tribune*, March 21, 1866, in James, *Framing*, p. 110.
5. *Nation*, April 5, 12, 1866.
6. Richard William Leopold, *Robert Dale Owen. A Biography* (Cambridge: Harvard University Press, 1940), pp. 356–57.
7. Robert Dale Owen, "Political Results of the Varioloid," *Atlantic Monthly* (June 1875), pp. 660–70.
8. *Cincinnati Commercial*, April 30, 1866, quoted in James, *Framing*, p. 108.
9. Owen, "Varioloid," p. 666.
10. The delegation, while not adopting a formal resolution, prepared a four-part proposition to present to the committee as that which would be acceptable. *New York Times*, April 27, 1866.
11. James, *Framing*, pp. 111–12.
12. Owen, "Varioloid," p. 664.
13. Ibid., p. 666.
14. Orville Hickman Browning, *The Diary of Orville Hickman Browning*, ed. James G. Randall, 2 vols. (Springfield: Illinois State Historical Library, 1933), 2:73.
15. William Salter, *The Life of James W. Grimes* (New York: D. Appleton & Co., 1876), p. 292.
16. James, *Framing*, p. 120.
17. *New York Weekly Tribune*, May 5, 1866.
18. McPherson, *Struggle* p. 354.
19. James, *Framing*, p. 119.
20. Ibid., p. 122.
21. Quoted in McKitrick, *Johnson*, p. 351.
22. In fact, however, the words of Section 1 indicate that it is a limitation on the states rather than an explicit assertion of the power of Congress, in contrast to the original civil rights

amendment reported by Bingham in February.

23. House, *Congressional Globe*, 39th Cong., 1st sess., 1866, 36, pt. 3:2459–60.
24. Ibid., pp. 2502–3.
25. Ibid., pp. 2537–39.
26. Ibid., pp. 2541–44.
27. Ibid., pp. 2544–45.
28. James, *Framing*, p. 131.
29. Grimes to Mrs. Grimes, May 11, 1866, Salter, *Grimes*, p. 297.
30. Quoted in James, *Framing*, p. 132.
31. Ibid., p. 133.
32. Ibid., p. 135.
33. House, *Congressional Globe*, 39th Cong., 1st sess., 1866, 36, pt. 3:2598–99.
34. James, *Framing*, p. 134.
35. *Nation*, June 5, 1866; Kendrick, *Joint Committee*, pp. 330–31.
36. Senate, *Congressional Globe*, 39th Cong., 1st sess., 1866, 36, pt. 3:2764–68.
37. Ibid., pp. 2768–69.
38. This is the interpretation of Joseph James. See *Framing*, p. 140.
39. Senate, *Congressional Globe*, 39th Cong., 1st sess., 1866, 36, pt. 3:2804.
40. Kendrick, *Joint Committee*, p. 312.
41. Senate, *Congressional Globe*, 39th Cong., 1st sess., 1866, 36, pt. 3:2788–2803.
42. James, *Framing*, pp. 140–41; Welles, *Diary*, 2:516–17.
43. James, *Framing*, p. 141.
44. Senate, *Congressional Globe*, 39th Cong., 1st sess., 1866, 36, pt. 4:2896; James, *Framing*, p. 143; White, *Trumbull*, pp. 282–83.
45. Senate, *Congressional Globe*, 39th Cong., 1st sess., 1866, 36, pt. 4:2895.
46. James, *Framing*, pp. 146–49.
47. Senate, *Congressional Globe*,

39th Cong., 1st sess., 1866, 36, pt. 4:2938–41.
48. Ibid., p. 3148; James, *Framing*, pp. 150–51.
49. James, *Framing*, pp. 169–70; Kendrick, *Joint Committee*, pp. 327–37.
50. *Harper's Weekly*, June 9, 1866; James, *Framing*, pp. 145–46; McKitrick, *Johnson*, pp. 355–57.
51. *National Anti-Slavery Standard*, May 26, 1866.
52. Quoted in McPherson, *Struggle*, pp. 355–56.
53. *National Anti-Slavery Standard*, June 30, 1866.
54. McPherson, *Reconstruction*, p. 83. The president's comments on Seward undoubtedly manifest some disharmony in the cabinet about the secretary of state, a suspicion on the part of loyalists like Welles that he was not so loyal to the administration as he might have been. See *Welles*, Diary, 2:532–38.
55. Kendrick, *Joint Committee*, pp. 338–47.
56. McPherson, *Reconstruction*, pp. 147–51.
57. Ibid., p. 194.

Chapter 7:
The Meaning of the Amendment—
For Contemporaries and Historians

1. For a brilliant analysis of the progressive historians, see Richard Hofstadter, *The Progressive Historians: Turner, Beard, Parrington* (New York: Alfred A. Knopf, 1968).
2. Charles A. Beard, *Contemporary American History, 1877–1913* (1914; reprint ed., Port Washington, N.Y.: Kennikat Press, 1971), pp. 54–59.
3. Howard Jay Graham, "The 'Conspiracy Theory' of the Fourteenth

Amendment," *Yale Law Review* (1938), 47:371–403; 48:171–94. In preparing this account I have consulted the editions of 1930 and 1945. See vol. 2 of both editions, pp. 111–14.

4. For a perceptive treatment of another legend, this one emanating from the Dunning school of Reconstruction history, see Stampp, *The Era of Reconstruction*, chapter 1.

5. Hofstadter, *Progressive Historians*, p. 303; Thomas J. Pressly, *Americans Interpret Their Civil War* (Princeton: Princeton University Press, 1954), p. 208.

6. Hofstadter, *Progressive Historians*, pp. 464–65.

7. Beale, *Critical Year*, pp. 216–19.

8. See, for example, Stanley Coben, "Northeastern Business and Radical Reconstruction: A Reexamination," *Mississippi Valley Historical Review* 46 (1959):67–90.

9. Howard K. Beale, "On Rewriting Reconstruction History," *American Historical Review* 45 (1940):818–19.

10. Carl Schurz, "The True Problem," *Atlantic Monthly* (March 1867), pp. 372–73.

11. George W. Julian, *Political Recollections, 1840 to 1872*. (Chicago: Jansen, McClurg & Co., 1884), pp. 272–73.

12. *Nation*, May 1, 1866.

13. Schurz, "True Problem," p. 372.

14. William Gillette, *The Right to Vote: Politics and the Passage of the Fifteenth Amendment* (Baltimore: Johns Hopkins Press, 1965), pp. 25–29.

15. V. Jacque Voegeli, *Free But Not Equal: The Midwest and the Negro During the Civil War* (Chicago: University of Chicago Press, 1967), pp. 44–46.

16. George M. Fredrickson, *The Black Image in the White Mind: The Debate on Afro-American Character and Destiny, 1817–1914* (New York: Harper and Row, 1971), p. 174.

17. James McPherson, in *The Struggle for Equality*, has given an admirable account of these dedicated men, but it does seem that he fails to show the limitations placed upon the politicians that were no hindrance to protagonists such as Phillips, Higginson, or Stearns.

18. Hans L. Trefousse, *Benjamin Franklin Wade: Radical Republican from Ohio* (New York: Twayne Publishers, 1963), pp. 284–85.

19. Donald, *Sumner and Rights of Man*, pp. 251–52.

20. Julian, *Political Recollections*, pp. 324–25; Riddleberger, *George Washington Julian*, pp. 228–29. In December 1868, Julian submitted an amendment to the Constitution declaring "the right of suffrage to be based on citizenship . . . without any distinction or discrimination . . . founded on race, color, or sex." But that was two years hence, after the victory of Congress over Andrew Johnson.

21. *National Anti-Slavery Standard*, December 30, 1865.

22. Kendrick, *Joint Committee*, p. 283.

23. See Irwin Unger, *The Greenback Era: A Social and Political History of American Finance, 1865–1879* (Princeton: Princeton University Press, 1964), for an excellent summary of economic conditions and economic thought at the end of the Civil War.

24. Coben, "Northeastern Business and Radical Reconstruction," passim.

25. Unger, *Greenback Era*, p. 76.

26. James, *Framing*, p. 185.

27. Schurz, "True Problem," p. 372.
28. Beale, *Critical Year*, pp. 147, 150.
29. McKitrick, *Johnson*, p. 95.
30. Kendrick, *Joint Committee*, p. 338.
31. Brock, *American Crisis*, p. 147, quoting Stevens's Bedford, Pa., speech of September 4, 1866.
32. Senate, *Congressional Globe*, 39th Cong., 1st sess., 1866, 36, pt. 1:128.
33. Rhodes, *History of the United States*, 6:91.
34. Burgess, *Reconstruction and the Constitution*, pp. 86–87.
35. Schurz, "True Problem," p. 378.
36. C. Vann Woodward, "Seeds of Failure in Radical Race Policy," in Harold M. Hyman, ed., *New Frontiers of the American Reconstruction* (Urbana: University of Illinois Press, 1966), p. 134.
37. William R. Brock has summed up the actions of Congress with clarity and compassion. Admitting that the manner in which the Fourteenth Amendment was presented to the southern states was a "cruel error," Brock goes on to say that it would be "unjust to blame Congress too much for its acts and omissions . . . [for] Congress had faithfully mirrored [both the] certainties and doubts" of northern opinion. "The motive force behind policy," he concludes, "had its origin deep in the Northern society; decision-making in Congress had given it legislative form, but the politicians had been significant only when their ideas echoed those of substantial groups among the Northern people. Thus the first attempt at Reconstruction by Congress is a fascinating study of the interplay between political opinion and political leadership; its faults and its weaknesses were not those of a revolutionary minority but those of a democratic society stirred with idealism, bitterness, and bewilderment." (*American Crisis*, pp. 151–52) See also Patrick W. Riddleberger, "The Radicals' Abandonment of the Negro During Reconstruction," *Journal of Negro History* 45 (1960), 88–102.

Chapter 8:
The Memphis and New Orleans Riots

1. *Memphis Daily Appeal*, quoted in Jack D. L. Holmes, "The Underlying Causes of the Memphis Race Riot of 1866," *Tennessee Historical Quarterly* (September 1958), p. 207.
2. *Memphis Daily Avalanche*, May 17, 1866, quoted in Holmes, "Underlying Causes," p. 205.
3. There were two additional conservative newspapers, the *Argus* and the *Public Ledger*, and two radical ones, the *Post* and the *Republican*.
4. James Welch Patton, *Unionism and Reconstruction in Tennessee, 1860–1869* (1934; reprinted., Gloucester, Mass.: Peter Smith, 1966), p. 134.
5. Thomas B. Alexander, *Political Reconstruction in Tennessee* (1950; reprint ed., New York: Russell & Russell, 1968), p. 128.
6. U.S., Congress, House, Select Committee on the Memphis Riots, *Memphis Riots and Massacres*, 39th Cong., 1st sess., 1866, H. Rept. 101, pp. 6–7.
7. Ibid., pp. 89–90; Lawrence E. Devall, "The Memphis Riot of 1866" (Seminar paper, Southern Illinois University at Edwardsville, 1974). In preparing this account of the Memphis riot I am indebted to Mr. Devall for

some content and for bibliographical suggestions.

8. House, Select Committee, *Memphis Riots and Massacres*, pp. 2–3, 50–53.
9. Ibid., p. 277.
10. Ibid., p. 36.
11. Ibid., pp. 54–55, 75.
12. Devall, "Memphis Riot," p. 15; *New York Times*, June 29, 1866.
13. *Chicago Tribune*, May 9, 1866.
14. *Harper's Weekly*, June 2, 1866.
15. *New York Tribune*, May 23, 1866.
16. Fred Harvey Harrington, *Fighting Politician: Major General N. P. Banks* (Philadelphia: University of Pennsylvania Press, 1948), pp. 143–44.
17. Ibid., pp. 147–48; Willie M. Caskey, *Secession and Restoration in Louisiana* (1938; reprint ed., New York: DaCapo Press, 1970), pp. 116–21.
18. Caskey, *Secession and Restoration*, pp. 124, 132.
19. Quoted in Caskey, *Secession and Restoration*, p. 130.
20. Roger W. Shugg, *Origins of Class Struggle in Louisiana* (1939; reprinted, Baton Rouge: Louisiana State University Press, 1968), pp. 198–210.
21. Quoted in Caskey, *Secession and Restoration*, p. 140.
22. Ibid., p. 140; Shugg, *Origins*, p. 210.
23. Shugg, *Origins*, p. 211; John R. Ficklen, *History of Reconstruction in Louisiana, through 1868* (Baltimore: Johns Hopkins Press, 1910), p. 82.
24. Caskey, *Secession and Restoration*, pp. 138–39.
25. Quoted in Caskey, *Secession and Restoration*, pp. 166–67.
26. Ibid., p. 180.
27. Ibid., pp. 180–83.
28. Quoted in Ficklen, *Reconstruction in Louisiana*, p. 140.

29. Ibid., p. 109; Fleming, *Documentary History of Reconstruction*, 1:229–30. Donald E. Reynolds, "The New Orleans Riot of 1866, Reconsidered," *Louisiana History* 5 (Winter 1964): 7.
30. Ficklen, *Reconstruction in Louisiana*, pp. 145, 148–49.
31. Reynolds, "New Orleans Riot," p. 6.
32. U.S., Congress, House, Select Committee on New Orleans Riots, *New Orleans Riots*, 39th Cong., 2d sess., 1866–67, H. Rept. 16, p. 56; Ficklen, *Reconstruction in Louisiana*, pp. 155–59; Reynolds, "New Orleans Riot," p. 8. In Washington Howell talked with people in and out of Congress, among them General Banks, Thaddeus Stevens, Boutwell, and Shellabarger.
33. G. Granger to Johnson, Johnson MSS, Series 1, June 11, 866.
34. House, Select Committee, *New Orleans Riots*, pp. 441–42.
35. Ibid., p. 458.
36. Ibid., p. 451.
37. Beale, *Critical Year*, p. 349.
38. James E. Sefton, *The United States Army and Reconstruction, 1865–1877.* (Baton Rouge: Louisiana State University Press, 1967), pp. 85–87.
39. Benjamin P. Thomas and Harold M. Hyman, *Stanton: The Life and Times of Lincoln's Secretary of War* (New York: Alfred A. Knopf, 1962), pp. 496–97.
40. Joe Gray Taylor, *Louisiana Reconstructed, 1863–1877* (Baton Rouge: Louisiana State University Press, 1974), p. 107.
41. Fleming, *Documentary History of Reconstruction*, 1:232; Ficklen, *Reconstruction in Louisiana*, pp. 161–62; Caskey, *Secession and Restoration*, pp. 220–21; Taylor, *Louisiana*, p. 108.

42. Taylor, *Louisiana,* p. 108.
43. Quoted in Reynolds, "New Orleans Riot," p. 10–11.
44. For eyewitness accounts of the riot see House, Select Committee, *New Orleans Riots,* passim. Richard Taylor was near the convention hall and noted the large number of boys in the crowd. Taylor, *Destruction and Reconstruction: Personal Experiences of the Late War* (1879; reprint ed., Waltham, Mass.: Blaisdell Publishing Co.,

1968), p. 249. The best secondary account in Reynolds, "New Orleans Riot," p. 11–13; see also Ficklen, *Reconstruction in Louisiana,* pp. 165–69.
45. House, Select Committee, *New Orleans Riots,* p. 348.
46. Ibid., p. 444.
47. Ibid., p. 12. A detailed breakdown of those killed and wounded, by classes, was presented to the committee by Dr. Albert Harstuff, Assistant Surgeon, U.S.A.

	Killed	Wounded Severely	Wounded Slightly	Total Wounded	Pistol Wounds	Incised Wounds	Contusions
Members of convention	1	4	4	8	4	1	3
White citizens, loyal	2	4	5	9	3	2	4
Colored citizens	24	40	79	119	44	30	45
Policemen			10	10	7	1	2
White citizens, disloyal	1						

48. House, Select Committee, *New Orleans Riots,* pp. 352, 437–45; McKitrick, *Johnson,* pp. 426–27; Philip H. Sheridan, *Personal Memoirs of P. H. Sheridan, General, United States Army,* 2 vols. (New York: Charles L. Webster & Co., 1888), 2:235–42.
49. House, Select Committee, *New Orleans Riots,* pp. 349, 351.
50. Welles, *Diary,* 2:569–70.
51. House, Select Committee, *New Orleans Riots,* pp. 60–61.
52. Caskey, *Secession and Restoration,* pp. 222–31.
53. Ficklen, *Reconstruction in Louisiana,* pp. 172–74.

54. House, Select Committee, *New Orleans Riots,* p. 40; Reynolds, "New Orleans Riot," p. 19.
55. Reynolds, "New Orleans Riot," p. 20; House, Select Committee, *New Orleans Riots,* p. 263.
56. Taylor, *Louisiana,* pp. 111–12.

Chapter 9:
The Voice of the Electorate

1. See especially Beale, *Critical Year.*
2. Blaine, *Twenty Years,* 2:217.
3. *New York Tribune,* September 27, 1866.

4. *New York Herald*, June 23, 1866.
5. Mary R. Dearing, *Veterans in Politics: The Story of the G.A.R.* (Baton Rouge: Louisiana State University Press, 1952), pp. 98–100, 115–16.
6. *New York Herald*, January 29, February 11, 1866, McKitrick, *Johnson*, p. 364–66.
7. *New York Herald*, April 19, 1866, quoted in McKitrick, *Johnson*, p. 399.
8. McKitrick, *Johnson*, p. 404; Welles, *Diary*, 2:528–29.
9. Browning, *Diary*, 2:79.
10. Welles, *Diary*, 2:528–29.
11. Ibid., pp. 529–30.
12. Beale, *Critical Year*, p. 127; Welles, *Diary*, 2:538–42.
13. Welles, *Diary*, 2:573. The new cabinet appointees were A. W. Randall of Wisconsin, Henry Stanbery of Ohio, and Orville H. Browning of Illinois.
14. McPherson, *Reconstruction*, pp. 118–19.
15. Henry W. Raymond, ed., "Extracts from the Journal of Henry J. Raymond," *Scribner's Monthly* 20 (1880):277.
16. Cox, *Politics, Principle, and Prejudice*, quoting *New York Herald* of August 29, 1866, p. 101.
17. Browning, *Diary*, 2:84–85.
18. McKitrick, *Johnson*, pp. 412–16; Ellis Paxson Oberholtzer, *A History of the United States Since the Civil War*, 5 vols. (New York: Macmillan Co., 1917), 1:386–88.
19. Raymond, "Journal of Henry J. Raymond," pp. 276–77.
20. Ibid., pp. 279–80; Augustus Maverick, *Henry J. Raymond and the New York Press for Thirty Years* (Hartford, Conn.: A. S. Hale and Co., 1870), pp. 459–60.
21. Maverick, *Raymond*, pp. 448–60.
22. Johnson MSS, Series 1, August 16, 1866.
23. Beale, *Critical Year*, 137.
24. Robert W. Winston, *Andrew Johnson, Plebeian and Patriot* (1928; reprinted., New York: Barnes and Noble, 1969), pp. 356–57.
25. McPherson, *Reconstruction*, pp. 127–29.
26. Blaine, *Twenty Years*, 2:226.
27. Ibid., pp. 227–28.
28. *New York Herald*, September 4, 1866.
29. Julian, *Political Recollections*, p. 303; Beale, *Critical Year*, pp. 184–85.
30. Quoted in Current, *Old Thad Stevens*, pp. 257–58.
31. *New York Herald*, September 4, 1866.
32. Blaine, *Twenty Years*, 2:238.
33. Welles, *Diary*, 2:587.
34. Beale, *Critical Year*, p. 368.
35. *New York Herald*, August 20, 1866.
36. *North American Review*, October 1866, p. 525.
37. Edward L. Pierce, *Memoir and Letters of Charles Sumner*, 4 vols. (Boston: Roberts Brothers, 1893), 4:298–99.
38. Oberholtzer, *History*, 1:412; *Nation*, September 20, 1866.
39. William E. Smith, *The Francis Preston Blair Family in Politics*, 2 vols. (New York: Macmillan Co., 1933), 2:365–66.
40. Welles, *Diary*, 2:592–95.
41. McPherson, *Reconstruction*, pp. 134–36; Oberholtzer, *History*, 1:404–5.
42. McPherson, *Reconstruction*, pp. 136–37.
43. McKitrick, *Johnson*, pp. 436–37; Beale, *Critical Year*, pp. 366–67; Oberholtzer, *History*, 1:407–9; Welles, *Diary*, 2:592–94; *New York Herald*, September 7, 11, 14, 1866.
44. Oberholtzer, *History*, 1:413.
45. Beale, *Critical Year*, quoting *New York Herald* of October 3, 24, 1866.

46. Beale, *Critical Year*, p. 361.
47. *Cincinnati Commercial*, October 8, 1866.
48. Beale, *Critical Year*, quoting *New York Herald*, August 20, 1866.
49. *Harper's Weekly*, September 29, 1866.
50. Ibid., September 8, November 3, 1866.
51. David Ross Locke [Petroleum V. Nasby], *Swingin Round the Circle* (Boston: Lee and Shepard, 1867), pp. 198–200, 211–12, 228.
52. Welles, *Diary*, 2:590; Winston, *Johnson*, pp. 369–70.
53. McKitrick, *Johnson*, pp. 416–17; Homer A. Stebbins, *A Political History of the State of New York 1865–1869* (New York: Columbia University Press, 1913), pp. 99–106, 112.
54. Maverick, *Raymond*, pp. 185–90; McKitrick, *Johnson*, pp. 416, 419–20.
55. Maverick, *Raymond*, p. 174; Stebbins, *Political History*, p. 86.
56. Taylor, *Destruction and Reconstruction*, p. 255.
57. *New York Herald*, September 6, 1866.
58. Ibid., September 8, 1866.
59. Ibid., September 10, 1866.
60. Ibid., September 12, 1866.
61. Ibid., September 19, 27, 28, 29, 1866.
62. Quoted in McKitrick, *Johnson*, p. 447.
63. Republican majorities were 42 to 11 in the Senate and 143 to 49 in the House.
64. Dearing, *Veterans*, pp. 102–3.
65. Oberholtzer, *History*, 1:416–17.
66. W. Sherman to J. Sherman, October 20, 1866; J. Sherman to W. Sherman, October 26, 1866, in Thorndike, ed., *Sherman Letters*, pp. 277–79; *Cincinnati Commercial*, October 21, 1866.
67. Dearing, *Veterans*, pp. 105–6.
68. Oberholtzer, *History*, 1:417–18, quoting Johnson to Stanton, November 1, 1866.
69. Ernest Duvergier de Hauranne, "Le Président Johnson et le congrès américain," *Revue des Deux Mondes* (December 1866), p. 786.

Chapter 10:
How Johnson Lost—
The Historical Debate

1. Beale, *Critical Year*, pp. 113–15, 299.
2. Ibid., pp. 7–9.
3. Quoted in Beale, *Critical Year*, p. 120.
4. Ibid., pp. 120–21.
5. Brock, *American Crisis*, p. 162.
6. Krug, *Lyman Trumbull*, pp. 244–45; Rhodes, *History of the United States*, 6:106; McKitrick, *Johnson*, pp. 386–87; see also letters to Trumbull in Trumbull MSS, May 2, 16, 31, 1866.
7. McKitrick, *Johnson*, p. 379.
8. Brock, *American Crisis*, pp. 164–65.
9. Davis R. Dewey, *Financial History of the United States*, American Citizen Series, A. B. Hart, ed. (N.p.: N.p., n.d.), pp. 332–33; Unger, *Greenback Era*, pp. 14–17.
10. Unger, *Greenback Era*, pp. 18–19; Dewey, *Financial History*, pp. 326–28, 385.
11. Robert P. Sharkey, *Money, Class and Party: An Economic Study of Civil War and Reconstruction* (Baltimore: Johns Hopkins Press, 1959), pp. 58–59.
12. McCulloch, *Men and Measures*, pp. 201–2. Italics added.
13. Ibid.
14. Unger, *Greenback Era*, p. 41.
15. Sharkey, *Money, Class and Party*, pp. 67–69.
16. Ibid., pp. 69–74.

17. John Sherman, *Recollections*, 1:379–83.
18. McCulloch, *Men and Measures*, p. 211; Sharkey, *Money, Class and Party*, p. 80.
19. Dewey, *Financial History*, p. 343.
20. Unger, *Greenback Era*, pp. 60–67.
21. Frank W. Taussig, *The Tariff History of the United States* (1892; reprint ed., New York: G. P. Putnam's Sons, Capricorn Books, 1964), pp. 158–59. Sidney Ratner, *The Tariff in American History* (New York: D. Van Nostrand Co., 1972), pp. 28–29.
22. Taussig, *Tariff History*, pp. 167–68; Ratner, *Tariff*, pp. 30–31.
23. Ratner, *Tariff*, pp. 31–32; Edward Stanwood, *American Tariff Controversies in the Nineteenth Century*, 2 vols. (Boston and New York: Houghton Mifflin Co., 1903), 2:150–52.
24. Beale, *Critical Year*, pp. 236–44.
25. Ibid., pp. 245–47.
26. Ibid., pp. 247–53; Richardson, ed., *Messages and Papers*, 6:678–79.
27. Beale, *Critical Year*, pp. 273–74.

28. Ibid., pp. 279–84.
29. Coben, "Northeastern Business and Radical Reconstruction," pp. 67–90.
30. Ibid., p. 78.
31. Ibid., p. 78.
32. Ibid., pp. 79–82.
33. Ibid., pp. 89–90.
34. McKitrick, *Johnson*, p. 368.
35. Ibid., pp. 369–73.
36. Ibid., pp. 374–77.
37. *New York Herald*, June 23, August 18, September 3, 17, 1866.
38. *Harper's Weekly*, July 14, 1866.
39. McKitrick, *Johnson*, p. 375.
40. The reader will have noted how heavily I have relied on the works of Professors Unger and Sharkey in writing this chapter. Neither of them discussed directly the economic aspects of the election of 1866, but their analysis of monetary and currency matters is so full of perception and substance as to make these two books, published after McKitrick's *Johnson*, indispensible to further scholarship on the subject. Beale, *Critical Year*, pp. 247–53; Unger, *Greenback Era*, pp. 60–67.

Selected Bibliography

Primary Sources

Manuscript Collections

William Pitt Fessenden MSS, Bowdoin College, Brunswick, Me.
Joshua R. Giddings–George W. Julian MSS, Library of Congress, Washington, D.C.
Andrew Johnson MSS, Library of Congress, Washington, D.C.
Justin S. Morrill MSS, Library of Congress, Washington, D.C.
Lyman Trumbull MSS, Library of Congress, Washington, D.C.
Benjamin F. Wade MSS, Library of Congress, Washington, D.C.

Printed Source Collections and Official Documents

Congressional Globe, 39th Congress, 1865–66.
Fleming, Walter L., ed. *Documentary History of Reconstruction*. 2 vols. 1906–7. Reprint. New York: McGraw-Hill Book Co., 1966.
McPherson, Edward. *The Political History of the United States of America during the Period of Reconstruction, from April 15, 1865, to July 15, 1870.* 1875. Reprint. New York: Greenwood Press for the Negro Universities Press, 1969.
Richardson, James D., ed. *A Compilation of the Messages and Papers of the Presidents, 1789–1897.* 10 vols. Washiongton D.C.: Bureau of National Literature and Art, 1896–99.
U.S., Congress, House, Joint Committee on Reconstruction. *Report of the Joint Committee on Reconstruction.* 39th Cong., 1st sess., 1866, H. Rept. 30.
U.S., Congress, House, Select Committee on the Memphis Riots. *Memphis Riots and Massacres.* 39th Cong., 1st sess., 1866, H. Rept. 101.
U.S., Congress, House, Select Committee on New Orleans Riots. *New Orleans Riots.* 39th Cong., 2d sess., 1866–67, H. Rept. 16.
U.S., Congress, Senate. *Report of Carl Schurz on the States of South Carolina, Georgia, Alabama, Mississippi, and Louisiana.* 39th Cong., 1st sess., 1865, Senate Executive Document 2.

Newspapers and Journals

Chicago Tribune
Cincinnati Commercial
Harper's Weekly

Nation
National Anti-Slavery Standard
New York Herald
New York Times
New York Tribune

Diaries, Memoirs, Books, and Articles by Contemporaries

Andrews, Sidney. *The South Since the War*. 1866. Reprint. New York: Arno Press and the *New York Times*, 1969.

Blaine, James. G. *Twenty Years in Congress: From Lincoln to Garfield, with a Review of the Events which Led to the Political Revolution of 1860*. 2 vols. Norwich, Conn. Henry Bill Publishing Co., 1893.

Boutwell, George S. *Reminiscences of Sixth Years in Public Affairs*. 1902. Reprint. New York: Greenwood Press, 1968.

Browning, Orville Hickman. *The Diary of Orville Hickman Browning*. Edited by James G. Randall. 2 vols. Springfield: Illinois State Historical Library, 1933.

Chandler, Pelig W. *Memoir of Governor Andrew with Personal Reminiscences*. Boston: Roberts Brothers, 1880.

Clemenceau, Georges. *American Reconstruction, 1865–1870*. Edited with an introduction by Fernand Baldensperger. Translated by Margaret Mac-Veagh. New York: Lincoln MacVeagh, Dial Press, 1928.

Cullom, Shelby M. *Fifty Years of Public Service*. Chicago: A. C. McClurg and Co., 1911.

Dennett, John Richard. *The South As It Is: 1865–1866*. Edited by Henry M. Christman. New York: Viking Press, Compass Books, 1967.

Fessenden, Francis. *Life and Public Services of William Pitt Fessenden*. 2 vols. Boston: Houghton Mifflin Co., 1907.

Hauranne, Ernest Duvergier de. "Le Président Johnson et le congrès Américain." *Revue des Deux Mondes* (December 1866), pp. 785–828.

Hinsdale, Mary L., ed. *Garfield-Hinsdale Letters: Correspondence Between James Abram Garfield and Burke Aaron Hinsdale*. Ann Arbor: University of Michigan Press, 1949.

Howard, Oliver Otis. *Autobiography of Oliver Otis Howard*. 2 vols. New York: Baker & Taylor, 1908.

Julian, George W. *Political Recollections, 1840 to 1872*. Chicago: Jansen, McClurg & Co., 1884.

Locke, David Ross [Petroleum V. Nasby]. *Swingin Round the Circle*. Boston: Lee and Shepard, 1867.

Lowell, James Russell. "The Seward-Johnson Reaction." *North American Review* (October 1866), pp. 520–49

McClure, Alexander K. *Abraham Lincoln and Men of War-Times*. Philadelphia: Times Publishing Co., 1892.

———. *Colonel Alexander McClure's Recollections of Half a Century*. Salem, Mass., 1902.

McCulloch, Hugh. *Men and Measures of Half a Century: Sketches and Comments*. New York: Charles Scribner's Sons, 1888.

Maverick, Augustus. *Henry J. Raymond and the New York Press for Thirty Years*. Hartford, Conn. A. S. Hale and Co., 1870.

Moore, W. G. "Notes of Colonel W. G. Moore, Private Secretary to President Johnson, 1866–1868." *American Historical Review* 19 (October 1913), pp. 98–132.

Owen, Robert Dale. "Political Results of the Varioloid." *Atlantic Monthly* (June 1875), pp. 660–70.

Pierce, Edward L. "The Freedmen at Port Royal." *Atlantic Monthly* 12 (September 1863): 291–315.

———. *Memoir and Letters of Charles Sumner.* 4 vols. Boston: Roberts Brothers, 1893.

Raymond, Henry W., ed. "Extracts from the Journal of Henry J. Raymond." *Scribner's Monthly* 20 (1880):275–80.

Reid, Whitlaw. *After the War: A Tour of the Southern States, 1865–1866.* 1866. Reprint. New York: Harper and Row, Harper Torchbooks, 1965.

Richardson, Joe M., ed. "The Memphis Race Riot and Its Aftermath: Report by a Northern Missionary." *Tennessee Historical Quarterly* (Spring 1965), pp. 63–69.

Salter, William. *The Life of James W. Grimes.* New York: D. Appleton & Co., 1876.

Schuckers, J. W. *The Life and Public Services of Salmon Portland Chase.* New York: D. Appleton & Co., 1874.

Schurz, Carl. *Speeches, Correspondence and Political Papers of Carl Schurz.* Edited by Frederic Bancroft. 6 vols. New York: G. P. Putnam's Sons, 1913.

———."The True Problem." *Atlantic Monthly* (March 1867), pp. 371–78.

Sheridan, Philip H. *Personal Memoirs of P. H. Sheridan, General, United States Army.* 2 vols. New York: Charles L. Webster & Co., 1888.

Sherman, John. *John Sherman's Recollections of Forty Years in the House, Senate, and Cabinet.* 2 vols. New York: Werner Co., 1895.

Stewart, William M. *Reminiscences of Senator William M. Stewart of Neveda.* Edited by George Rothwell Brown. New York: Neale Publishing Co., 1908.

Sumner, Charles, "Clemency and Common Sense." *Atlantic Monthly* 16 (December 1865), pp. 745–60.

Taylor, Richard. *Destruction and Reconstruction: Personal Experiences of the Late War.* 1879. Reprint. Edited by Charles P. Roland. Waltham, Mass.: Blaisdell Publishing Co., 1968.

Thorndike, Rachel Sherman, ed. *The Sherman Letters: Correspondence Between General and Senator Sherman from 1837 to 1891.* New York: Charles Scribner's Sons, 1894.

Trefousse, Hans L., ed. *Background for Radical Reconstruction: Testimony Taken from the Hearings of the Joint Committee on Reconstruction.* Boston: Little, Brown and Co., 1970.

Trowbridge, John T. *The Desolate South, 1865–1866: A Picture of the Battlefields and of the Devastated Confederacy.* 1866. Reprint. Boston: Little, Brown and Co., 1956.

Vattel, Emmerich de. *The Law of Nations or the Principles of Natural Law Applied to the Conduct and the Affairs of Nations and of Sovereigns.* Translation of the edition of 1758 by Charles G. Fenwick. Washington, D.C.: Carnegie Institution, 1916.

Warmouth, Henry Clay. *War, Politics and Reconstruction: Stormy Days in Louisiana.* New York: Macmillan Co., 1930.

Welles, Gideon. *Diary of Gideon Welles*. 3 vols. Boston and New York: Houghton Mifflin Co., 1909–10.

Secondary Sources

Alexander, Thomas B. *Political Reconstruction in Tennessee*. 1950. Reprint. New York: Russell & Russell, 1968.

Barrett, Don C. *The Greenbacks and Resumption of Specie Payments, 1862–1879*. 1931. Reprint. Gloucester, Mass.: Peter Smith, 1965.

Beale, Howard K. *The Critical Year: A Study of Andrew Johnson and Reconstruction*. New York: Harcourt, Brace & Co., 1930.

————. "The Tariff and Reconstruction." *American Historical Review* 35 (January 1930):276–94.

Beard, Charles A. *Contemporary American History, 1877–1913*. 1914. Reprint. Port Washington, N.Y.: Kennikat Press, 1971.

Beard, Charles A., and Beard, Mary R. *The Rise of American Civilization*. Two volumes in one. New York: Macmillan Co., 1927.

Belz, Herman. *Reconstructing the Union: Theory and Practice During the Civil War*. Ithaca, N.Y.: Cornell University Press, 1969.

Bentley, George R. *A History of the Freedmen's Bureau*. 1955. Reprint. New York: Farrar, Straus & Giroux, Octagon Books, 1970.

Berwanger, Eugene H. *The Frontier Against Slavery: Western Anti-Negro Prejudice and the Slavery Extension Controversy*. Urbana: University of Illinois Press, 1967.

Brock, William R. *An American Crisis: Congress and Reconstruction, 1865–1867*. London: Macmillan & Co., 1963.

Brodie, Fawn M. *Thaddeus Stevens: Scourge of the South*. New York: W. W. Norton, 1959.

Burgess, John W. *Reconstruction and the Constitution, 1866–1876*. New York: Charles Scribner's Sons, 1902.

Capers, Gerald M. *Occupied City: New Orleans Under the Federals, 1862–1865*. Lexington: University of Kentucky Press, 1965.

Caskey, Willie M. *Secession and Restoration in Louisiana*. 1938. Reprint. New York: DaCapo Press, 1970.

Coben, Stanley. "Northeastern Business and Radical Reconstruction: A Re-examination." *Mississippi Valley Historical Review* 46 (1959):67–90.

Cox, Lawanda. "The Promise of Land For The Freedmen." *Mississippi Valley Historical Review* 45 (1958): 413–40.

Cox, Lawanda, and Cox, John H. "Andrew Johnson and His Ghost Writers: An Analysis of the Freedmen's Bureau and Civil Rights Veto Messages." *Mississippi Valley Historical Review* 48 (1961):460–79.

————. "General O. O. Howard and the 'Misrepresented Bureau.' " *Journal of Southern History* 19 (1953): 427–56.

————. *Politics, Principle, and Prejudice, 1865–1866*. London and New York: Macmillan, Free Press, 1963.

Current, Richard N. *Old Thad Stevens, A Story of Ambition*. Madison: University of Wisconsin Press, 1942.

Dearing, Mary R. *Veterans in Politics: The Story of the G. A. R.* Baton Rouge: Louisiana State University Press, 1952.

Devall, Lawrence E. "The Memphis Riot of 1866." Seminar paper, Southern
Illinois University at Edwardsville, 1974.

Dewey, Davis R. *Financial History of the United States.* American Citizen
Series, A. B. Hart, ed. (N.p.: N.p., n.d.).

Dewitt, David M. *The Impeachment and Trial of Andrew Johnson,
Seventeenth President of the United States. A History.* New York:
Macmillan Co., 1903.

Donald, David. *Charles Sumner and the Rights of Man.* New York: Alfred A.
Knopf, 1970.

Dorris, Jonathan T. *Pardon and Amnesty Under Lincoln and Johnson.* Chapel
Hill: University of North Carolina Press, 1953.

DuBois, W. E. Burghardt. "The Freedmen's Bureau." *Atlantic Monthly* 87
(1901): 354–65.

Dunning, William A. *Essays on the Civil War and Reconstruction.* 1897.
Reprint. Gloucester, Mass.: Peter Smith, 1931.

————. *Reconstruction, Political and Economic, 1865–1877.* 1907. Reprint.
New York: Harper and Row, Harper Torchbooks, 1962.

Ficklen, John Rose. *History of Reconstruction in Louisiana Through 1868.*
Baltimore: Johns Hopkins Press, 1910.

Flack, Horace E. *The Adoption of the Fourteenth Amendment.* 1908. Reprint.
Gloucester, Mass.: Peter Smith, 1965.

Foulke, William D. *Life of Oliver P. Morton.* 2 vols. Indianapolis:
Bowen-Merrill Co., 1899.

Fredrickson, George M. *The Black Image in the White Mind: The Debate on
Afro-American Character and Destiny, 1817–1914.* New York: Harper
and Row, 1971.

Gates, Paul W. "Federal Land Policy in the South, 1866–1888." *Journal of
Southern History* 6 (1940), 303–30.

Gillette, William. *The Right to Vote: Politics and the Passage of the Fifteenth
Amendment.* Baltimore: Johns Hopkins Press, 1965.

Graham, Howard Jay. "The 'Conspiracy Theory' of the Fourteenth
Amendment." *Yale Law Review* (1938), 47:371–403; 48:171–94.

Harrington, Fred Harvey. *Fighting Politician: Major General N. P. Banks.*
Philadelphia: University of Pennsylvania Press, 1948.

Hofstadter, Richard. *The Progressive Historians: Turner, Beard, Parrington.*
New York: Alfred A. Knopf, 1968.

Holmes, Jack D. L. "The Underlying Causes of the Memphis Riot of 1866."
Tennessee Historical Quarterly (September 1958), pp. 195–221.

Hunt, Gaillard. *Israel, Elihu, and Cadwellader Washburne.* New York:
Macmillan Co., 1925.

Hyman, Harold M. *A More Perfect Union: The Impact of the Civil War and
Reconstruction on the Constitution.* New York: Alfred A. Knopf, 1973.

————, ed. *New Frontiers of the American Reconstruction.* Urbana:
University of Illinois Press, 1966.

James, Joseph B. *The Framing of the Fourteenth Amendment.* Urbana:
University of Illinois Press, 1956.

Jellison, Charles A. *Fessenden of Maine: Civil War Senator.* Syracuse:
University Press, 1962. Syracuse

Kelly, Alfred H., and Harbison, Winfred A. *The American Constitution.* New
York: W. W. Norton, 1963.

Kendrick, Benjamin B. *The Journal of the Joint Committee of Fifteen on Reconstruction, 39th Congress, 1865–1867.* New York: Columbia University Press, 1914.

Krug, Mark M. *Lyman Trumbull: Conservative Radical.* New York: A. S. Barnes and Co., 1965.

Leopold, Richard William. *Robert Dale Owen. A Biography.* Cambridge: Harvard University Press, 1940.

McFeely, William S. *Yankee Stepfather: General O. O. Howard and the Freedmen.* New Haven: Yale University Press, 1968.

McKitrick, Eric L. *Andrew Johnson and Reconstruction.* Chicago: University of Chicago Press, 1960.

McPherson, James M. *The Struggle for Equality: Abolitionists and the Negro in the Civil War and Reconstruction.* Princeton, N.J.: Princeton University Press, 1964.

Magdol, Edward. *A Right to the Land: Essays on the Freedmen's Community.* Westport, Conn.: Greenwood Press, 1977.

Meyer, Howard N. *The Amendment that Refused to Die.* Radnor, Pa.: Chilton Book Co., 1973.

Milton, George Fort. *The Age of Hate: Andrew Johnson and the Radicals.* New York: Coward-McCann, 1930.

Nugent, Walter T. K. *Money and American Society, 1865–1880.* New York: Free Press, 1968.

Oberholtzer, Ellis Paxon. *A History of the United States Since the Civil War.* 5 vols. New York: Macmillan Co., 1971.

Patrick, Rembert W. *The Reconstruction of the Nation.* New York: Oxford University Press, 1967.

Patton, James Welch. *Unionism and Reconstruction in Tennessee, 1860–1869.* 1934. Reprint. Gloucester, Mass.: Peter Smith, 1966.

Peirce, Paul Skeels. *The Freedmen's Bureau: A Chapter in the History of Reconstruction.* Iowa City: State University of Iowa, 1904.

Pressly, Thomas J. *Americans Interpret Their Civil War.* Princeton, N.J.: Princeton University Press, 1954.

Randall, J. G., and Donald, David. *The Civil War and Reconstruction.* 2d ed. Lexington, Mass.: D. C. Heath, 1969.

Ratner, Sidney. *The Tariff in American History.* New York: D. Van Nostrand Co., 1972.

Reynolds, Donald E. "The New Orleans Riot, Reconsidered." *Louisiana History* 5 (Winter 1964):5–27.

Rhodes, James Ford. *History of the United States from the Compromise of 1850 to the McKinley-Bryan Campaign of 1896.* 8 vols. New York: Macmillan Co., 1920.

Riddleberger, Patrick W. *George Washington Julian, Radical Republican.* Indianapolis: Indiana Historical Bureau, 1966.

———. "The Radicals' Abandonment of the Negro During Reconstruction." *Journal of Negro History* 45 (1960):88–102.

Rose, Willie Lee. *Rehearsal for Reconstruction: The Port Royal Experiment.* 1964. Reprint. New York: Knopf, Vintage Books, n.d.

Roseboom, Eugene H. *The Civil War Era, 1850–1873.* Columbus: Ohio State Archaeological and Historical Society, 1944.

Schwartz, Bernard, ed. *The Fourteenth Amendment: Centennial Volume.* New York: New York University Press, 1970.

Sefton, James E. *The United States Army and Reconstruction, 1865–1877.* Baton Rouge: Louisiana State University Press, 1967.

Sharkey, Robert P. *Money, Class, and Party: An Economic Study of Civil War and Reconstruction.* Baltimore: Johns Hopkins Press, 1959.

Shugg, Roger W. *Origins of Class Struggle in Louisiana.* 1939. Reprint. Baton Rouge: Louisiana State University Press, 1968.

Slotkin, Richard. *Regeneration Through Violence: The Mythology of the American Frontier, 1600–1860.* Middletown, Connecticut: Wesleyan University Press, 1973.

Smith, William E. *The Francis Preston Blair Family in Politics.* 2 vols. New York: Macmillan Co., 1933.

Sproat, John G. "Blueprint for Radical Reconstruction." *Journal of Southern History* 23 (1957):25–44.

Stampp, Kenneth M. *The Era of Reconstruction.* New York: Alfred A. Knopf, 1965.

Stampp, Kenneth M., and Litwack, Leon F., eds. *Reconstruction: An Anthology of Revisionist Writings.* Baton Rouge: Louisiana State University Press, 1969.

Stanwood, Edward. *American Tariff Controversies in the Nineteenth Century.* 2 vols. Boston and New York: Houghton Mifflin Co., 1903.

Stebbins, Homer A. *A Political History of the State of New York, 1865–1869.* New York: Columbia University Press, 1913.

Swint, Henry Lee. *The Northern Teacher in the South, 1862–1870.* Nashville, Tenn.: Vanderbilt University Press, 1941.

Taussig, Frank W. *The Tariff History of the United States.* 1892. Reprint New York: G. P. Putnam's Sons, Capricorn Books, 1964.

Taylor, Joe Gray. *Louisiana Reconstructed, 1863–1877.* Baton Rouge: Louisiana State University Press, 1974.

ten Broek, Jacobus. *Equal Under Law.* New York: Macmillan, Collier Books, 1965. Originally published, 1951, as *The Antislavery Origins of the Fourteenth Amendment.*

Thomas, Benjamin P., and Hyman, Harold M. *Stanton: The Life and Times of Lincoln's Secretary of War.* New York: Alfred A. Knopf, 1962.

Trefousse, Hans L. *Benjamin Franklin Wade: Radical Republican from Ohio.* New York: Twayne Publishers, 1963.

———. *The Radical Republicans: Lincoln's Vanguard for Radical Justice.* Baton Rouge: Louisiana State University Press, 1968.

Unger, Irwin. *The Greenback Era: A. Social and Political History of American Finance, 1865–1879.* Princeton, N.J.: Princeton University Press, 1964.

Voegeli, V. Jacque. *Free but Not Equal: The Midwest and the Negro During the Civil War.* Chicago: University of Chicago Press, 1967.

White, Horace. *The Life of Lyman Trumbull.* Boston and New York: Houghton Mifflin Co., 1913.

White, Howard A. *The Freedmen's Bureau in Louisiana.* Baton Rouge: Louisiana State University Press, 1970.

Winston, Robert W. *Andrew Johnson, Plebeian and Patriot.* 1928. Reprint. New York: Barnes and Noble, 1969.

Woodward C. Vann. "Seeds of Failure in Radical Race Policy." In Hyman, Harold, ed., *New Frontiers of the American Reconstruction*. Urbana: University of Illinois Press, 1966.

Index